Situational Analysis of Women in Politics

Situational Analysis of Women in Politics

Alka Saxena

AKHAND PUBLISHING HOUSE
NEW DELHI (INDIA)

Published by

AKHAND PUBLISHING HOUSE
L-9 A, IST FLOOR, STREET NO. 42
SADATPUR EXTENSION
DELHI-110094 (INDIA)
CELL- 0-9013387535, 0-9968628081

Situational Analysis of Women in Politics

Edition 2011
ISBN 978-81-910525-8-9

Printed in India
at Asian Offset Printers, Delhi

Preface

The position of women has improved down the ages and there is hardly any field without a woman's touch and politics is no exception. Women enjoy a share in politics but not a good share or one equal to men—the dilatory tactics on the women's Reservation Bill for instance. In a party, the presence of women members just means and mostly stops with the formation of a 'Mahila Samaj' and carrying out its activities. The decision making power always vests on men. Moreover, the candidates fielded by the parties are mostly men and the women account for only to 5 to 10 per cent. The Congress party with a woman as president which backs the Women's Reservation Bill has only a minimal of 10 per cent women candidates. There are women, who played and are playing a significant role in Indian politics. The most prominent woman Indira Gandhi was a clear example.

The women in India are more committed to becoming house wives and good mothers than involving themselves in politics. Politics and leadership requires an enigmatic charisma. Most of the women candidates find it difficult to establish themselves even within the party until they present themselves as 'Bahus or Betis' from a rich political background. This results in 'leaders without excellence'. The passing and approval of the Reservation Bill or giving equal priority alone is not the only criteria but the elegance and prowess of the women that matters. This is a clear indication of the Indian politics requires a giant leap.

The present book has taken into account the status of women politics, especially in the Indian context. It has made a humble attempt to make analysis of the role of women in central as well as local political spheres. The present book will definitely be a significant addition to the existing literature on women and politics.

Alka Saxena

Contents

1

Women in Parliament

When women in different parts of the world struggled to win the right to vote, they expected that the right to vote would inevitably lead to greater women's representation. Their expectations were not met. Instead, women embarked on another long and difficult struggle to actually get women elected to parliament. Part of this effort involved convincing women voters to support women as their representatives. In most countries, much of the work centred on political parties, the typical channels of entry to national legislatures. Women inside and outside political parties organised and mobilised themselves to change long-established party methods of political recruitment.

Once women entered parliament, their struggle was far from over. In parliament, women enter a male domain. Parliaments were established, organised and dominated by men, acting in their own interest and establishing procedures for their own convenience. There was no deliberate conspiracy to exclude women. It was not even an issue. Most long-established parliaments were a product of political processes that were male-dominated or exclusively male. Subsequent legislatures were, for the most part, modelled on these established assemblies. Inevitably, these male-dominated organisations reflect certain male biases, the precise kind varying by country and culture.

Until recently, this "institutional masculinity" has been an invisible characteristic of legislatures; it was embedded, pervasive and taken for granted. Only recently have legislatures' masculine biases come under scrutiny. Indeed, in most countries, the political role of women in legislatures became a public issue only in the second half of the twentieth century.

In 2002, women constitute 14.3 percent of legislative members worldwide. In the Nordic countries, their numbers are highest at 38.8 percent, while in the Arab states their representation is only 4.6 percent. As with previous efforts to try to get women elected to parliament, today women inside parliament are organising, mobilising, motivating and advancing women from inside the world's legislatures. They are devising strategies and taking action to promote issues relevant to women and facilitate changes in legislation.

The actual impact women parliamentarians can make will depend on a number of variables that vary from country to country. These include the political context in which the assembly functions, the type and number of women who are in parliament and the rules of the parliamentary game. Each of these factors has a significant bearing on the extent to which women MPs can make a difference once elected. Because these factors vary significantly from country to country, it is difficult to make generalisations that are universally relevant regarding how women MPs can maximise their impact.

In addition, there is very little research and information available on what sort of impact women have made. Underscoring the need for more knowledge and understanding in this particular field of women and decision-making, the UN Commission on the Status of Women (CSW) said in a report that there is an urgent need for case studies on "women making a difference" in politics.

The extent of women's impact will depend very much on the number of women in parliament who are motivated to represent women's issues and concerns.Feminists often argue that pioneer women parliamentarians became surrogate men – that they were socialised into the legislature and became indistinguishable from the men they replaced. We doubt this. Men are known to behave differently when women are absent. Because it upsets gender boundaries, the presence of even one woman will alter male behavior; the presence of several women will alter it even further. West European experience shows that where women MPs have a mission to effect change even small numbers can produce significant results.

While the presence of even one woman can make a difference, long-term significant change will largely be realised when there is a sufficient number of women in parliament who are motivated to represent women's concerns. This need for a significant minority of women to affect political change has been referred to by feminist political scientists as "critical mass". According to Drude Dahlerup, the test that a critical mass of women is present is the acceleration of the development of women's representation through acts that improve the situation for themselves and for women in general. These actions are critical acts of empowerment.

In her studies of women MPs in Scandinavia, Dahlerup found that women politicians worked to recruit other women and developed new legislation and institutions to benefit women. As their numbers grew it became easier to be a woman politician and public perceptions of women politicians changed.

1.1. Changing Rules

The full development to maximise women's impact on the legislative process requires a critical mass of women working on and promoting women's concerns. Simply put, the strategy consists of three parts: learning the rules, using the rules and changing the rules. By rules we mean the customs, conventions, informal practices and specific regulations that govern the way a legislature functions.

These include law-making processes, division of labor in the assembly, hierarchy structures, ceremonies, disciplines, traditions, habits and the norms of the assembly including its internal functioning and its relationship to other parts of the government and to the nation it has been elected to serve.

This strategy of learning, using and changing the rules is based on the belief that there is a need for change and that an objective in electing women MPs is to secure change. There are essentially four types of change that will make a difference to women. They can be categorised as institutional/procedural change, representation change, influence on output and discourse.

1. *Institutional/procedural change* refers to measures that alter the nature of the institution to make it more "woman-friendly". Cultural changes, such as greater gender awareness, should be accompanied by procedural changes designed to accommodate women members. Increased gender awareness is not simply a

matter of including women, but also a sensitivity that women are no more a universal category than are men and that class, age, ethnicity, race, physical ability, sexuality, parenting and life stage, have a determining effect on women's lives, much the same as they do on men's lives.

2. *Representation change* involves specific actions to secure women's continued and enhanced access to the legislature. These include encouragement of women candidates; a conscious use of role model capacities; the promotion of sex equality legislation, parity or equality regulations; and appropriate changes in electoral and campaigning laws. Representation change also includes actions in parliament that are designed to place women in important parliamentary positions and to secure their presence in government. It must also include changes in political parties that bring more women to legislatures. Parliamentary women often use the power their representative status gives them to support improving political opportunities for women in their parties. Similarly, parliamentary women may organise to support women for higher office. Parliaments constitute a crucial pool of recruitment to higher office.

3. *Impact/Influence on output* refers specifically to the "feminisation" of legislation and other policy outputs, i.e., the extent to which laws and policies have been altered or influenced in women's favor. This includes both putting women's issues on the agenda and ensuring that all legislation is woman-friendly or gender-sensitive.

4. *Discourse change* involves changes both inside and outside of parliament. Not only should efforts be made to alter parliamentary language so that women's perspectives are normalised, it is also necessary to make use of the parliamentary platform to alter public attitudes and to change the discourse of politics so that a political woman becomes as normal a concept as a political man. Such "speaking out the window" uses the parliamentary opportunity of greater access to the mass media and to the general public to raise awareness of women's issues and of women's political capacities in public debate.

1.2. Ways to Become Effective Parliamentarians

The first step is for women MPs to understand how the legislature works in order to be able to use this knowledge to operate more effectively.

Legislatures debate policies, make laws, examine their implementation and effects, provide a recruitment pool for government and scrutinise the activities of government. Most legislatures have a budgetary function; they are responsible for both the formal allocation of the budget and for auditing government spending. They are organised into front and back benches, government and opposition and functional and procedural committees. Through such structures, debate, monitoring, interrogation and interpolation are organised. MPs tend to specialise in particular issue areas and make their parliamentary reputations on the basis of their performance in the various structures and processes of the legislatures.

For women to be effective parliamentarians, they must clearly understand the functions of the legislature and they must learn the rules of the game – both the written and unwritten codes, procedures and mechanisms on how to get things done in parliament. They must first learn the internal practices of parliament in order to equip themselves to utilise these rules better and to devise effective strategies to change the rules to advance women's interests and goals. These ideas are elaborated below, grouped under each of the four main areas of change, namely institutional/procedural, representation, influence on output and discourse.

The first step is for women MPs to understand how the legislature works in order to be able to use this knowledge to operate more effectively within the legislature. MPs can acquire this knowledge in a variety of ways, including specific training and orientation programes as well as more general socialisation processes. For example, it is common for legislative leaders and other officials to offer orientation to new members on how the assembly works. Often, political parties also provide such training. Training by political parties is particularly useful since it offers insight into how the MP's party understands the procedures and how the party itself fits into the procedures. Since the organisation of legislative work often depends on party composition, parties have a significant influence on procedures. In some parts of the world political parties offer special skills training especially for women, since they may be less experienced in legislative procedures than men. However, in many parts of the developing world most parties do not have the resources, nor the willingness, to offer such training. In fact, as many of the case studies point out, very often party allegiance can handicap the development of political discourse in general and of any assistance to women MPs in particular. Political parties in Egypt, Jordan and Lebanon, for example, do not allow for any structural improvements and still operate with the assumption that women's perspectives and women's issues do not deserve any specific priority. This has obvious repercussions on the procedure inter-party, as well as intra-party and within parliament itself.

Networking is a crucial mechanism of training and socialisation for women MPs. Networking provides quick access to knowledge that may otherwise take years of experience to acquire and enables women MPs to come together to discuss their concerns and share their knowledge and expertise, thus greatly enhancing their potential for effectiveness. Networking of women MPs across party lines has been successful in a number of countries including Sweden, France, the Netherlands, South Africa and Egypt. The issues are as diverse as rape laws, electoral reform, personal status and other country-specific issues (such as women's rights to issue passports without their husbands' permission in Egypt and social, political and economic rights for Dalits in India). Also noteworthy is the formation of "support groups" composed of women professionals and MPs, especially from European countries. In the words of one Finnish MP, Riitta Uosukainen: "The fact that these women are able to get together across party lines, across professional areas and support each other not only personally, but also seek to do so professionally, is invaluable."

Mentoring (i.e. supervising, befriending and giving advice and guidance) by more experienced women MPs is another important way of providing special training for women MPs. In the Netherlands, for example, a system of "shadowing" has been developed whereby women who are hesitant to be nominated for elected office are assisted by elected members to gain confidence.

One structure that seeks to provide a space for women to exchange ideas and strategies across nations is the International Forum of Women Speakers of Parliament. This body works to enhance the visibility and effectiveness of women locally and internationally and also provides mentoring and support not only to each other, but also to other women MPs.

In addition to programes especially geared for women, orientation exercises involving both men and women are also important. In joint training sessions, women are encouraged to address their areas of interest and to network with male counterparts, as well as to learn how to break through established "codes of conduct". At the same time, male deputies are made aware of women's issues and the importance of enabling women deputies to act effectively in the legislature. The latter in particular is an important step in overcoming the sense of threat that many male deputies feel vis-à-vis women colleagues, since it provides an opportunity not only to raise awareness of gender issues, but to indicate the extent to which they are interlinked with most other social, economic and political concerns. Thus training and orientation of male parliamentarians plays an important role in the mainstreaming of women's issues and perspectives.

In addition to information about both the written and unwritten rules and procedures of parliament, women may also find training in voice projection and public speaking particularly helpful. Many women have difficulty speaking authoritatively and some find it difficult to make themselves heard in large legislative chambers. New entrants, in particular those in developing democracies, confess that they find it difficult to be given the opportunity to speak and to know the ins and outs of parliamentary speaking procedures. The effectiveness of former actress Glenda Jackson in the British House of Commons, for example, proves that a trained woman's voice can have as much impact as a man's. Some women MPs in established democracies have also organised media-training sessions. This involves, among other things, seminars and workshops where MPs are informed about "media-speak" and advised on how to network with media personalities and on which ones are more sympathetic to women's issues.

Institutional rules, customs and procedures determine the key legislative positions and functions such as committee assignments and participation in floor debates. Recruitment to these important positions may depend on any one or a combination of factors including party position, seniority and faction, ability, support for the government, national or local profile and issue expertise. While the appropriate strategy will depend to some extent on the number of women in the legislature, at a minimum women should identify key positions and functions and strategise on ways to get women into these positions. If existing channels are not open to promoting women into key positions, new avenues should be developed. In some countries, such avenues could be parliamentary or governmental women's committees. In other cases, nationwide umbrella organisations (non-governmental) or strong grassroots organisations can act as catalysts to get women into key areas. Further avenues could be opened through training and educational programes, or through pressure for representation by the media. International pressure could also be used to encourage governments to include women at all levels of power and decision-making. Knowledge about these positions and ways to get women in can be shared by mentoring, caucusing and networking. This enables women MPs to maximise their impact. Sympathetic men in crucial positions are invaluable allies.

Women in key positions not only enhance their own ability to make an impact but they also facilitate opportunities for other women to speak out. For example, a study of the Colorado State legislature measured differences in the speaking behavior of members of legislative committees by sex, seniority, interest and party. In one study it was found that women did better at controlling the dialogue and making themselves heard when other women were present, visible (sitting where they could be seen) and in positions of authority. This research also showed that male dominance of conversation, discussion and meetings enhanced their power and undermined that of women even where the formal positions of men and women legislators were equal.

One way of building women's careers and thus their advancement into key positions is by learning how to use the media to increase the visibility and confidence of women parliamentarians. Since women employed in the media field have their own problems of self-establishment and advancement they may be sympathetic to MPs interested in women's concerns. In fact, one of the key problems in the media is the lack of women in decision-making posts, which effectively means that decisions concerning editorial content and production issues are largely controlled by men. Hence there may be room for women MPs and media personalities to network on the basis of common interests and concerns.

Typically, women's interests have led them to what is still perceived as the less prestigious (and less powerful) social policy areas of specialisation, i.e., committee assignments such as education, health and family affairs. Many women MPs believe it is necessary to establish women's presence in the more prestigious and traditionally influential sites within parliaments, such as finance and foreign affairs. Others argue that the distinction itself cannot be justified.

Norwegian political scientists have made the important point that describing "soft" values as weak values ignores the facts that these areas, in which Nordic women are most active and in the majority, account for the largest share of public expenditure education, health and social services at local and regional levels. Women choose these areas because they prefer them and they accept making the very difficult decisions such as whether to prioritise care of the elderly or day care. The traditional distinction between "hard" and "soft" values is old-fashioned and inaccurate and should be contested by women representatives. Ideally a twofold strategy must be developed: on the one hand, the importance of such areas needs to be continually stressed; on the other hand, simultaneous efforts should be made to ensure women's active participation in all policy areas.

In order to discuss the impact of women representatives it is useful to make a distinction between women's issues and women's perspectives. Women's issues are issues that mainly affect women, either for biological reasons or for social reasons (e.g. sex equality or childcare policy). Women's perspectives are women's views on all political concerns. Some research indicates that although broadly the same issues are significant for both sexes, women's perspective on issues differs from that of men. For example, research carried out in Britain in 1996 showed that although both women and men prioritised economic issues, women were more concerned about part-time work, low pay and pension rights, while men were more concerned about unemployment.

MPs need to have knowledge and understanding about both women's issues and women's perspectives if only, as most contributors to this volume have expressed, to see the other half of reality in order to produce output that has a favorable impact on women. The kind of impact MPs will wish to have will inevitably vary by party. Professor Skjeie found that women representatives from different political parties emphasise women's issues such as childcare, but they do so from different perspectives and with different policy implications. Hence, conservative women, for example, stress women's needs as mothers, while those from the socialist parties stress their roles as workers.

But the need for knowledge and information exists regardless of party perspective. Women MPs have successfully used various means of becoming informed about women's issues and perspectives. Most important in this regard is what contributors to this volume have highlighted: maintaining close links with women's organisations of all kinds and drawing on their expertise and resources. Such linkages with the women's movement also enhance the legitimacy of MPs and keep them in touch with changing, often varying, women's concerns. Other sources of information are academic experts on different issue areas, particularly those working with women's studies, who are often willing to make their knowledge of issues available.

European parliamentarians have made use of the goodwill and knowledge of academic experts to draft policies on such matters as domestic violence, female bondage, care of children and the aged, pensions and women's health issues. Some of the most active pro-women European Union Commissioners, such as Swedish Anita Gradin, make a point of involving non-governmental organisations (NGOs) and academic experts in their work to further the women's issues through their respective portfolios and agendas. Some politicians keep themselves informed by sponsoring seminar series on the issues, a process that also extends their contacts and networks within the women's movement. Research on policy issues is a major political tool and can be gathered and used by MPs by participating in conferences organised by women's organisations, experts and politicians and by caucusing with other MPs who have similar interests. Caucusing by women MPs is part of both learning and using the rules. Deputies interested in a particular issue, for example employment or women's health, might meet to identify important upcoming votes and committee discussions and decide on tactics and strategies to influence the outcome.

Parliaments have their own distinct language, a product both of their specialised tasks and functions and also of their culture and their traditional male membership. For example, in Britain the House of Commons has a discourse characterised by a formal set of titles, modes of address and rules of debate. It has also acquired, from many years of male domination, a barracking, sexist and lavatorial "humour" that women MPs find offensive, especially when it is used on them. Familiarity with speaking and debating techniques can help to curtail such "yahoo" heckling. British women have successfully used the media to draw attention to the sexism in the House of Commons by revealing these practices to women in the media and to other journalists eager to criticise ill-behaved MPs. The result was a series of press and broadcasting items about the childish and sexist behavior of male MPs. The public, previously unaware of this, disapproved of their MPs' behavior.

1.3. Using the Rules

By learning how to use the rules, women can seize opportunities to participate on key committees and positions, make themselves heard in discussions and debates and fully utilise their skills and abilities.

Gaining familiarity with the rules is the first part of a longer term process to enhance women's position and to highlight women's issues and perspectives. The next step is to learn how to use the rules for maximum impact. One of the problems that many women parliamentarians face is that they are not allocated time in discussions and debates and they are not given the opportunity to participate on key committees and in key positions. Thus they are not able to fully utilise their skills and abilities and their contribution cannot be accurately assessed. By learning how to use the rules, together with other women deputies and the media, women can break this vicious circle. Many of the tactics for using the rules, discussed below, can be shared across national boundaries.

Intergovernmental organisations such as the Council of Europe, the Commonwealth Secretariat, the European Union, the United Nations and international NGOs can play a vital role in helping women learn how to use the rules by facilitating the sharing of information. Their meetings bring together experts and politicians to network and exchange ideas and their publications make these discussions about women's needs, strategies and achievements available to a wider audience.

Formal and informal parliamentary roles are often allocated by established rules and procedures. There is, nevertheless, some room for influence and intervention which women should maximise. For example, women MPs should make a point of nominating and voting for women in internal elections, of suggesting women's names for informal positions, and of drawing attention to the absence or relative absence of women in key positions. Particular attention should be given to opportunities available in committee work, as there is considerable evidence from the long-established democracies that women do better in committee work than in debating chambers. Having said this, women should not abandon debating chambers since this is where parliamentary reputations are often made and where the media often direct their sustained attention.

The skill of debating in general is a particularly important one and can be encouraged and sponsored through parliamentary networks linked up to schools, that is, through the curricula, as well as through leadership institutions. Women's parliamentary networks can also play a crucial role in supporting women speakers and in changing to less adversarial styles of debate. Since government careers tend to follow from legislative careers, the advancement of women through the range of committees and through the legislative hierarchy is an important component in their qualification for high office. Equal opportunity positions in government and ministries for women's affairs and their shadow counterparts in opposition parties, are other positions that have been well used by women politicians to advance their interests and their careers. For example, between 1992 and 1997 four Labor women MPs in the UK were shadow ministers for women. All four were appointed to important government positions (two at cabinet level) when Labor won the elections in 1997. This indicates that such positions need not be a ghetto for women, but may instead be a means of advancement.

Rules have been used to increase women's representation in a number of ways. In this area, a three-track strategy has proven effective:

— Pressure political parties to ensure that women are nominated for winnable seats in the legislature.
— Design procedural mechanisms to ensure the presence of women in the full range of parliamentary positions.
— Design legislation that creates new structures to ensure that women's interests are represented.

The expansion of political structures has proven an especially useful means of securing women's representation. In the Indian Government of June 1997, four posts were created in the central Government Ministry to introduce women into the newly created positions. In Britain, during the 1990s, the shadow cabinet was an elected body. Following pressure from women's advocates, Labor increased the size of the shadow cabinet and introduced a requirement that all ballots cast in shadow cabinet elections must include a minimum number of votes for women (first three, later expanded to four) or they would be invalid. This mechanism both ensured women's membership of the cabinet and their representation of various constituencies. When Labor won the general election in 1997, women members of the shadow cabinet were given full cabinet positions.

In Costa Rica, a practice that the Vice-President should be a woman has been established. Dutch experience shows that the creation of parliamentary committees on women's issues is one way of making positions available for women. Such committees scrutinise all legislation for their gendered content and thereby aid the extension of women's agendas. They also enhance awareness of the gendered nature of many political issues. The committees feed into the legislative process and also play a part in generating public discussion on such issues.

Concern has been expressed by women deputies in many countries that such devices may serve only to separate and "ghettoise" women's issues and the politicians who support them. Although ghettoisation may be a risk in the short term, experience indicates that over time, such work becomes accepted and, in fact, affirms and legitimises broader gender issues. Moreover women gain valuable experience by serving on women's committees, reserved places and women's ministries.

They may then extend their influence by working with other committees on different issues, for example by monitoring the implementation of the "Beijing Platform for Action" or the "European Union Medium-Term Action Plans on Equality between Women and Men". Women's committees need not be seen as permanent structures, but while in existence they enable women to display their skills and thus serve as launching platforms for careers in other political areas. Moreover, women who have experience on sex equality portfolios carry this increased awareness and knowledge of women's issues to other ministries, thus advancing the process of mainstreaming women's concerns.

How much can be accomplished necessarily depends on the number of women who are actually elected to parliament. But even small numbers of women MPs can have a major impact. Where there are only a few women the advantage of high visibility can be used both in placing women in key positions and in raising women's issues. High visibility sometimes brings unexpected benefits. One example is when UK Labor opposition leader Neil Kinnock was unable to subject Prime Minister Margaret Thatcher to sustained pressure, because although a gifted orator and debater, he felt inhibited by Thatcher's sex and his own ingrained habits of courtesy toward women. While he used his skills against powerful male adversaries, he was never able to direct them at her. Such benefits are likely only to be a temporary advantage.

Knowledge of procedural rules has frequently been used to influence the parliamentary agenda by introducing women's concerns into otherwise gender-blind debates – forcing debates on issues such as reproductive rights, equal pay, childcare– as well as by proposing sex equality legislation and amendments. Parliamentarians have established public enquiries into omen's status and condition, then used the results to push through legislative programes. Once the issues are on the agenda, the behavior of other politicians changes. After all, it is more difficult politically to come out against equality for women than it is to prevent equality issues from getting onto the agenda in the first place. The classic example of this occurred in the American Congress debate on the 1964 Civil Rights Bill. In order to prevent the bill from becoming law, anticivil-rights representatives proposed that sex equality be added to the race equality provisions of the bill. Their belief was that sex equality would help to sink the bill. In fact, once the sex equality amendment was accepted, few politicians were willing to oppose it publicly. Ironically, sex equality provisions may have helped the bill to pass. In some cases, activities such as co-sponsorship, speech-making and sponsorship of bills by women have been much more effective than their actual votes. One study looking at the support for women's issues in the 101st U.S. Congress found that, although differences in roll call voting on feminist issues between women and men were small, women were significantly more likely than men to co-sponsor feminist bills, to make speeches on behalf of feminist legislation and to sponsor feminist legislation.

There are many instances in some parts of the developing world however, where women MPs shy away from any association with bills on women. This is largely due to the lack of a critical mass, as explained earlier, as well as to a certain stigma associated with "those feminists". This further underscores the need for raising awareness about the interlinkage between women's issues and every other issue handled by parliament. The budgetary and economic interests for example, are not and should not be seen as only "male" concerns since they affect everyone. Similarly, health, social welfare and education do not only affect women. It is interesting to note that such limited perceptions of social issues may actually reflect an old political hierarchy which places "external affairs" on a higher pedestal than the internal condition of citizens – a reason why the current and largely scholarly, concern with issues of citizenship deserves the attention of both men and women deputies.

In certain countries, cultural norms of equality between men and women, or discourse on rights, meritocracy and conventions about representation may be avenues that can be used to alter parliamentary balances. For example, research in the U.S. on legislative elections following the Anita Hill– Clarence Thomas hearings reveals a major increase in the number of women candidates, in support for women candidates from women voters and in public and media attention that women candidates received. Public discussions of the Hill–Thomas hearings highlighted the absence of women from the Senate and from other high offices, the research suggests. Images of a male Senate committee cross-examining Anita Hill about her experiences of sexual harassment contributed to making the representation of women in government a major theme of the subsequent election in 1992, which the press dubbed the "year of the woman".

Danish women deputies have also succeeded in altering the parliamentary discourse. Drude Dahlerup notes how prior to the entry of significant numbers of women into the Scandinavian parliaments, most politicians did not have the vocabulary to speak about issues such as discrimination, inequality, sexual harassment or sexual violence. Most had problems even using the word for women and preferred to use euphemisms. Today, Nordic politicians know how to say the word for woman. Over time in the Nordic states the increased presence of women has altered the style of campaigning, bringing in expressions of warmth and compassion as well as family references. This does render it less adversarial. In the Netherlands, study of legislative debates reveals how women's interventions have been associated with changing the way in which abortion policy is debated, notably its shift from a medical or religious issue to an issue of choice.

The participation of women politicians in major international conferences has also had an important effect on challenging public notions of what women can do. One example is the way in which perceptions about the women's movement in Egypt and in other Arab countries changed following the International Conference on Population and Development (ICPD) that was held in Cairo in September 1994. Prior to this conference, many Egyptian women MPs and indeed the general public, had at best been ignorant of the women's movement and at worst been downright disdainful of its capabilities. Those involved in the women's movement held a similar view of women parliamentarians. The ICPD was an opportunity for women MPs to actually witness what women's NGOs had managed to accomplish and to network with them on issues of common interest. It also enabled the women's movement to realise that they could have potential allies in women MPs since they shared many interests and goals. Regardless of what may have actually happened later on, at least there was a perceptible change in awareness on the part of both the MPs and the women's organisations. Equally important was a shift in public awareness and perception of women as activists and as politicians. The ICPD demonstrated to the general public that women's issues (whether it was changes in family law, reproductive rights, or female circumcision) were part of their general concerns and that rather than a bunch of loose women ciamouring for change, those articulating these concerns were capable and intelligent women who deserved to be listened to and taken seriously. Women's issues and the women's perceptions gained a certain credibility that was not on the agenda of public consciousness prior to this international networking event.

1.4. Women's Parliamentary Roles

Women's experiences in a variety of parliamentary roles will build up political capital which can be used to secure further advancement, to help change existing rules and structures and to assist new generations of women politicians.

The presence of women and the introduction of women's concerns will inevitably challenge existing arrangements and procedures. At a minimum, parliamentary timetables, places of meeting, childcare provisions, working hours and travel arrangements may be changed to make these more suitable for women.

Changes in parliamentary structures and procedures might include the introduction of proportionality norms for men's and women's membership in committees, the establishment of women's whips (responsible for organising the parliamentary votes of women in a particular party) and formal or informal quotas for women in various legislative positions.

Quota systems have been used effectively in Germany at local and national levels and via political parties in France and Belgium. In countries where compulsory quotas are politically difficult, voluntary targets can be set. These should be dated with realistic timetables for implementation. Mechanisms to monitor the implementation of quotas that are accountable to the assembly should be established. This ensures that regular discussions on progress are part of the parliamentary timetable. Setting up committees on women's issues and national sex-equality offices that are also accountable to parliament have similar effects.

Accountability to parliament ensures that their work is scrutinised, debated and publicised, providing numerous additional opportunities for discussion of women's concerns. For example, the

South African government has implemented a national machinery that proposes changes in legislation and which supervises and ensures implementation, through a system of checks and balances. The case of South Africa reveals how simultaneous functions, both inside and outside parliament, can operate – in South Africa a new constitution was drafted, a woman's empowerment programe was set up in consultation with women parliamentarians and an Office for the Status of Women was created to mainstream women's concerns and ensure follow-up.

A Commission on Gender Equality was also established in 1997 to promote gender equality and to advise and make recommendations to Parliament or any other legislature with regard to any laws or proposed legislation which affects gender equality and the status of women. An important challenge is to ensure that these institutional mechanisms maintain their links with grassroots activists, so that MPs are aware of what takes place outside parliamentary walls.

Changes in procedure can be effective in and of themselves and they can also have a wider impact on society. For example, Janet Beilstein formerly from the United Nations Department for the Advancement of Women (UNDAW) reported to the August 1997 International IDEA conference in Stockholm that when a woman raises her hand to speak in discussions in the German Bundestag she is automatically shifted to the top of the list of male speakers. This practice seeks to overcome women's diffidence about speaking in male-dominated groups by maximising their opportunities to participate.

It has become so ingrained in MPs that they repeat the practice even when they are outside of parliament. More fundamental changes involve changing the way in which certain issues, namely those closer to women's concerns and in which women have an expertise (e.g. education, welfare policy, family policy) are viewed in the parliamentary hierarchy. The distinction between "hard" and "soft" issues is difficult to sustain and is likely to break down. This process will develop from increased interest in "soft" issues by all politicians, as women deputies become more successful in pushing them up the parliamentary agenda. Agenda changes are closely related to output changes.

Networks of women MPs have been successful in changing candidate selection rules to assist women's access to political office. Special measures such as quotas or minimum proportion rules for both sexes on candidate lists, reserved places for women and earmarked public funds for political parties have been operationalised. Political parties have been at the centre of most of the effective strategies to enhance women's representative capacities. Parties have developed strategies to promote women internally into decision-making positions in the party organisation and externally into elected assemblies and public appointments. Generally they have been more radical, committed and imaginative in devising policies to bring women into internal party positions than to nominate women as candidates for elected office. Their most effective action has been the introduction of various kinds of quota.

Quotas are, in most cases, temporary measures designed to overcome imbalances that exist between men and women. They are an effort to change the political equilibrium between women and men. In 1992, quotas were used by at least 56 political parties in 34 countries according to the Inter-Parliamentary Union. The two countries with the highest levels of women's representation in 2002 (Sweden and Denmark), both include parties that have used voluntary quotas of some kind. Often quotas are introduced in a two-stage process. First, minimum proportions of women are set for internal bodies; then, with the support of the newly installed women officials, they are extended to the party's lists of candidates.

— In Denmark, the first party to introduce quotas was the People's Socialist Party, which agreed in 1977 that all party bodies and electoral assemblies should have a minimum representation of 40 percent from each sex. In 1979, 64 percent of the party's representatives in parliament were women. In 1984, quotas were introduced for the selection of candidates for the European Parliament and in 1988 they were introduced for local elections.

— Norway also began with quotas for women for party boards, which made it much easier later to adopt quotas for elected bodies.

Both the level of compulsion and the size of a quota can be raised incrementally as the idea gains acceptance.

— The German Sozialdemokratische Partei Deutschlands (SPD) has a quota of 40 percent for internal party councils and committees. Since 1998, the SPD has sought to achieve a minimum 40 percent representation of each gender in all functions and mandates within the party.

— The Dutch Labor Party adopted a recommendation that 25 percent of all seats inside and outside the party should be held by women. In 1985, the recommendation was strengthened to become an official quota. The quota was raised in the 1990s to 30 percent representation and in 1998 the Party Board adopted a further recommendation that 50 percent of candidates' lists at the national level should be comprised of women.

— The British Labor Party agreed in 1989 to introduce quotas for women on all internal bodies, sometimes by increasing the size of the body, sometimes not. By 1993 it was possible to introduce a policy of all women short-lists in half of the party's vacant winnable seats, a policy that was overturned by the courts at the beginning of 1996.

Mechanisms for quotas vary by the type of electoral system. In single-member constituency first-past-the-post systems there are relatively few options, but in party list systems devices such as women's lists, placing women at high positions on closed lists and "zip lists" (a woman in every other position) are often used. The policy to enhance women's representation is most controversial where the introduction of new women means displacing men who are already established.

One way of avoiding such displacement is by increasing the size of the relevant representative body; another way is to create new organisations for women. When the British Labor Party introduced compulsory votes for women into its shadow cabinet election rules it also increased the size of the shadow cabinet. Similarly when it introduced new regional policy forums, these had minimum proportions of women members. This effect extends well beyond legislation as parliaments have been used to promote media discussion of feminist and other women's issues in the media. The spread of images of political women has increased public expectations that there will be a substantial "feminisation" of parliament, which will in turn result in discussions on equal political representation.

In general, European governments have been reluctant to introduce laws compelling quotas of women in electoral office. France and Belgium are exceptions.

In June 1999, the French constitution was amended, whereby the law now "favors the equal access of women and men to electoral mandates and elected offices and positions". The parity principle requires that 50 percent of candidates on lists forwarded for election must be women, otherwise lists of candidates will be rejected, or political parties will face financial sanctions.

One clear indication that women have influenced output is the fact that quotas exist for women in political parties and parliament. Output changes are inevitable as women become more and more effective in promoting women's issues and concerns. Once women's issues are raised and sustained on the agenda, they rapidly secure the interest of all politicians. This interest can apply to a wide host of issues: political, economic, social and even cultural.

Recent research indicates that the most effective way to influence output and promote women's equality is to provide financial incentives to programes geared towards women. For example, to enhance the education of girls, the Indian Government pledged to match and double any contribution made to the building of girls' schools. The Dutch Government previously used the system of public funding of political parties to earmark special funding for the promotion of women candidates by all parties. South Africa has introduced a women's budget to fund projects that cater to the particular needs and interests of women.

The most important change affecting discourse has been the overturning of implicit rules limiting appropriate topics of debate to matters in the "public" sphere. In cooperation with women's movements, parliamentarians in some countries have extended the agenda of legislatures to discussions of domestic violence, stalking, rape, consent in marriage and the rights of lesbian mothers. Further change in the area of discourse can come about once women themselves become increasingly proud of their identities as women. In her article in a Dutch feminist magasine, European parliamentarian Hedy D'Ancona surveys some of the mcst influential women Euro-MPs. She argues that by not being shy of their "womanhood", but rather being proud of their identity as women, women have enhanced their work, impact and performance. Women are often apologetic rather than proud or assertive of their identity as women. A change in a woman politician's self- perception, Shvedova maintains, remains key to changing public perception and reaction to women and their contributions.

A woman's sex identity and her "outsider" status can even enhance electoral attractiveness, particularly in times of constitutional crisis. As new political entrants, women are often not associated with the corrupt and autocratic practices of collapsing regimes. Instead they can become symbols of modernity, honesty, democracy and caring, all images that are invaluable to reform movements.

The process of increasing the proportion of women in legislatures is part of a larger phenomenon of changing political images so that politics starts to be regarded as a normal activity for women. To take hold, such an attitude-shift requires reinforcement in the mass media and agreement within the women's movement that politics is an appropriate activity for women.

1.5. Measuring Women's Performance

To claim that women representatives make a difference in political processes, it is necessary to establish clear criteria to measure their impact. A fundamental component of such criteria is that women parliamentarians act, at least some of the time, in women's interests. In formulating such criteria, it should also be recognised that: (1) there are many, sometimes conflicting, women's interests to be represented; and (2) that the very presence of women in a traditional male environment creates gender awareness and alters expectations.

What women can actually achieve will vary according to their numbers in parliament. Numbers are always an important, a necessary, if not sufficient criteria for sustained impact. As Dahlerup has said, it takes a substantial minority of women to ensure that critical acts of representation are undertaken. As the numbers of women grow we should expect increased participation by women in all aspects of parliamentary life, including interventions in debate, the proposing and sponsoring of legislation, access to parliamentary resources and occupancy of leading positions.

One criteria for determining success is that women's impact must be detectable in legislation on women's issues; this will become more prominent and frequent as women become more and more active and effective. Furthermore, with women's growing effectiveness, all legislation will increasingly take women's perspectives into account. An especially telling indication of women's impact will be an increase in men raising women's issues and exhibiting sensitivity to women's perspectives.

An important facet of success will involve interaction between the different agents of change: governments, women MPs, women's organisations and other members of civil society, locally, regionally and internationally. It should always be remembered that partnership between women and men is a key ingredient in the process of change and impact. Many women MPs openly acknowledge that to attempt to work alone, without men, is not feasible.

1.6. Strategies to Enhance Impact

The following are some of the main strategies to help women maximise their power and effectiveness as representatives

1. *Raise awareness*. Campaigns with the media should focus public attention on the importance of balanced participation and representation of women and men. Political parties or women's organisations could be financed to mount such campaigns and related activities. NGOs interested in encouraging the participation of women in political life have often been active in awareness raising. To encourage such campaigns, women and men politicians must be proactive in identifying and establishing relations and promoting these issues with key members of civil society as well as with media producers and presenters. An example of this is the "Movement for Equal Rights – Equal Responsibilities" in Cyprus which aims to promote public awareness that women can be politicians.

2. *Work in partnership with men*. This entails designing programes, whether inside or outside specific political forums, that take into account men's concerns and perspectives with respect to solidarity with women politicians. This idea is now gaining credibility with the growing realisation that women need the

support of their male colleagues, partners and electorate to enhance the effectiveness of their strategies and increase the value of their social and political message.

3. *Enlarge the pool of eligible*, aspirant women. This means enhancing women's interest in becoming politicians as well as increasing their involvement in politics. Eligibility for and involvement in politics are partly a matter of access to general resources such as education, income and time; and partly a matter of specific resources such as knowledge and information about politics and political experience. Policies to enhance women's access to higher education, to paid employment and to various social and economic organisations provide a context for political participation that is increasingly hospitable to women. However, even where they lack adequate resources to participate politically, women are devising creative strategies to mobilise resources that would facilitate their access. For example, in India, some women draw upon transitional networks of extended family, neighbourhood links and other "women-centred" spheres to enable them to gather the resources they may require.
4. *Take positive action*. Quotas have been particularly effective in increasing women's presence in legislatures. In Sweden, women used several means to press their parties to nominate women candidates and place them in favorable positions on party lists. One way was to simply put forward women's names, a tactic that was very important in the early stages. They also conducted campaigns to promote women candidates and issued proposals to get women into better positions on party lists. Finally, they acted as watchdogs and protested whenever reversals occurred. This process of securing substantial increases in women's electoral fortunes was achieved without recourse to formal compulsory quotas. Recommendations, arguments and the threat to press for quotas succeeded in setting targets requiring women to get 40 percent of the nominations. Once these targets were set, considerable progress was achieved.
5. *Amend laws to allow positive discrimination*. Such practices are rare in politics. In general, governments do not use the law to compel parties to promote women, not least because such policies often run against other legal principles. The latest defeat in the

British courts of the British Labor Party's policy of "forcing" women onto their lists (simply because they are women) in order to increase their numbers in parliament and in the party itself is not unusual. In Italy, the 1993 law to impose quotas of women on candidate's lists was overturned by the constitutional court in 1995; a similar regulation by the French Socialist Party was overturned in 1982. However, some countries have introduced laws requiring that women hold a certain proportion of seats on government-appointed bodies. Such laws were introduced in Denmark in 1985, Finland in 1987, Sweden in 1987, Norway in the 1980s, the Netherlands in 1992 and Germany in 1994. Published statistics in these countries indicate that women's participation in such bodies has risen steadily since. Governments can also use incentives. This is particularly easy where there is state funding of political parties. For example, the Dutch Government was able to make financial support for political parties dependent on their efforts to increase the proportion of women in their electoral bodies.

6. *Raise the general standard of living and access to resources of all women.* The high achievements of Scandinavian women stem from a combination of government policy, party initiative and demographic changes. The remarkable position of women in Scandinavian politics rests on social/demographic foundations involving considerable changes in the structure of women's family, economic and social lives. These are probably irreversible. The policies on equality of representation have included government equality reforms operating in conjunction with the influence of the women's movement, functioning both autonomously and through the political parties. To some extent there is feedback between demographic and political change as policies have included explicit attempts to change demographics and the gendered division of labor both in the family and in paid employment.

7. *Build and maintain links with women's organisations.* The maintenance of ties to the women's movement is crucial both for their support and for information on issues; similarly, the women's movement needs bases in political parties and in the legislature.

8. *Caucus and network.* This allows women MPs to share information, ideas, resources and support. Networks may be party-based, cross party (very rare), local, regional and international. Meetings, conferences, seminars, newsletters and electronic mail links are useful networking devices. Consultations with women's organisations and research gauging the needs of women (demand) and their practical constraints (supply), enable women MPs to target their efforts to activities that will be most useful and effective.
9. *Use the mass media effectively.* Women MPs must use the mass media, particularly the resources offered by organised media women broadcasters, editors and journalists, to communicate their concerns and highlight relevant issues. As well as enhancing the image of women MPs and promoting their political ideas, the mass media is instrumental in educating and mobilising voters, particularly in rural areas – an important concern particularly in developing countries where women, with limited resources, may have difficulty reaching out to these voters.
10. *Establish women's committees and other machinery accountable to the legislature.* This provides opportunities for women deputies to gain experience and for women's issues and perspectives to be debated and publicised.
11. *Collect, monitor and disseminate statistics and facts about women's political participation and representation.* This enables women's advocates in parliament to analyse the position of women in decision-making and to define problems, devise appropriate solutions and seek political support for their preferred solutions. In particular, a collation of data on how women MPs have actually managed to make a difference through their legislatures is an ongoing need.
12. *Mainstream gender issues.* Ensure that gender issues are integrated within different political, social and economic concerns, in order to reveal the interdependency and linkages with other issue areas.

The ultimate objective of enhancing the quality of women's political participation is a goal that must be worked towards constantly. Much the same way as men's political input is in constant need of improvement, women should not be complacent about their contributions to the political process; nor should they take whatever gains achieved for granted. Political participation is a process that is evolving and developing. The actors involved in this process should be prepared always to strive to keep ahead of the changes. The women and men involved in this process should work together to be agents of change, constantly aware that obstacles are but means to realise new and evolving strategies. Women and men politicians have achieved a great deal in the area of women's participation. Politicians of both sexes have contributed to advancing women's political participation in general and within legislative structures in particular. Although the road ahead is long, the lessons learned from the accumulation of experiences, can and will, significantly illuminate and facilitate the many paths ahead.

1.7. Strengthening Women's Participation in Parliament

The Inter-Parliamentary Union (IPU) works to enhance and promote democracy by strengthening the institution of parliament. Created in 1889, it brings together more than 140 national parliaments from across the globe.

The IPU believes that the balanced participation of men and women in the management of public affairs is central to any democracy. Article 4 of its 1997 Universal Declaration of Democracy states that:

> The achievement of democracy presupposes a genuine partnership between men and women in the conduct of the affairs of society in which they work in equality and complementarity, drawing mutual enrichment from their differences.

This principle guides the organisation's work; over the past 30 years, the IPU has developed numerous activities aimed at promoting women's participation in, and bolstering the contribution that they can make to, parliament. It conducts surveys and produces research on women in parliament; it monitors the percentage of women in national parliaments and publishes a monthly status report; it facilitates contact between women parliamentarians and encourages them to share their experiences; and it organises technical assistance projects in specific countries. Finally, it promotes the participation of women parliamentarians within its own structures, the ultimate goal being equality in participation, as enshrined in its statutes.

Indeed, the IPU is one of the few international organisations if not the only one to have adopted specific measures and mechanisms to promote gender equality within its ranks. In December 2004, women made up a mere 15 percent of parliamentarians worldwide. In contrast, at the last IPU Assembly, held in Geneva, Switzerland, in October 2004, 28.7 percent of participants were women, close to the 30 percent target set by the United Nations (UN).

The participation of women within the IPU has never been as strong as it is today. This is due to the existence of a strong movement complemented with specific actions, which can be regarded as affirmative action measures or quotas.

1.7.1. IPU's Position on Quotas

The IPU does not see quotas as the prime means of enhancing women's participation in politics. It prefers gradual change to mandatory measures. However, the organisation recognises that, when faced with deadlock and slow change, quotas, insofar as they are temporary special measures, are sometimes the only way forward.

The organisation's position on affirmative action and quotas is set out in its Plan of Action to correct imbalances in the participation of men and women in political life, adopted by the Inter-Parliamentary Council in 1994. The Plan of Action states that:

> On a strictly interim basis, these measures may include affirmative action measures. Wherever the measure chosen is a quota system, it is proposed that the quota should not target women but that, in a spirit of equity, it may be established that neither sex may occupy a proportion of seats inferior to a given percentage.

In 1994, this represented quite an important stand for an international organisation to take. The balanced approach to women's participation is noteworthy, and is consistent with the IPU's promotion of gender partnership. It is also in keeping with the Convention on the Elimination of Ali Forms of Discrimination against Women (CEDAW), which also introduces, in Article 4, the notion of 'temporary special measures aimed at accelerating de facto equality between men and women'.

Since 1994, the IPU's position on quotas has not changed. Its resolutions regularly mention affirmative action measures, and even set targets to achieve gender equality in politics. In a resolution adopted as recently as October 2004, on parliament's role in implementing the Beijing objectives, the IPU 'strongly urges parliamentarians to promote a stronger presence of women in political parties and at all levels of decision-making through the adoption, for example, of quota systems or other forms of affirmative action'.

Clearly, the IPU considers quotas and affirmative action measures to be useful mechanisms to make progress in areas characterised by gridlock and to encourage women's participation in parliament.

However, utilising such mechanisms within the IPU has required time, effort and persuasive argument. Indeed, when the idea was raised in the IPU, in the early 1990s, it led to much debate and opposition. This was also the case in 1999 when the subject resurfaced. Affirmative action at any rate can be a controversial issue, all the more so in the context of an international organisation.

At that time, though, one thing had become clear to the IPU: women's participation within the organisation was not increasing at a satisfactory pace.

In 1947, women made up only 1.2 percent of delegates at the conference in Cairo, Egypt. Some improvement had been made by 1975, with women comprising 7.8 percent of delegates at the 62nd conference in London. Progress remained slow up to 1990, when the figure stood at 12 percent.

Women's participation was also extremely weak and unsatisfactory in the IPU's other decision-making bodies, the Executive Committee and the Governing Council. The first woman to be elected to the Executive Committee was Marina Molina Rubio of Guatemala, in October 1987, almost a century after the organisation was established. It was not until 1999 that a woman, Najma Heptulla, Speaker ad interim of the Indian Upper House, was elected President of the IPU.

Furthermore, no significant progress was made in the number of women participating at the national level. Although the organisation had only a limited direct impact on women's participation in national parliaments, it was clear that reform within the IPU could also serve as an incentive to promote women's participation nationally and internationally. Ensuring greater participation of women parliamentarians within the IPU:

— Set an example at the international level;

— Encouraged change at the national level; and

— Led to improvements in the functioning and work of the IPU.

1.7.2. Affirmative Action Measures

Following a three-year consultative process, the IPU adopted, in 2001, a number of affirmative action measures and quotas intended to strengthen women's participation within the organisation:

— A straightforward quota system was introduced for elections to the Executive Committee – 20 percent of its elected members must now be women;

— A gender-neutral target was adopted for the Governing Council, which, if strictly applied ensures that representatives of each sex account for at least 30 percent of its members. Each delegation is entitled to three members (and, therefore, three votes), provided that men and women are included in the delegation. Where this is not the case, the Member Parliament's voting rights and number of delegates on the Council are reduced by one (i.e. one-third of the total); and

— Delegations that attend IPU Assemblies without representatives of both sexes on three consecutive occasions lose some of their voting rights and see their officially registered numbers reduced.

It must also be pointed out that the IPU statutes also limit participation in the Executive Committee to MPs from states that have granted women the right to vote and to stand for election.

These measures seek to enhance women's participation in the IPU quantitatively and qualitatively.

1.7.3. Participatory Process

What factors are behind the increase in women's participation in the IPU? Simply put, strong political will has been in evidence within the IPU, and there has been greater awareness of the need for, and the benefits of, gender equality within the parliaments of member states.

Several of the measures adopted in 2001 by IPU bodies had already been proposed in one form or another a decade earlier, mainly by women parliamentarians. At that time, these proposals were seen as too forceful and thus were rejected. Ten years later, the context was very different, and definitely more favorable to the adoption of such measures.

By 2001, there was a general framework that was conducive to change within the IPU. The existence of a strong women's movement and the necessary political will was crucial. The process was also an inclusive and transparent one.

1.7.4. Women's Movement

The increased presence and influence of women within the IPU cannot be dissociated from the recent adoption of quota measures. The women's movement in the IPU has grown over the years and today is an important element in the IPU's decision-making process. It all began with the establishment of the regular Meeting of Women Parliamentarians, which was the product of some ten years of struggle. The first Meeting of Women Parliamentarians was held in 1985. This served as a concrete incentive to send more women to IPU meetings and, as a result, the percentage of women MPs in IPU meetings rose slightly in the late 1980s before slowing down again. The Meeting of Women Parliamentarians brings together women parliamentarians from around the world to discuss specific gender issues and to make an impact on the work of the IPU. Its action and support was vital to the adoption of quota measures by the IPU.

1.7.5. Political Support at Highest Level

At its highest decision-making level, the IPU could not be more politically supportive of greater participation by women within the organisation. Participation by women has been high on the agenda of all recent IPU presidents. Their approach has always been one of partnership and gender equality. The IPU President Sergio Páez Verdugo (Chile), under whose leadership the affirmative action measures were adopted, stated that: 'Modern societies will only be more humane and more equitable when all of their subjects are actively involved in the decision-making process'.

It must also be noted that the question of women's participation within the IPU has become increasingly prominent over the years. Reports on the number of women participants, the number of 'single-sex delegations' and the qualitative participation of women, have been regularly presented and discussed in the plenary session of the Governing Council raising awareness among delegates.

1.7.6. Gender Equality

Many of the measures encouraging women's participation in the IPU were introduced as part of a broader reform package. Gender equality was one of several items proposed with a view to improving the functioning of the IPU. Hence it was discussed by all concerned, and was seen as the responsibility of all.

The Gender Partnership Group, itself comprising two men and two women members of the IPU Executive Committee, spearheaded the affirmative action measures linked to participation in the IPU Assembly. Set up in 1997, this body was charged with ensuring that the policies and functioning of the IPU took into account the needs of both men and women on an equal basis. It started by examining the participation of women in delegations to IPU meetings. At that time, the novelty of the Meeting of Women Parliamentarians was beginning to wear off and the rate of women's participation at IPU events was starting to level off. Including men in the process to elaborate and adopt affirmative action measures proved critical. It made it possible to avoid marginalisation of the issue and to incorporate the perspective of men.

1.7.7. Inclusive and Consultative Process

The affirmative action measures were adopted following an inclusive and consultative three-year process, ending in 2001. Initially, the Gender Partnership Group's recommendations were not far reaching, merely encouraging delegations to include women. Gradually, it began to discuss affirmative action measures and the possibility of imposing sanctions for non-compliance. These ideas were shared with the IPU membership at three assemblies. Members' comments were widely circulated and the Gender Partnership Group discussed them. Some suggestions were accepted while others were rejected. When a proposal was rejected, an explanation was given to all members.

The consultative process revealed a wide range of opinions on how best to ensure women's participation and gender balance at IPU events. Many IPU members were opposed to insisting that delegations to the conference/assembly have a specific gender composition, and instead called for a voluntary system. Others felt that only a more rigid and mandatory system (involving sanctions) would be effective. The IPU therefore devised a hybrid system, which would not impose a mandatory quota on each delegation, but would introduce sanctions if a delegation consistently ignored the need to ensure gender balance.

Consequently, a consultative and transparent process turned out to be key to the adoption of the quota measures. These could hardly be contested, as they were the product of the work of the entire IPU membership. The process also had to be consultative and transparent in order to take into account the various points of view of the IPU membership, and to reflect differences in cultures and traditions.

The affirmative action measures were adopted in 2002 and restrictions on voting rights and representation were applied as early as October 2003. While it is too early to draw any conclusions on the effect of these measures, the following observations can be made:

— The participation of women in IPU Assemblies and on the Governing Council and the Executive Committee has increased significantly over the past five years or since the process was launched. The participation of women in the IPU Assembly almost reached 30 percent in 2004. However, what is most notable is the decrease in the number of 'single-sex delegations'. True, some parliaments send delegations with only one female member in order to avoid sanctions and the ultimate objective of equal representation within delegations has yet to be met;
— Putting the question of women's participation in the IPU on the organisation's agenda (especially within the framework of its

reform process) has raised IPU members' awareness of gender equality in politics. Today, gender equality is more prominent in IPU debates, although there is still room for improvement;

— These measures have had an indirect effect on the composition of elected bodies and positions within the IPU. Greater effort is now made to ensure that appointed posts are gender balanced (for instance, the members of drafting committees and the rapporteurs of standing committees).

Interestingly, the main reservations expressed vis-à-vis the mechanisms in place at the IPU focus on sanctioning as opposed to facilitating change. While the first option (sanctioning) was eventually adopted, the second approach was nevertheless considered necessary to encourage more long-term change at the IPU and in national parliaments.

To maximise the impact at the national level, the IPU has been active in different areas. The Gender Partnership Group has initiated a series of hearings with delegations from national parliaments that have no women members. The aim is to establish a dialogue, assess difficulties, encourage progress, evaluate needs and identify if and how the IPU can aid women's participation. Preliminary hearings have been held with parliaments from the Gulf States and those Pacific Island states where no women are present in parliament.

1.7.8. From the International to the National Scene

Quotas are not the only solution available. A number of other measures to facilitate women's participation should complement them, both within the IPU and in national parliaments. After all, that is the ultimate goal.

The IPU has thus attempted to encourage debate on the means of promoting women's participation in parliament. IPU meetings, particularly the Meeting of Women Parliamentarians, serve as useful forums for the exchange of ideas and for debate on the effectiveness of steps taken at the national level. These meetings are also useful for disseminating data and ensuring that men and women are aware of tools that exist in this field. The quota database of the International Institute for Democracy and Electoral Assistance (IDEA) is an excellent example of a tool that is of value to MPs, politicians and parliamentary staff considering what measures to develop in their own countries.

It is also important to provide MPs with a broader approach to quotas and to focus on how to justify such measures and implement them. A better understanding of the rights included in CEDAW can be helpful. The IPU has produced, with the UN, a handbook for parliamentarians The Convention for the Elimination of All Forms of Discrimination against Women and it Optional Protocol — a handbook for parliamentarians on that particular subject and organises seminars for MPs grappling with the issue.

Quotas must not be an objective per se, but a mechanism to ensure the participation of a greater number of women in politics or within the IPU. They provide for a quantitative leap, to attain the goal of effective gender equality in politics, and need to be accompanied by a series of other measures, which range from awareness-raising to the training of women and the development of gender-sensitive environments both within national parliaments and the IPU

The IPU has therefore developed more comprehensive programes for women in parliament at the national level. These may include the development of quotas, but this is just one initiative. National technical assistance projects to support women in politics have also been established.

References

Dahlerup, Drude. 1988. "From a Small to a Large Minority: Theory of Critical Mass", *Scandinavian Political Studies*. Vol. 11. No. 4. pp. 275–298.

Dodson, Debra L. 1991. *Gender and Policy Making: Studies of Women in Office*. New Jersey: Centre for the American Woman and Politics, Eagleton Institute, Rutgers University.

Karvonen L. and Per Selle. eds. 1995. *Women in Nordic Politics: Closing the Gap*. London: Dartmouth Press. Inter-Parliamentary Union. 1997. *Men and Women in Politics: Democracy Still in the Making*. Geneva.

Leijenaar, Monique. 1996. *How to Create a Gender Balance in Political Decision Making*. Brussels: European Commission.

2

Women in Local Government

The role of women in leadership positions has been the focus of much debate in the last two decades. At the international level, the United Nations conferences on women have, in particular, advocated the need to increase the number of women in decision-making positions, not only to ensure that women's interests are represented but also because of growing evidence that women's involvement improves the way in which leadership and decision-making is practised.

Within the Asia and Pacific region the initiatives to encourage women's political participation have, up until now, focused mainly on women's leadership at central government level. However, women have always been an integral part of their communities and they take a very active role in village life, community organisations, towns and cities. Local government is much closer to this level of participation and is often a first step into a political decision making arena in which real differences can be made.

This chapter draws a picture of women's involvement in local government in the Asia and Pacific region. It is based on 13 country reports prepared for the United Nations Economic and Social Commission for Asia and the Pacific and highlights continuing barriers to women's involvement in local government, initiatives that have increased women's participation and the transformative leadership that women provide in local government. It also discusses regional and country-level strategies for increasing women's involvement in local government.

The participation and representation of women in local government has been poorly documented in Asia and the Pacific, as it has been internationally. In recognising the importance of women's involvement in decision-making in this tier of government and the need to develop local and regional strategies to increase this involvement, the United Nations Economic and Social Commission for Asia and the Pacific initiated a project in 2000 to document and increase awareness of the current situation as well as to identify strategies that will increase the number of women in local government. An Expert Group was established to prepare State of Women in Local Government reports for selected countries in South and East Asia and the Pacific. The Expert Group comprised selected women from the following countries: Australia, Bangladesh, China, India, Indonesia, Japan, Malaysia, Nepal, New Zealand, Pakistan, Philippines, Sri Lanka, Thailand and Vietnam. This group met in Thailand in June 2000 to discuss preparation of these reports.The objective of these country reports was to document the situation and the perspectives of women in local government; to increase the awareness of the transformative role women can play in local government; and highlight the issues and constraints they face while working with and leading local government. The details of the studies are described in ths chapter.

International data collected on the extent of women's participation in government at both local and central levels shows that, despite some improvements in some parts of the world in the last two decades, women are still profoundly under-represented. For women in Asia and the Pacific, the picture is similar. The highest percentage of women in local government seats is 33.3 percent and the lowest is 2 percent. Women have had the most success in the South Asia and the East Asia and Pacific sub-regions while the South-East Asia sub-region has the lowest numbers of women. As the following discussion will show the reasons for this are related to a number of factors:

— The length of time women have had the right to vote and participate;
— Political and electoral arrangements;
— Whether or not there is a quota of reserved seats for women;
— The level of development in a country; and the social and economic circumstances in which women live.

2.1. Women in Local Bodies of South Asia

As Table 1. shows, in three countries in this sub -region (India, Nepal and Bangladesh) women hold between 24 and 33 percent of seats in local authorities. These statistics are directly related to the introduction of quota systems for women in the local government systems in these countries. The impact of these quotas can be seen when compared with the much lower percentages of women in other levels of government and in management positions.

Table 1. Women in Local Government in South Asia, 2000

Country	Year women were eligible to vote and stand for Local Government	Women in Local Government seats (% of total)	Women Mayors (% of total)	Women in senior manag-ment po-sitions	Women in Central Govern-ment (% of total)
Sri Lanka	1938	2	0	13.7	5.3
India	1947	33.3	-	-	7.9
Pakistan	1970	33	-	-	2.9
Nepal	1955	24.1	0	2.3	7.9
Bangladesh	1947	33.3	0	3.8	11.2

2.1.1. Sri Lanka

At the local government level, Sri Lanka has both provincial and local government. There are three types of local authorities at the local level: 14 Municipal Councils, 37 Urban Councils and 258 Pradeshiya Sabhas, the alter being rurally based. Elections are run on a proportional representation system and there is a requirement that 40 percent of the candidates on the nomination lists are required to be between the ages of 18 and 35 years. This is to ensure youth representation on local authorities. Women hold 4 percent of provincial council seats and 2 percent of municipal and urban council seats. So far there have been 3 women mayors although there are none at present. Slightly more women have been appointed to management positions in local government an average of 9.5 percent at provincial level and 23.3 percent at local level (13.7 percent in the top positions). At central government level there are 12 women MPs (5.3 percent), the highest decision-making positions (President and, until recently, the Prime Minister) are held by women, and two other women hold ministerial responsibilities for women's affairs, social services, health, trade and food.

2.1.2. India

India has three types of urban local government: municipal corporations for cities with more than 0.3 million people; municipal councils for towns smaller than this; and nagar panchayats for villages in transition to becoming towns. These local bodies are all elected. There are also three tiers of rural local authorities: the district council for about 1,000 villages; the block panchayat samiti for about 100 villages; and the village panchayat at the village level. The rural local bodies are funded by and act as implementing agencies for state governments. Elections to both the urban and rural local bodies in India are ward based with one third of the wards being reserved for women candidates. Some other wards are reserved for candidates from socially underprivileged sections. There are about 1 million elected women representatives in panchayats and municipal bodies in India. There is also a one third reservation for women for the position of chairperson on these local bodies. Only 5.7 percent of the total number of government administration positions are filled by women. At central and state government levels in India, women occupy 7.9 percent of the parliamentary seats and approximately 5 percent of state level seats. In the past 50 years since independence the number of women elected to state legislatures has averaged 3 to 5 percent while at parliamentary level the average has been between 5 to 7 percent. At the national level there is currently one woman Cabinet Minister and 8 Ministers of State in a Cabinet of 70.

2.1.3. Pakistan

On the western side of this sub-region, Pakistan consists of four provinces: Punjab, Sindh, North Western Frontier Province and Balochistan. Local government is established within these provinces with rural areas being divided into Zila councils (districts), Tehsil councils (sub-districts) and Union councils (village level). Elections have until recently only been held infrequently. However under a Devolution of Power Plan introduced in 2000, elections have now been held for Union councils. At all levels of local government 33 percent of seats are now reserved for women and 20 percent reserved for workers/ peasants. These reserved seats are filled through direct election on Union councils while on district and sub-district level councils, these reserved seats are indirectly elected. At central government level there are 9 women elected to 304 seats (2.9 percent): 7 in the 217 seat National Assembly (3 percent) and 2 in the 87 seat Senate (2.3 percent). At the ministerial level there is currently one woman minister of state (1 out of a total of 21). At provincial level there are only 2 women elected to the 483 provincial assemblies seats (0.4 percent) and no women ministers.

2.1.4. Nepal

Nepal has 58 municipalities and 3,995 village development committees. Municipal councillors are elected on a ward basis and mayors elected at-large. Women have had the right to exercise and contest the franchise since 1955 and one woman was elected to the Kathmandu City Municipal Board in the very first local elections. A quota of 20 percent of seats has been allocated to women as an acknowledgement of their need to participate in the decision-making process in local bodies. The Local Bodies Act states that at least one of every five seats in each ward of the municipality should be reserved for a woman. In addition there are also six seats reserved for social workers, disadvantaged, caste and aboriginal groups. Currently there are 806 elected women (24.1 percent) in municipal government. At central government level the Parliament has both an upper and lower house. Overall there are currently 21 women in parliament (7.9 percent): 9 in the National Assembly – the upper house (15 percent) and 12 in the House of Representatives the lower house (5.8 percent). There are few women in the civil service at senior management or special class level (2.3 percent).

2.1.5. Bangladesh

Bangladesh is divided into six administrative divisions within which are districts and Thanas or sub-districts. Local government is divided into 225 urban based municipalities or Pourashava and 4,451 rural micro areas known as unions and about 80,000 grams or villages. Elections are held for urban local government with councilors/ commissioners elected on a ward basis while mayors and chairmen are elected at-large. While elections are held every five years, at present, due to political reasons, many Purashavas, municipalities and city corporations' terms are over and elections have not been held. Local authorities are strictly controlled by central government and totally dependent on government funding. One third of municipal and union seats are reserved for women and in the last elections in 1997 for union seats nearly 48,000 women stood for seats. Currently Bangladesh has a woman Prime Minister and a woman leader of the opposition. However their high position in politics is not a reflection of women's political position overall in this country as both women come from political families and their election has not led to a great number of other women being elected. There are 300 seats in the national parliament and 30 of these are reserved for women.

2.2. Women in Local Bodies of South-East Asia

Overall the numbers of women in decision-making positions in local government in this sub-region are the lowest in this comparative report (Table 2). All the countries in this sub-region have three levels of government, central, state or province and local.

Table 2. Women in Local Government in South East Asia, 2000

Country	Year women were eligible to vote and stand for Local Government	Women in Local Government seats (% of total)	Women Mayors (% of total)	Women in senior manag-ment po-sitions	Women in Central Govern-ment (% of total)
Thailand	1932	6.7	0.5	0.06	7.8
Malaysia	1957	9.8	0.7	0	14.1
Philippines	1937	16.5	18	32.5	12

2.2.1. Thailand

Thailand has three levels of government: central, provincial and local. At central government level the bicameral parliament has an appointed Senate of 200 members and an elected House of Representatives with 500 members. Provincial government is based on 75 provinces that are divided into districts, sub-districts and villages. At local government level there are cities and municipalities that govern urban centre in the provinces. As well there is the Bangkok Metropolitan Administration administered by an elected governor and divided in 38 districts. Some positions in local government are elected and some appointed but this is changing. The first election held for a mayor resulted in a woman being elected in Prathumthani. Currently there are 8 women mayors (0.53 percent) and women fill approximately 6.79 percent of local government seats in Thailand. 30 percent of city clerks are women as are 40 percent of executives. There are 44 women in the National Parliament (7.8 percent): 22 women in the Senate (10.9 percent) and 22 in the House of Representatives (6.1percent).

2.2.2. Malaysia

Malaysia also has three levels of government: central, state and local. The bicameral National Parliament has a 43 seat Senate and a 193 seat House of Representatives. All central government seats are elected as are the 373 seats at state level. While there are also 2,921 seats at local government level, elections to local authorities have been suspended since the 1960s. The 1976 Local Government Act replaced the system of elected representatives with one in which local councilors are now appointed. These appointments are political ones made by supporters of the Front, the party in government. In 1998 there were 285 women in local government seats (9.8 percent) and one woman mayor (0.7 percent). In state legislatures there are currently 21 women (5.6 percent) and at national government level there are 39 women (14.1 percent), 18 in the senate (29 percent) and 21 in the House of Representatives (9.8 percent). There are also two women in the Cabinet. Within the public service the gap between men and women widens as they move into higher grades. The distribution is fairest in the managerial and professional group.

2.2.3. Philippines

In the Philippines central government consists of a bicameral legislature with 24 senators and a 220 member House of Representatives. At provincial and local levels there are 78 provinces, 87 cities, 1,534 municipalities and 42,000 barangays. Currently 2,102 women councilors have been elected to the 12,680 contested seats (16.5 percent) and women fill almost 18 percent of mayoral posts and 12.7 percent of vice-mayoral positions. At the gubernational level women are in 233 of the 1544 positions (21.3 percent). At central government level there are 29 women (12 percent): 2 in the Senate (8.3 percent) and 27 in the House of Representatives (12.2 percent). The Philippines has a woman President and 2 women in the cabinet heading social welfare and tourism departments. Within the government bureaucracy there are more women than men. Women are in 32.5 percent of the highest level positions, 72.2 percent of second level positions and 34 percent of third level positions.

2.3. Women in Local Bodies of East Asia and the Pacific

The number of women in political positions in local and central government in the East Asia and the Pacific sub-region is comparatively high compared to the other sub-regions in the study. In Australia and New Zealand all local body representatives are elected, in Japan and Vietnam the majority are elected and China has a system of direct and indirect election. The current situation is shown in Table 3.

2.3.1. China

China's local government consists of a system of local people's congresses at provincial, prefecture, city and county levels. Those above the county level are elected indirectly by people's congresses at a lower level while counties and cities are elected directly by the people. The number of women on these local congresses range from 4,524 at provincial level (21.5 percent) and 144,367 at the county level (22.1 percent). There are a large number of women mayors in city level government in China – 463 (69.3 percent). At central government level the National People's Congress has 650 women delegates (21.8 percent).

Table 3. Women in Local Government in East Asia and the Pacific, 2000

Country	Year women were eligible to vote and stand for Local Government	Women in Local Government seats (% of total)	Women Mayors (% of total)	Women in senior manag-ment po-sitions	Women in Central Govern-ment (% of total)
China	1949	22.1	69.3	NK	21.8
Vietnam	1946	19.8	3	2.1	26.2
Japan	1946	6.2	0.5	3	10.7
Australia	1908	26.3	15	5.1	25
New Zealand	1910	31.5	26	5.8	30.8

2.3.2. Vietnam

Local government in Vietnam consists of people's councils and people's committees at provincial, district, commune, ward and township level. People's councils consist of locally elected people. People's committees are elected by the people's councils as they are the executive of people's councils as well as administrative bodies of the State in localities. Women have clearly had more success at being elected to people's councils than appointed to people's committees. Currently the percentage of women on people's councils at provincial level is 22.5 percent, 20.7 percent at district level and 16.3 percent at commune level. Data on women on people's committees at these levels of local government show a range between 4.5 percent and 6.4 percent. At the central government level women have been elected to 26.2 percent of seats in the National Assembly, there is a woman vice President and five women ministers (11.9 percent). On the administration side there are 46 women chiefs of government departments or institutes (13 percent).

2.3.3. Japan

Japan has a two-tiered system of local government with 47 prefectures at the regional level and municipalities at the local level. Of these municipalities, 12 are designated cities with populations of over one million, 659 cities, 23 special wards of Tokyo and 2,558 towns and villages. In total there are 3,872 women in local government seats at this time (6.2 percent). There are 158 on prefecture assemblies (5.5 percent), 1,821 on city assemblies (9.8 percent), 1,702 on town and village assemblies (4.2 percent) and 191 on special wards assemblies (19.7 percent). Heads of each local government (mayors and governors) and representatives of its assembly are directly elected. Deputy heads of local government (deputy mayors and vice governors) are appointed and are usually high-ranking officials, either of the central government or the respective local governments. Currently there are 2 women governors, 3 women mayors, 2 women town heads and 1 woman village head while 10 women are deputy leaders (7 vice governors and 3 deputy mayors). At senior management level the numbers of women are also low – 3.4 percent in prefecture offices and 2.9 percent in specially designated city offices. At the national government level there are 43 women elected in the upper house, the House of Councilors (17.1 percent) and 35 in the lower house, the House of Representatives (7.3 percent).

2.3.4. Australia

A federal state, Australia has a national government, 8 state/territory governments and 683 units of local government, 254 of which are urban councils. Of 6,637 local politicians, 1,745 are women (26.3 percent). All councils are headed by a Mayor or President who is either directly elected by the people or by the other councilors. Currently there are 122 women mayors (15 percent). At central government level there are 22 women in the Senate (28.9 percent) and 34 in the House of Representatives (23 percent). Within the state government there are a total of 37 women in the upper houses (23.6 percent) and 94 in lower houses (21.4 percent). In total there are 29 women at ministry levels in the federal and state governments. While women's employment within the senior public service is increasing there are no women chief executives at federal level and 7 at State/ territory levels. There are 35 women chief executives in local governments (5.1 percent).

2.3.5. New Zealand

There are 86 units of local government in New Zealand, 74 of which are territorial authorities (city and district councils) and 12 regional councils. Some of these local authorities also have community boards. All territorial authorities have an elected mayor while regional councils elect a chairperson from among those already elected to the council. Currently there are 19 women mayors (26 percent). In total there are 596 elected women in local government at present (31.5 percent), 259 of them being on city and district councils, 37 on regional councils, 281 on community boards and 19 mayors. At central government level there are 37 women MPs in the 120 seat Parliament (30.8 percent). New Zealand has a woman Prime Minister and a woman Leader of the Opposition and 11 women hold ministerial portfolios (50 percent of women elected in the governing parties), 7 of them in Cabinet. Within the public service 23.9 percent of chief executives are women. Women have not been as successful on the senior management side of local government as only 5 chief executives are women (5.8 percent).

2.4. Factors Affecting Women's Involvement in Local Government

While women are underrepresented in positions of political power worldwide they have clearly had more success at gaining access to local level decision-making positions than to those at central government level. The reason for this has been attributed largely to the everyday realities of women's lives. Participation in local government is easier for women to fit into their lives, along with family, household responsibilities and employment. Local government is also seen as more accessible as there are more positions available and less competition for places than in state and central parliaments. Local government can also be less intimidating as it is an extension of the great deal of involvement that women already have within their communities. As a result of more women being elected to local government councils, the environment has become more open to them being there, to women's issues being on the agenda and to equal employment opportunities for staff. Much of this acceptance has been aided in the last two decades by a very active women's movement, campaigns developed to increase the numbers and, in some instances, by the statutory requirement for quotas of women.

Despite this progress, however, there are still fewer women in local government than men. Part of the reason for this is historical as originally only land and property owners could vote or stand for office and as early laws prohibited women from owning land, local government has inherently been very male. In some countries in Asia and the Pacific women have had the right to vote and stand for political office for only about 50 years. Cultural and traditional barriers to women's involvement in public life can run alongside limits on other basic rights such as education, health care, and employment opportunities as well as political freedom and safety. Further barriers to participation can include discrimination against women candidates by political parties and by electors; the difficulty of being elected within first-past-the -post electoral systems as opposed to proportional representation systems and in at-large districts as opposed to ward systems; the costs of being involved and the need to juggle other responsibilities alongside the commitments of public office; and the fact that women are just not prepared to stand for local government because of the adversarial nature of politics.

The State of Women in Local Government country reports, on which this comparative analysis is based, all provide specific details on the laws, practices and initiatives that ensure women have the right to participate, and the constraints and issues that remain in each country. All country reporters were asked to provide in-depth analysis of the factors that help and hinder women's participation and access to decision-making positions in local government. An overview of much of this information follows.

One crucial point to be made first though is that all of the 13 countries in this analysis have statutory provisions that guarantee women the right to participate and all have signed the United Nations Convention on the Elimination of All Forms of Discrimination Against Women (CEDAW) which guarantees political and civil rights for women, although there are some reservations to this.

2.4.1. South-Asia

Laws and Practices that Ensure the Right to Participate All countries in this sub -region have constitutions that guarantee rights to equality and freedom. Sri Lanka's constitution guarantees freedom of speech, expression and association and while there are no laws that promote women's participation in urban local government the Constitution stipulates that no person shall be discriminated against on the grounds of sex. There is also a special provision for the advancement of women, children and disabled persons. In elections for local authorities the law requires that at least 40 percent of candidates on nomination lists are between the age of 18 and 35 years, this being to ensure youth representation in this tier of government. In 1998 a Commission of Inquiry on Local Government Reforms received submissions requesting that similar provisions be made for women's representation. While this Commission of Inquiry rejected this proposal on democratic grounds it did recommend that election of representatives to local bodies should be based on a ward system. Other recommendations proposed by this Commission to ensure women's participation in local authorities were the creation of forums for dialogue between elected councilors and youth and women's groups, compulsory inclusion of women and youth on various committees and opportunities for women, youth and other special groups to contest elections. There are several government-run programes for training employees and those elected to local authorities, although most of these programes are not gender specific. The Sri Lanka Institute of Local Governance was recently established to provide this training.

In *India* the constitution includes prohibition of discrimination on the grounds of religion, race, caste, sex and place of birth and equality of opportunity in matters of employment. In 1992 the 73rd and 74th Amendments to the Indian Constitution reserved one third of all seats for women in local government in urban areas and a one third reservation of all chairpersons' positions on these local bodies for women. This legislative move was seen as a major breakthrough in ensuring women's equal access and increased participation in local government. It was also seen as ensuring democracy and effectiveness within local government. While these amendments were introduced only at local government level there is now a very active campaign to also have quotas for women at other levels of government activity.

Reservation of a quota of seats for women, however, is only the first step in ensuring that a certain number of women are involved in local government. The next step has been to ensure they have the capacity to fulfil the role and make a difference. To this end most local governments run orientation / training programes on all aspects of local government, including legislation, budgeting, services and management. As well, Urban Development Programes at both central and state government levels organise training programes on municipal administration, urban development and capacity building. All levels of government in India also collect gender-disaggregated data for use in policy and programe formulation and quantitative and qualitative data on the number of women and men employed in the various levels of government and on elected women's participation rates.

Pakistan's constitution states that women and men have equal rights and guarantees equality of citizens before the law, forbidding discrimination on the basis of sex alone and providing for affirmative action for women. The Principles of Policy state that steps will be taken to ensure the full participation of women in all spheres of national life. This policy provides for reserved seats for women with about 10 percent of seats reserved for women in the National Assembly and 5 percent in Provincial Assemblies. There is also provision for 33 percent reserved seats for women in local government.

While *Nepal* also has a constitution that guarantees formal equality for women, the government is currently initiating new policies to promote women's opportunities in education, employment and political decision-making in order to overcome some of the inequities that continue for women in this country. As part of this, Local Government legislation requires that a minimum of 20 percent of all elected positions be reserved for women. As well, there are legal provisions to reserve 6 seats on local authorities for members representing social workers, disadvantages, deprived caste and aboriginal groups. The municipalities also develop programes to increase women's participation in their decision-making processes and other activities. Special provisions have also been implemented to enable more women to be employed in the civil service and the Ministry of Women, Children and Social Welfare has a role in training women to take on these jobs.

In *Bangladesh* the constitution provides for formal equality of women and men with women being entitled to the same fundamental rights as men. Article 10 of the constitution ensures the participation of women in all spheres of national life; Article 65(3) provides for reserved seats for women in parliament and Article 9 provides for the special representation of women in local government. One third of seats on local councils are reserved for women commissioners and there is a 10 percent quota for women in the civil service. However difficulties have been experienced with these reservations as the responsibilities of women ward commissioners are not gazetted and the resulting confusion over their roles has undermined the status of these elected women. To date, they have mainly dealt with women's issues, particularly micro-credit programes, handicrafts and professional training programes. The spin off is that women are becoming more concerned about their rights and this has led to local government being compelled to introduce services for women such as transport, childcare and violence against women.

Programes and Initiatives that Support Women's Involvement

Initiatives and support for women in Sri Lanka have come mainly from within local government itself. While some NGOs have launched programes to increase women's participation and political parties have provided basic political education, a few local authorities have set up women's organisations and training programes have been implemented for both elected and employed women. These training programes include different aspects of gender and gender equity.

NGOs and the women's movement in India have been strong advocates for change. They have emphasised the need to strengthen women's participation and leadership, have provided training and support for women and they work on consciousness raising, their aim being to change women's perceptions about the need to be involved and to transform politics. Local governments have also set up orientation and training programes to encourage women to participate in local governance. This training has specifically included material on municipal legislation, budgeting and taxation, service delivery systems (solid waste management, water supply, sewerage, health care services, traffic and transportation), poverty alleviation schemes, community and environmental management, shelter committees, reforms in municipal administration, functioning of ward committees, communication skills and women and development. Similar training programes and workshops are organised by Urban Development departments at central and state levels. These include, in particular, capacity building programes for elected women members and diploma courses on aspects of municipal administration for women employed in local government. Among the many groups providing training for elected women in local government is the All India Institute of Local Self Government, one of the premier training institutions. Women mayors meet during meetings organised by the All India Council of Mayors and have set up a formal association for support and interaction in order to exchange ideas and effective urban service delivery. There are also associations for women officials.

While one political party in *Pakistan*, Jamat-I-Islami, has started a training programe for women, it is at the NGO le vel that strategies for increasing women's participation in local government have been based. The Aurat Foundation, a women's organisation committed to the empowerment of women in governance roles, initiated a campaign based on public meetings, the preparation and distribution of information and intensive lobbying to increase the number of women in local government. As a result quotas for women were bought in for local government seats in the Punjab and Balochistan provinces and for the first time in Pakistan's history individuals and groups were involved in the Local Government Plan 2000 which focused on devolving power and include opportunities for training of councilors. Under this plan elections for local council were held between December 2000 and August 2001, with direct election for all seats and 33 percent of all seats being reserved for women. As a result the Aurat Foundation and several other organisations have started a campaign called the "Citizens' Campaign for Women's Representation in Local Government" as it was expected that at least 20,000 to 25,000 women would be elected to the lowest tier of the Union Council alone and these women would need support for campaigning as candidates and for effective participation once elected.

In *Nepal* the Municipal Association of Nepal, a non-governmental federation of urban local bodies, has conducted an orientation programe for local women on their role and the development of leadership. The Urban Development Training Centre has conducted similar programes for women and different municipalities provide their own local courses.

In *Bangladesh* women are encouraged to participate by women's wings within political parties, NGOs, women's groups and civil society organisations, most of which run workshops and seminars which highlight the initiatives needed to improve the position of women. One NGO, Nijera Kori, organised women and encouraged them to participate in local elections. Local government has also encouraged women's participation through different programes. In particular, the National Institute for Local Government conducts training programes for women commissioners. These programes focus on empowerment of women, gender and development and women's rights.

2.4.1.1. Barriers to Participation

Demographic data from countries in the South Asia sub-region shows the inequitable position women are in when compared to men and this lack of real equality creates major barriers to women's participation in public life. In most cases women's lives are constrained by obstacles such as culture and tradition (the view that men are superior to women), religion, political turmoil, violence, money and lack of opportunities. Demographic statistics show low literacy rates, poor health rates and poverty.

For women in *Sri Lanka* increased access to education, employment and health care over the last 40 to 50 years has opened up opportunities for greater participation in the social life of this country. However, several constraints continue to prevent women from participating equally with men. These have been identified as gender inequality within families caused by male dominance and an inequitable division of labor within households which means that women's responsibilities to their family and children prevent them from participating fully in outside activities. As well, assumptions about gender roles assign political and community affairs to men and exclude women from what are perceived to be unsuitable activities for women. As a result women feel vulnerable to intimidation as they are more likely to be publicly criticised for their activities than men are.

The demographic figures for women in India also show considerable disparities between women and men, these differences being the result of the traditional view that men are superior to women. Women's work is confined to the household and rearing of children and women's identity is attached to her father, husband and son. Women make up about 28 percent of the labor force and overall literacy rates show that for women the rate is 39.3 percent and for men 64.1 percent. While considerably more women are participating in formal politics (as a result of the quota system) and in grass roots political movements, obstacles such as the cost of standing for election and the abusive political environment remain. Even the smallest of elections requires money to stand as a candidate and women candidates face intimidation, violence and slander combined with ongoing opposition from men. Few electoral opportunities and a desire to field a winning candidate make most political parties shy away from fielding more than a token number of women candidates. Even if they are chosen, kinship and affinity factors play a major role. If elected, political representatives in local government find the role is demanding and all "new recruits" need time to gain experience and learn the rules and procedures. Effective participation can be hampered by a lack of understanding of urban development issues and municipal laws and administration; no knowledge or experience in dealing with the complexities of civic issues and urban service delivery systems; a lack of support and co-operation from colleagues and officials; the lack of money and resources; fear and insecurity; a lack of confidence and family responsibilities. As well, many women have found that they are often not equipped to become members of political parties as they have difficulty in attending meetings on policy issues as they are expected to fit in with the established structure and ideology of the party. While traditional values and attitudes prevail, women's issues are not part of the political agenda.

In *Pakistan* nearly two thirds of the adult population cannot read or write and nearly half of the population does not have access to basic primary health care and safe drinking water. Only 19.1 percent of women in rural areas are literate compared to 48.6 percent of men and in urban areas 52.2 percent of women are literate compared to 74.6 percent of men. Women have on average 8 children and both maternal and infant mortality rates are high. It is estimated that the maternal mortality rate is 340 for every 100,000 live births and the infant mortality rate for girls between the ages of 1 and 4 years is 66 percent higher than for boys. Pakistani society is so entrenched in culture that customary and traditional laws and practices usually override statutory law. Political turmoil, economic instability, martial law, war and internal strife have all affected the development of a democratic political culture, norms of sexual equality and respect for human rights and the rule of law. All of these social, cultural, economic and historical factors have directly and indirectly affected the status and rights of women at every level of society and have negatively impacted on opportunities to participate in decision-making.

While the constitution guarantees equality, protection and non-discrimination, socio-cultural norms and religious interpretations are frequently used for challenging and re-deciding women's rights and creating insecurity for women. And although women have equal political rights to participate as voters and representatives, in reality they are actively discouraged to do so. They are prevented from exercising their right to vote by their families, tribes, clans, and local and spiritual leaders. Identification requirements also place hurdles in the way of them voting and agreements are made between candidates and political parties to restrain women from casting their vote. Even when they manage to be selected for local government seats, women face further barriers through the need to please the chairperson and other male councilors or they have no access to development projects and are unable to meet the needs of their constituencies. A highly patriarchal society enforces a set of rules, responsibilities and behavior for women and subjects them to levels of abuse and public humiliation that enforce these norms, affect their self-confidence, limits their access to information and skills and reinforces their lower status.

Women in *Nepal* are in a similar position in that their literary rate is 30 percent as compared to 66 percent for men, their health status is poor with 70 to 80 percent of women being anemic, and infant and maternal mortality rates are high (the maternal mortality rate is 515 out of 100,000 live births). With the average life for women being 53.5 years as opposed to 55 for men, Nepal is one of the few countries in the world where life expectancy is lower for women than for men. The patriarchal structure within this country gives priority to the male child because he will earn the livelihood for the family, be responsible for elderly parents and ultimately be the decision-maker. Girls are socialised to be gentle, unassertive and to make sacrifices. Self-esteem, assertiveness and decision-making are not skills that are encouraged as girls are confined to the inside world of the home and lack access to the outside world of information, knowledge and resources. Religious belief places restrictions on young women, out of concern for the preservation of their chastity. As a result they face early marriage (in rural areas marriage can occur between the age of 12 and 14) and the perils of early pregnancies.

The purity of women is also an issue in *Bangladesh*, one of the poorest countries in the world. The reproductive years of 13 to 45 are a crucial part of women's lives and are a major determinant of their inability to participate in public life. Bangladesh women suffer from poverty, poor health (the maternal mortality rate is 850 per 100,000 births), a lack of awareness of the value of education and other social stigmas. Both primary and lower secondary schooling is free for girls but the dropout rate is significant after this with statistics showing that the number of boys far exceeds the number of girls in secondary and tertiary education.

While considerable progress has been made in the election of women to local government positions in Bangladesh through the reservation of one third of all seats, reserved seats are not seen as having the same value as general ones. As well, once elected as women ward commissioners many women have found further obstacles as their positions are not equal to those filled by men. The fund they receive to do their work is comparatively lower than that received by male commissioners and as none of their work responsibilities have been gazetted for these women they cannot take development initiatives and actions without the permission of other ward commissioners, many of whom have been uncooperative. This is often due to the fact that male ward commissioners are opposed to women being in these positions and are not keen to share their financial or political power. On top of this is the reality for these women of having to juggle their local government role with their domestic schedules so making it difficult for them to take on committee leadership positions.

2.4.1.2. Impact of Political System

While all countries in this sub-region have processes that formally guarantee the rights to participate in political activities, the informal practices that continue to support traditional and cultural inequities remain strong and create significant barriers for women. All of these countries have introduced quota systems within their local government systems in an attempt to break down these barriers: a legal requirement that takes a big picture approach rather than just attempting to chip away at the problem. For women in these countries a fundamental shift in numbers and thinking was needed rather than a case of getting a few more women into politics. For instance, since India gained independence in 1947 the development of a political system with equal rights and opportunities has neither resulted in women gaining access to decision-making positions as of right nor led to women's issues being part of the political agenda. For women in this country constitutional guarantees have not meant effective participation or political equality. The demand for a quota of 33 1/3 percent of elected seats for women was not based on the concept of advantage or privilege for women but rather it was seen by women to be a vital measure that ensured they became part of the mainstream of politics and development.

In *Nepal* where socio-economic and cultural discrimination is strong, quotas were introduced because of the belief that women have political rights and that reserved seats ensured their participation.

For women in *Bangladesh*, reserved seats for women commissioners and quotas for women in the civil service has meant the difference between almost no women in these positions and the recognition that women have the right to be there.

While the implementation of quota systems has resulted in considerably more women being elected and employed in local government than before, there are still barriers that continue to act against their effective participation. For example, when compared with directly elected positions reserved seats can be seen as having an inferior status and a lack of constituency. As well, the ability to be part of decision-making can still be blocked from within the system. Considerable support and training is needed to assist women to learn the way in which the political environment works and support is also needed to help them fulfil both their public and private roles.

Another factor that has had an impact on women's participation rates is family connections. Many women in politics, particularly in parliamentary leadership roles, have achieved these positions, albeit indirectly, through personal associations with male politicians. This trend is also seen in local government. For example, in Bangladesh, of the 20 women commissioners who participated in this country's survey, 18 had family members who were or had been in central or local government or were active in political parties and all of them had been politically conscious from childhood and had been involved in politics for a long time. There is no doubt that while kinship can be responsible for political participation it also provides an environment for learning political skills and competition. And this environment is often very different to that in which other women in the same country are socialised. For women without such connections, barriers to participation remain while political environments are still inherently male and traditional.

The reality of women's lives in this sub-region is that while they have constitutional rights, they are not seen as equal, their roles are closely tied to their reproductive and household activities, and politics and community affairs are seen as unsuitable for them. In some cases the increasing corruption in politics has added to this as growing disillusionment over the inability of political parties to deliver and a lack of faith in the electoral process itself has resulted in a general downward trend in overall voter turnout. In Pakistan the reported voting rate of 61.9 percent had decreased to 35.4 percent by 1997.

2.4.2. South-East Asia

Laws and Practices that Ensure the Right to Participate All countries in the South-East Asia sub-region have constitutions that guarantee citizens the right to participate. Thailand's constitution guarantees women the right of vote. It has also ratified the Convention on the Political Rights of Women that guarantees political freedom. Formal barriers to the advancement of women in the civil service were removed in 1991 when the government ordered all government agencies to review their discriminatory regulations so that female civil servants could hold any positions except those related to national security. The National Women's Coordination Board, a government agency, has been set up to strengthen the potential of women, but at present their work has been mainly restricted to urban areas. At village level the Community Development Department promotes women's roles and works to set up women's groups but these are currently more focused on the economic aspects of women's lives rather than their political role. At local government level local organisations have been established to strengthen communities and encourage participation and development. These provide women with the chance to be elected as a community leader. They also can lead to the setting up of women's development groups that help strengthen communities and women's role in that improvement. The Thailand Municipal League has attempted to promote the role of women in local administration. In particular, the Phitsanulok Municipalitiy supports women to join the administration and as a result of this council objective there are currently three women, a deputy mayor and two councilors who have had the opportunity to learn and participate in local government.

In *Malaysia* the Federal Constitution ensures all Malaysians of all races and gender freedom to choose representatives of the people; freedom of movement; freedom of speech, assembly and association which includes the right to form and join associations, trade unions, political parties; freedom of religion and rights in respect of education. However there are neither laws nor policies mandating women's representation in local government nor any affirmative action programes for the recruitment of women into public service employment at local government level. And while Malaysia has signed the United Nations Convention on the Elimination of All Forms of Discrimination Against Women they have a reservation to Article 7 (b) on the right to participate in the formulation of government policy.

The Women's Affairs department within the Prime Minister's Department and NGOs promote women's participation in development. The Women's Affairs department also plays a significant role in gender sensitisation at government and non-government levels through training programes and research on women's needs to ensure these are incorporated in policy development. Liaison officers have been appointed at state and district levels to monitor the implementation and impact of projects for women.

The *Philippines'* Constitution recognises the fundamental equality of women and men and the New Family Code of 1987 affirms women's rights, such as participation of women in major decision making activities in the community and in their homes. Much progress was made on gender and development under the leadership of President Corazon Aquino. In particular, the Philippines Plan for Gender Responsive Development 1995-2025 was adopted. This is the government's 30 year blueprint of policies, programes, projects and strategies wherein women are both major participants and beneficiaries in national development. Since 1996 the GAD or women's budget directs all government agencies to allocate five percent of their budgets to address gender issues. Women's concerns have also been integrated into the government poverty alleviation programes through projects designed to spread economic opportunities, stopping violence measures and the setting up of day-care centre.

Under the Philippines Development Plan for Women, the National Commission on the Role of Filipino women undertakes programes to raise the consciousness and train people in the government on gender analysis and sensitivity in planning and date collection.

A deliberate effort has also been made to have women represented in all decision-making bodies. The Department of Interior and Local Governments issued an administrative order stipulating 30 percent representation of women in all barangay assemblies and in all mandatory consultations within local and central government. As well the Local Government Code provides for a sectoral representative for women in the different local government units. And several local government have set up Focal Points for Gender and Development in order to mainstream women's concerns in the bureaucracy. Currently the House of Representatives is considering legislation that would mandate that one third of appointive positions in both local and national government be reserved for women and that political parties reserve one third of their party slate of official candidates for women in elections for the municipality/city councils and provincial boards.

Programes and Initiatives that Support Women's Involvement The National Council of Women of Thailand works to promote women's participation in public and local activities in order to increase knowledge of the political system and to encourage and support women to take part in political activities and to work together to find solutions which will improve the lives of women. The focus is on improving access to and the quality of education, employment, family life, health and Thai culture for women.

The focus of the National Council of Women in Malaysia is on legislative reform that will ensure equality of opportunity for women rather than on undertaking initiatives which will increase women's participation in local elections. However the Women's wings within political parties have lobbied their parties to increase women's representation at all levels of government as women are a big part of the membership of political parties. They have used forums such as closed-door meetings, dialogues and the annual National Assembly of their respective parties to make such calls to the leadership. Government seminars are held for all new councilors on their roles and responsibilities and these assist in equipping both female and male councilors with skills to perform effectively.

In the *Philippines* there are many NGOs that support women in local government within the broader framework of women in politics and decision-making. These include the Women's Legal Bureau which conducts legal training for elected official and advocacy campaigns for women in politics. Also, a coalition of 13 women's networks for politics, the Sama-samang Inisyatiba so Pagbabagong Batas at Lipunan has committed itself to advancing a legislative agenda on women's issues.

The Centre for Asia-Pacific Women in Politics, based in the Philippines, advances women's political participation through training and support programes and the Centre for Legislative Development provides training for staff, legislators and NGOs. The Women's Empowerment Lobby Group was recently formed to lobby for budget allocations for women's programes in local government. Gender awareness training is provided by several organisations for both elected representatives and for those employed in local authorities. Women in local government have also set up their own networks. The Provincial Women's Commission is pioneering integrating women and gender concerns and the Women Municipal Mayors' League has also been established.

2.4.2.1. Barriers to Participation

Traditional views on women's role in the family are strong in this sub-region. In Thailand such views have resulted in women not being perceived as credible leaders, this belief continuing to inhibit women's political participation. According to the old Thai tradition there is a belief that a woman is not strong enough to stand by herself and so had to stay at home and participate only in household traditions. Political involvement was strictly for men only. Women face economic, social and cultural obstacles and as a group they are forced into a passive role in society. Although NGOs work to involve women in development and community administration in towns the reality of women's lives makes this particularly difficult. While literacy rates are high and educational opportunities are increasing for women, girls from very poor families may start earning a living after six years of schooling to help her family, thus losing the chance to continue to a higher educational level.

The lack of quality education at a high level is a factor identified in *Malaysia* that has limited both women's involvement and their ability to speak effectively once elected. However this is changing as a result of an emphasis on equal opportunities in education and more women having access to tertiary education. Family responsibilities and the practical difficulties of balancing family commitments act as barriers to participation and to furthering their careers. Those appointed to local authorities have had to work long and hard as a party worker at the grassroots level and at senior levels within the women's wing of the party at the division, state and even federal levels before being considered for appointment. This climb to the top is not an easy one, their struggle often not being rewarded until they are between 40 and 60 years of age. Academic achievement is also a prerequisite for entry into local government as is the necessity to perform well at the selection interview. Even within the various women's wings training is not provided on leadership or local government.

The multiple roles of women were also identified as a barrier that significantly affects women's participation in the *Philippines*. They have little time to attend and participate in major decision-making and many still believe that such decisions should be made by their male counterparts. This in turn contributes to women's belief that they will not be heard, that their concerns are less important and that they lack knowledge on aspects of urban governance. There is little awareness of women's legal rights in terms of access to resources and membership of decision-making bodies. Some survey respondents, in identifying barriers that restricted women from entering local government, pointed to attitudes that put politics and decision-making into the male preserve – women were seen to be physically and intellectually incapable of managing towns. Such beliefs come from the Filippino culture which did not regard women as important agents of change. As well, traditional governance practices, such as making important decisions during evening drinking sprees, excluded women from fully participating.

2.4.2.2. Impact of Political System

A major barrier to women's participation in *Malaysia* is the closed political system at local government level. While elections are held for representatives at central and state level, elections to local authorities have been suspended since the 1960s. Currently political appointments to councils are made by supporters of the ruling party, with the result that less than 10 percent of nominated members are women. As well, there are no laws that mandate a quota for women's representation nor are there any affirmative action policies for the recruitment of women into employment at local government level. While the civil service at Federal and State levels operate within an open system the support services at the local government level is a closed system and the workforce is not transferable. With few women in the council they are not able to form a strong and united voice to speak on women's issues and concerns.

Electoral systems can be a major determinant of women's success in elections. Research has shown that proportional representation systems can result in more women being elected, one reason being that they come in on party lists rather than on electorate seats. The Philippines party list system enables under-represented groups, including women, to be elected to the Congress. The 1987 Philippines Constitution guaranteed that for three consecutive terms after the ratification of the constitution, one half of the seats allocated to party list representatives would be filled by those representing labor, peasant, urban poor, indigenous, cultural communities, women and youth groups. This led to the success in the 1988 elections for the House of Representatives of a women's party list organisation, the Abanse! Pinay party. The name Abanse! Pinay represents a commitment to advancing women's rights and welfare by fighting for women-friendly legislation. They are actively promoting legislation for women as well as the amendment of existing laws which discriminate against women. Currently government committees are scrutinising laws on trafficking in women and minors, women's empowerment and domestic violence.

Family connections have had a significant impact on women's access to political positions and there is evidence of this in parts of this sub-region. In the Philippines most of the women who participated in the survey came from politically connected families. For instance, the husband, father-in-law and mother-in-law of one mayor had been mayors of the town before her. Other women without such connections had previously proved their ability to manage their towns through a long record of public service. The influence and support of family members is also identified in Malaysia as contributing to political careers and to overall achievement. However the need to have family connections in order to access decision-making positions can also act as a barrier for women without such ties.

Political appointment as opposed to direct election can also impact on access to decision-making positions. In Malaysia where all local government seats are gained by political party appointment women's representation is less than 10 percent.

The collection of statistics on women highlights information on the realities of their lives and is useful for accurate policy and programe development. The Women's Affairs department in Malaysia collects gender-disaggregated data by sectors and agencies so that women's needs are identified.

2.4.3. East Asia and the Pacific

Laws and Practices that Ensure the Right to Participate All countries in the East Asia and Pacific sub-region have basic laws on the right to participate and have also signed commitments to international covenants that guarantee political and civil rights. China and Vietnam both have constitutions that provide guarantees for women. Article 48 of the Constitution of the People's Republic of China stipulates that women are to enjoy equal rights in political, economic, cultural and social affairs and in family life. The Constitution, along with Election Law and legislation which Guarantees the Rights and Interests of Women also guarantees the right to vote, to stand for election and to hold public posts regardless of nationally, race, gender, occupation, family background, religious belief, education, property and length of residency. Article 10 of the Law Concerning the Guarantee of the Rights and Interests of Women also states that all levels of government "shall have appropriate numbers of women deputies and try to gradually increase the proportions of women deputies. " And Article 11 when referring to the appointment and training of women cadres, states that "all State organs, social bodies, enterprises, and institutional units shall adhere to the principle of equality between men and women." A Program for the Development of Chinese Women (1995-2000) has been implemented with local government being urged to implement it. It's chief objective is to increase women's participation in decision-making and management of state and social affairs. Over the last five years national conferences have been held on the training and selection of cadres and five year plans have been established at provincial and local government levels. Selection and training is done at grassroots level and in college and polytechnics. Some provinces have established specific policies on women's participation that include a percentage of women in people's congresses within a specific timeframe. For example, Hebei Province set an objective of at least 25 percent women, this to be gradually expanded to 30 percent by 2000.

Vietnam's 1946 constitution also gives women and men equal rights to vote and to stand for election. And the amended Constitution 1992 Article 63 declares that "male and female citizens have equal rights in all fields – political, economic, cultural, social and family." Official documents such as the Politburo 04-ND/TW, July 1993, stipulate that there should be an increase in the number of women in positions of authority in all sectors within Party Committees and in the Government and there is other legislation on Marriage and the Family and the Penal Code 1992 which include references to political rights for women.

Once appointed or elected to local government in Vietnam all women and men are entitled to special training and to sit an examination at the Ho chi Minh National Political Academy. The personnel department within the local authority decides who shall attend this training and while the number of women trainees is still low (15 percent in 2000) special efforts are being made to increase this.

In *Japan* Article Five of the Basic Law for a Gender-Equal Society stipulates the importance of women's equal participation in decision-making processes and some individual local government have enacted local ordinances to promote gender equity. A few special measures have also been taken at both central and local government level to increase the numbers of women's employees. For instance, in 2000 the National Personnel Authority organised an unprecedented seminar to encourage female students to apply for national government officer positions and has encouraged Ministries to recruit and promote women.

As well as the basic right to vote and stand for election for all citizens over the age of 18 years, federal and state level legislation also protect women's rights in Australia. The Federal Affirmative Action (Equal Employment Opportunity for Women) Act, 1986, and similar state legislation prohibits discrimination against women in the workplace. EEO legislation also applies to employees of all local councils and to elected representatives in carrying out their duties. At the local government level, reforms in the 1990s resulted in new legislation for planning in which consultation with communities is required.

Democratic and civil rights in *New Zealand* are ensured through The Bill of Rights Act 1990, Section 12 on Electoral Rights which states that every New Zealand citizen who is 18 or over has the right to vote and is qualified to stand for election. This legislation ensures freedom of thought, expression, belief and association. Section 19 of this Bill also ensures that one's civil and political rights will be free from discrimination "on the ground of color, race, ethnic or national origins, sex, marital status, or religious or ethical belief" The Human Rights Act 1993 further enforces existing human rights legislation by establishing a Human Rights Commission which has both an educational and compliance function.

These Acts also affirm New Zealand's commitment to International Covenants on Civil and Political Rights, Human Rights and Discrimination against Women.

New Zealand's local government has, like Australia, been through significant reform in the last two decades, reform that has particularly stipulated that one of its purposes is the effective participation of local people and communities. The Local Government Official Information and Meetings Act 1987 requires all council meetings to be open to the public and the press and while some business can be held in committee there must be lawful reason for doing this and the Ombudsman can review such decisions. The Local Government Act 1974 requires all councils to prepare annual plans, detailing its policies, activities, performance targets and costs. The special consultative procedure requires local authorities to publish a draft of these annual plans, call for submissions from the public, publish an annual report which matches these policies and activities against the annual plan and be subject to independent audit.

Programes and Initiatives that Support Women's Involvement

All countries have NGOs that promote women's involvement in local government through gender awareness, training and affirmative action programes. The national organisation of women in China, the All-China Women's Federation, provides training and recommends women for appointments. This organisation uses all newspapers and magasines published by Women's Federations to publicise the contribution women can make to economic, political and cultural development and they support the training courses provided by schools and colleges. They have also established a database of women and recommend candidates for appointments in departments at all levels of government. Many women have been successful in achieving appointment. For example, of 1710 recommendations in the Guangxi Zhuang Autonomous Region between 1992 and 1997, 714 women were appointed to positions above the county level.

Within local government itself the China Association of Mayors has established a Branch of Women Mayors in response to an increasing number of women becoming leaders of local governments. Initially women mayors used this organisation to meet and share their personal experiences and developments as women leaders and to study the law and characteristics of women in management. More recently they have sponsored courses on economic theories for women mayors and on management and sustainable development.

In *Vietnam*, the Vietnam Women's Union and the National Committee for the Advancement of Women both represent the rights and interests of women. Prior to the 1999 People's Councils elections both of these organisations worked with local government to organise training for women candidates. This training focused on political, economic and cultural information, gender awareness and leadership skills. As well, the National Committee for the Advancement of Women ran campaigns to support women candidates, to encourage people to vote for them and to raise the issue of women in society in general. The success of this approach was seen through an increase in the number of women elected, attitudinal changes to women and leadership and increased self-confidence among elected women. A similar campaign will be used in future.

In *Japan* the League of Women Voters of Japan and the Ichikawa Fusae Memorial Association have taken leading roles in what has been called the "Japanese women's silent revolution", a movement which aims to change the belief that 'women are not politicians' and increase women's representation in politics. The League of Women Voters was initially established when Japanese women obtained the vote in 1945 and its focus has been on raising the awareness of women voters, clean election campaigns and monitoring policies on consumer issues and the environment. The Ichikawa Fusae Memorial Association provides both training and information on women in politics. Initially the Association ran a training course in 1994 for people who intending standing in the 1995 unified local elections. Of the 36 candidates on this course, 24 were elected. Since then this training course has expanded into two, one for new women candidates and the second for incumbent assembly members, both women and men. Training involves detail on election regulations, local politics and administration and effective campaigning. A campaign fund is also available. The Association also publishes a monthly journal and has a circulation of 10,000.

Other groups established for similar purposes include two that were set up following women's international and regional conferences. Two women who participated in the 1995 Fourth World Conference on Women in Beijing set up a Back-up School to Send Women to Assemblies. The electoral success of those who completed their first course resulted in 20 more prototypes being set up throughout Japan and a great number of course participants became local councilors / assembly members at the 1999 Unified Local Election. Training is provided on election law, campaigning, key issues in local government and the experiences of women who are already elected. Another network of women who had attended a regional Asia and Pacific Women in Politics forum in Manila in 1998 started a 'Campaign for Increasing Women in Politics" which focused on those prefectures and local councils where there was no women representative. An unusual feature of local government in Japan is the inclusion of consumer representatives. NGOs successfully lobbied for consumer groups to be part of metropolitan council in the 1970s and as the majority of consumer cooperative members are women, the majority of these representatives have been women.

In *Australia* and *New Zealand* the major initiatives at NGO level aimed at increasing and supporting women in local government have come from the Women's Electoral Lobby and women in local government themselves. The Women's Electoral Lobby is a feminist lobby group that aims to achieve social, economic, educational, political and sexual equality for women and works to increase the participation of women in politics and provide information to voters. When initially established in Australia in 1972 they surveyed all candidates for the federal election on their attitudes to feminist issues and published these results so that all voters could assess their candidates. This organisation has branches throughout Australia and lobbies politicians, unions, employers, educationalists on behalf of women and seeks to change societal attitudes and practices which discriminate against women.

New Zealand's Women's Electoral Lobby encourages women to vote, to be active in political parties and to stand for political office. In particular they have supported women candidates in practical ways by providing training, information and fundraising. They publish a quarterly national newsletter proving research and information for women, lobby at central and local government levels and hold public meeting and publicity campaigns.

Women within local government have also initiated programes to encourage women to participate. Many elected women participate in seminars talking about their experiences as councilors, what the issues are and how to stand for office,. Some have also approached women informally to encourage them to stand for office. The Australian Local Government Women's Association has been involved in a number of initiatives. The Queensland branch has initiated a mentoring programe for women and prior to the last elections targeted councils where women were either not represented or under represented by advertising in local papers for women candidates and then helping in the elections.

Some of these women were elected. The NSW branch regularly conducts pre election seminars in both urban and rural areas with very successful results. And the Tasmania branch has been involved in a joint initiative with local and state government to encourage women into local government by running seminars that provided information on local government and running campaigns. Victoria has the most comprehensive and well-funded programe to date. This was initiated in 1997 by a coalition of the Australian Local Government Women's Association, Women's Electoral Lobby, the Ladies of the City Action League, the Women's Planning Network (Victoria) and local authority organisations to strengthen local communities, local government democracy and good governance by increasing women's participation. Developed in three stages, the programe initially focused on practical assistance to women candidates such as developing an information kit containing practical advice, and case studies. The second stage involved the appointment of a project officer who conducted workshops, media campaigns, mentoring programes, set up a database, and established a website to monitor the elections. As a result women's representation was increased by 4.5 percent in March 2000. Stage three aims to support and enhance the skills of elected women and encourage them to take on leadership positions.

2.4.3.1. Barriers to Participation

While constitutions, legislation, policies and practices provide formal rights and equality, in practice there are many informal constraints or barriers that continue to prevent women from participating in local government. Within the East Asia and Pacific sub-district constraints range from institutional and political to cultural and societal barriers. Appointed women also face difficulties in being selected for senior positions.

Tradition, ideology and attitude are barriers for women in China, Vietnam and Japan. While there are officially no formal constraints on women participating equally with men and voicing their opinion, the tradition of male decision-makers is strong. In China traditional beliefs about the superiority of men have a negative impact on how women see themselves as decision-makers, as innovators and as being confident enough to be competitive. Particular evidence of this is seen in the election of village committees where cadres reject women to take up important posts. Women cadres who have worked hard or outperformed men cadres would usually be found fault with and rejected. Outdated methods of selecting women cadres make it difficult for outstanding talents to emerge and in some regions, particularly poverty-stricken regions, there are few women cadres. Women's role within the family also impact on their ability to participate in local government as there is still a strong belief that 'it is unruly for women to work all day away from home'. Some survey respondents identified the dual responsibility of families and public life as creating both work and psychological pressures as they just did not have the same support and time for keeping abreast of issues as men because of their family responsibilities. The fact that there were few women on decision-making bodies means that these women have to work within styles and modes that are acceptable to men. As a result women find they cannot be open about women's issues and social justice. Some also find they are judged harshly by society and by their colleagues as if they handle matters like a man they are said to be arrogant and seeking the limelight. Their achievements can also be treated suspiciously as some say they have attained these through special means or favor. In essence, legislative equality does not guarantee real equality as laws are not enforced, traditional attitudes prevail and prejudice and discrimination continues to occur.

In *Vietnam*, the remnants of Confucianism ideology, family responsibilities and lack of training all influence the level of success women have had at achieving public decision-making positions. Survey respondents cited outdated concepts of 'respect for men and disdain for women' as still existing and impacted significantly in elections. They see this attitude of disdain towards women as being responsible for the lack of confidence that voters have towards women candidates. Leadership positions, in particular, are seen as being men's positions as of right and this leads to prejudice when promotions to leading posts are made. A prevailing belief that women's work is to take care of their families while men participate in politics means that the family burden can constrain their involvement in public life. Families have to be supportive to enable women to take on the extra responsibilities and even when they are, the workload is high juggling both home and council work.

In *Japan* evidence of the tradition of male decision-makers is seen particularly in rural areas where more than half of the village and town assemblies and 10 percent of city councils have no women members. Survey respondents in Japan cited the patriarchal society which considers women as inappropriate to be politicians and so does not trust them with decision-making positions. As a result male governors and mayors do not appoint women to senior positions. Some women had faced gender-related discrimination when standing for election from their opponents, including mass dissemination of handbills that contained slanderous information on the women candidates. Once elected some assembly members also experienced discrimination from their male colleagues, including sexual harassment and antagonism over campaigns promoting gender equality and equality of children born to unmarried couples. Two of these women have formally complained. Other constraints for women are funding, insufficient training, the election system and a general lack of awareness about the need to increase women's participation in politics.

Barriers limiting women's participation in both *Australia* and *New Zealand* fit within four broad categories – attitudinal, financial, competing responsibilities and personal characteristics. Among survey respondents, attitudinal barriers were frequently mentioned with women pointing to the aggressive political culture, combative debate and personality conflicts as well as male colleagues who had difficulty coping with women and so belittled and personally attacked them. The few women employed at senior management level in local government have similar experiences. They found that conservative attitudes meant that women did not fit the image they had of a chief executive level job – the 'man in charge' concept. In Australia the harassment and intimidation of one woman chief executive resulted in a public enquiry and subsequent dismissal of the council. The enquiry found that "a lot of the hostility to, and prejudice against her [had], as one of its principal causes or roots, the fact that she is not only a women, but a forceful and successful one at that." The financial cost of campaigning, particularly for mayoral office, is seen as a deterrent as is the rate of remuneration for the almost full time positions on council, particularly for those who have no other source of income. Meeting times and lack of childcare support are also barriers to participation.

2.4.3.2. Impact of the Political System

On the whole, women in the East-Asia and Pacific sub-region have had the right to vote and stand for local government for a longer period than other countries in the Asia and Pacific region. For women in New Zealand and Australia this right was gained in the early 20th century while for women in Japan and Vietnam it was the 1940s. This period of time is, in itself, a factor in the greater level of success that women have had in gaining local government positions.

Electoral success is also dependent on the realities of women's lives, the system of local government and representation within a country, and the type of electoral system used for choosing decision-makers. In highly urbanised countries like Australia, New Zealand and Japan the high levels of participation in education and the labor force equate with increases in life expectancy. Put alongside the steady increase in the number of women in the public sphere and a growth in the women's movement, all of these factors have contributed to an increased number of women in local government.

The type of local government whether it is a second, third or even fourth level of government can be a factor in the relative importance of that decision-making body and so have an impact on the number of women who gain office. Local government positions at the community level are not always as valued as those in provincial, state and central governments. Whether mayors are elected or appointed can also impact on the number of women in these leadership positions.

The lack of official statistics and general information recorded on local government systems and elections, when compared to that known about central government, also reflects the relative lack of importance attributed to this level of government. In New Zealand the Department of Internal Affairs publishes election statistics after every local government election. These include comprehensive data on the representation of women. However, apart from information on chief executives, statistics on the number and the gender makeup of those employed in local government are not collated. In Japan national statistics on local politicians are collated by the Ministry of Home Affairs but any gender breakdown of this is only available through special request.

The electoral system used for electing representatives has had a significant impact on women's access to political office. Research on women's political participation has identified proportional representation party list systems of election as enhancing women's electoral success. Women's chance of election is increased if they are ranked highly on political party lists. There is clear evidence of this in the increase in women elected to New Zealand's Parliament since the Mixed Member Proportional system was introduced, a jump of almost 10 percent in just one election. There is currently a proposal to change to a single transferable voting system for local government elections in New Zealand. In Australia a preferential voting system is used for electing councilors and an optional preferential system when Mayors are elected.

There is also some evidence that at-large systems of election can disadvantage women as women tend to be known in their local communities through their involvement in local groups and community activity rather than throughout the whole city. Local elections that are based on ward representation can ensure that women candidates are known to voters. They can also encourage more women to stand for election as campaigning costs are not as high as in a city wide election.

Quotas to increase the number of women have not been favored in this sub-region. While quotas within political parties and parliaments were debated in Australia in the 1990s the Australian Labor Party was the only one to introduce a target of 35% for endorsement of women in winnable, generally safe, seats.

This target has not been reached and there is some doubt that it will be in the near future. Women are often the most vocal critics of what they see as a move away from a traditional 'merit-based' system. In Japan both national and local governments have set numerical and time bound targets for women's representation on advisory councils. While these targets have not been enforced they have been voluntarily implemented and in August 2000 the national government publicly announced it had reached its target of 20 percent. As a result of lobbying by women's organisations in Japan some of the political parties have taken initiatives to recruit women candidates. The Democratic Party has also established a special fund for women candidates

In New Zealand a considerable reduction in the number of local authorities and elected positions as a result of reforms in the last two decades has led to fewer opportunities to participate in community level decision-making, a tier of government in which women have historically had greater electoral success than in other areas of government. While the percentage of women elected has continued to rise, the actual number of women has decreased significantly. Added to this is the concern that many elected positions at community level have been replaced by appointed positions. Appointments for these boards are made by central government and there is clear evidence that fewer women are appointed than the number elected in the past. Added to this is a problem that not enough women stand for election. Election statistics show that women candidates have a greater chance of being elected than male candidates, particularly in urban areas but it is clear that women do not stand because of the cost and, also other commitments in their lives. There is also some evidence that the adversarial nature of politics is disliked by many women and that local government is still perceived as both male and conservative.

2.5. Women as Leaders

Much of the research on women and politics has had a quantitative focus, describing the number elected, the political environment and the factors that help and hinder women's ability to be involved. In more recent years, however, there has been growing recognition of the impact that women have on political institutions and agendas as well as on approaches to governance. It has become clear that while a small number of women have attained the highest political positions in their countries, a critical mass of women is still to be elected and there is no place in which women hold the same number of seats as men. Nevertheless it is also clear that many of the women who have succeeded have transformed the way in which politics is practised and they have changed the political agenda to include issues that improve women's lives. Some believe that "it is in the contradictory experience of progress and oppression that the transformative power of women's political work is located".

Consequently some recent initiatives that have focused on increasing the opportunities for women's political participation have worked from the basis that more women in government will mean better futures for other women and their children and for future generations. Such an approach also comes from the perspective that women with political power have a responsibility to work in a transformative way to ensure that their involvement makes a difference in terms of outcomes for women. One example of this in the Asia Pacific region is that developed by the Centre for Asia-Pacific Women in Politics whose vision of transformative politics is based on a new political paradigm: a politics that is both transformed and transformational. Within this framework politics are transformed to ensure that power is used to create change and develop people and communities; it is non-hierarchical and participatory; and it gives priority to disadvantaged sectors. Politics are seen as transformational when they work for economic, social and political equality for women within a humane and sustainable society.

> "This framework sees governance as adhering to excellence, integrity and accountability, gender equality, sustainable development and peace. It is also a framework that sees the necessity of creating a critical mass of competent, committed and effective women politicians in elective and appointive positions in government; and of developing a responsive women citizenry. It is the partnership of these two – the women in government positions and the women electorate, that will promote and put into practice the women's transformative political agenda that will: guarantee equal rights and opportunities to every member of society in charting the course of development, and always serve the common good as opposed to private means."

Questions about transformative leadership were included in the questionnaires that were used to collect information from women in local government for the individual country reports on which this comparative analysis is based. The criteria for selecting women to participate in this survey were based on the factors that contribute to good governance and the transformative role of women in local government. These factors were:

— Responsiveness and accountability to the local community
— Across the board ethics-based government
— Inclusive and consensus building policies – "power with rather than power over"

— Sustainability in terms of institutions and programes as well as the environment
— Gender equity
— Age and experience in local government.

In reality, selection was also based on the practical circumstances of these women's lives as with their very high workloads and the realities of juggling many roles it was difficult for many to have the time to participate in answering the questionnaire.

The intention was to highlight the impact of women's involvement on local government and the impact that more women might have. Women participants were asked whether they felt they had different concerns and priorities to men; whether increasing the number of women in local government would make a difference and what they had done during the time they had been in local government.

It is clear from the responses to these questionnaires that women believe that they do have an impact on local government and that they do practice transformative leadership. However, while the basic right to participate is continually undermined by the political system and through the barriers imposed by tradition and culture, some women are still dealing with the first hurdle of just getting into local government. This sometimes means they have to be start with a more conservative approach and work within party lines than have different agendas to promote. The exciting thing is that even in these repressive systems we see women making a difference even if only initially in small ways. A summary of much of the material in the questionnaire responses follows.

2.5.1. Difference Made by Women

Research has found that women in local government believe they make a difference as women leaders; they bring a different style to local government; and they consciously approach the job in a different way. Many also believe that increasing the number of women in local government will "accelerate the pace of change, promote collaborative styles of leadership and decision-making, broaden perspectives and move communities forward."

Evidence of this difference in countries in the Asia-Pacific region shows those women:

— Have a greater sense of the social issues and the well being and welfare of their communities and factor these into the decision-making process
— Promote policies and activities which strengthen communities · Encourage participation
— Emphasise the importance and the practice of good communication with the community
— Have a different approach to the way their local authority is governed
— Develop a team approach
— Set different priorities
— Bring the mediation skills that they have developed as mothers, the ability to have clear goals, to juggle many tasks at once, and to be practical.
— Are dedicated, responsible, practice what they preach and show a great deal of spirit
— Stimulate and encourage other women to be part of development

2.5.2. Different Agenda

Women's concerns and priorities are more likely than are those of men to centre around people's needs for safety and clean water supplies and for community facilities rather than just the traditional roads, rates and rubbish. Women also have a strong focus on women's issues and a human rights flavor in their goals for local government, suggesting that changes in local politics will lead to changes in society, less discrimination against women and greater flexibility in work and childcare. By bringing a grassroots perspective to local government, women make it more people orientated and closer to the community it serves. Some survey respondents suggested that:

— There are differences in the interests of female and male councilors in that women's interests focused on environmental issues, childcare, education and caring while men are more interested in construction, maintenance and planning for water supplies, sewerage, roads and urban development.

— Women are more concerned about the social implications of policies and give priority to issues which impact on people's lives such as employment, care of elderly, poverty elimination, the rights of women and children, education, health care and sanitation, family planning, quality of life and social support.

— Women are more concerned with social issues such as health services, poverty alleviation and community development. They also tended to work out the details and aim to achieve consensus on specific policies and programes rather than to politicise issues.

— When dealing with the needs and priorities of women in planning city development, local government women not only take into account the physical considerations but they also consider harmony in art and culture, the quality of life, a healthy city, and environmental development. And in their involvement with their communities, it is suggested that women actually contribute more at all levels of politics than men.

— Women ensure a more democratic and transparent form of governance by standing on a unified platform with other women to pressure municipal government to present information such as the budget in detail

— Women give importance to issues that men find trivial, such as family and marriage disputes and dowry problems. They also feel they work from their heart as their own experiences help them understand the causes and nature of gender discrimination.

— There is also a belief that women's work in the home and with their children has made them more concerned than men are about aspects of health, cleanliness, water, sanitation, housing conditions and the environment.

2.5.3. Different Style

The women suggest that they take a democratic approach to governance and management within their councils and with their communities, encouraging participation in decision-making. Their styles were described as being:

— More inclusive, collaborative and consultative

The style of some woman mayors was described as involving everyone, consulting and sharing power. Women also broaden the governance outlook and outcomes and they expect discipline from councilors. Women use more democratic forms of decision-making, preferring to consider debate and discuss with their colleagues rather than resort to orders.

— More tolerant of different points of view

Women work around the problem and look at it more fully rather than taking a confrontational approach to it. They don't always have fixed views and prefer win-win solutions.

— More caring, people orientated and respectful,

They facilitate opportunities for community representatives to make submissions to the council.

— Change focused, in particular wanting to clean up the dirty image of politics.

This approach is based on honesty and an effort to create a corruption free society.

— More open, informative and professional

Some women issue regular newsletters to report on their activities and the major issues being dealt with in their local authority.

— More innovative and conscientious

Some women have made bold and pioneering strides. They are practical and will stick with issues and projects throughout and they can put themselves in the place of others. They also take effective decisions and demonstrate self-confidence.

— More persistent, persuasive, committed and unafraid of challenging the structures.

2.5.4. Impact of Increasing the Numbers of Women

Successful and competent women act as role models and earn respect not only for themselves but also for women in general. Many women believe that being a role model helps demonstrate that women can participate effectively in local government. This in itself opens doors for more women. The range of issues considered by councils has also extended, council processes have changed because of different styles of women and community perceptions of the council have changed as a result of increased openness, accountability, breaking down the 'red tape' and a preparedness to listen. Some examples from the survey material suggest that:

— Women are particularly well-suited to coping with change itself and the diversity of issues that local government is now required to consider as their approach is distinctly different to that of many of their male colleagues. They have a strong sense of wanting to demonstrate a different way of 'doing' politics and not simply operating in the same way as many male politicians. These qualities, if possessed by significant numbers of people, have the capacity to transform the local government environment. Anecdotal evidence suggests that male councilors and appointed staff have observed and learnt from the examples that have been set by women colleagues.

— Women have a greater understanding of equity issues and the need for more women decision-makers results in an increased number of women participating, gender equity policies being mainstreamed and a greater diversity of role models for women being seen.

— The increasing numbers of women in local government has had a positive impact on the improvement of women's position in society as it creates an increased understanding of conditions for women and children and leads to policies, projects and funding for development and to promotion of other women to decision-making positions.

— Once women reach decision-making positions in urban local governments, more concern is shown for the improvement of living and working conditions of women. Women's activities become favorable and are included in the allocation of budgetary funds to women's work.

— Women's status has improved with increasing participation of women and more women in elected positions. In particular, the concept of 'respect for men and disdain for women' is gradually changing.

— In a political climate in which opportunities have been opened up for women and minorities to participate, women have been able to take advantage of these to provide women's services.

— Women in large numbers have come out against atrocities on women, in defence of their traditional control over crucial resources such as water, forests and land, mass literacy drives and other issues. They are also coming out against ecological degradation, price rises and protests against repression.

— In supporting women's groups and being part of their programes on health, cleanliness, environment, security and family issues, more women have become conscious of their own worth and ability.

— Women members participate more actively in women's issues – health, welfare, atrocities against women and violations of human rights.

— The environment in which local government operates has changed. It is more people friendly, more transparent and less corrupt. It has also changed in relation to the poor and women. Issues like familial disputes, dowry issues, domestic violence, mother-child healthcare, education opportunities, women's cooperatives, income earning and credit programes and emergency funds and relief in times of disaster have received special attention.

— For some women their most important achievement has been to make women more politically aware and active and to help them understand their political rights and capacity.

— Women's groups are working together collaboratively to promote women's participation in public life and the economic welfare of women.

2.5.5. Impact Women on their Communities

When asked what they had done to improve their local authorities women in the Asia and Pacific region had long lists. Some examples of programes initiated, continued or supported include:

— Women's centre, youth centre, arts centre, community owned child care centre, playground projects, petitions to oppose development that would impact negatively on the district, safety councils, trusts to deal with unemployment, urban and community projects, campaigns to improve local hospital and health services, environment projects, pensioner housing, landscape projects, swimming pools, independent economic development projects, EEO projects, urban and community renewal programes, a recreation review. Different processes were also initiated by some women in order to improve consultation, participation, planning, decision making, working as a team with council and develop a culture of cooperation and collaboration, changing the language and using more user friendly approaches

— Changes to council policies, land-use planning instruments and new and improved infrastructure, facilities and service. Specific projects relate to community services and facilities such as art galleries, parks, aquatic and sports centre, childcare and community centre. And apart from projects that involve their councils directly, women have had a significant influence on more broadly based initiatives through their work with community and business organisations or through their contacts and influence on state and federal committees and with state and federal politicians. Some of these projects are main street programes, revitalisation of central business districts, obtaining a sexual assault counsellor for the town, community festivals, business enterprise centre, projects to build relationships with indigenous and non-indigenous communities, crime prevention, community safety and health programes for older people.

— Gender equity policies have been implemented which provide for training and promotion of women employees and improve their working conditions, increase the number of women on advisory committees, consciousness raising and gender mainstreaming policies.

— Local programes and projects for the improvement of the urban environment, farm economy, garden, field and fruit tree development and programes to mobilise people in the construction of infrastructure, roads, electricity and safe water supply.

— The pace of civic construction has accelerated in order to provide basic and much needed facilities, water supplies, housing and controlling pollution. Cultural, educational and public health management projects have included a nine year compulsory education plan, welfare facilities, rest homes, libraries and centre for women's activities. Urban economic programes have targeted outside investment for local projects which build community infrastructure and activities.

— Increased development to districts has occurred through completion of projects on time and these improvements have not gone unnoticed. This has helped to secure more federal and state funding for the district, created the capacity to do more and developed community pride as the district as won awards for this transformation.

— Developed proposals for programes on energy and environmental concerns for women with the result that a recycled paper project has been set up to solve waste problems and increase the income in the community.

— The provision of clean water, waste management, city cleanliness has improved, street lighting provided, slum development, food packages for workers, programes that address the needs of poor children, such as noon meal centre.

— Projects which improve the municipality and assist its residents, such as programes for education and basic needs for internally displaced and a housing and resettlement programe. This has also included successfully fighting for a significant percentage of the city budget.

— Initiating and actively supporting public utility services such as provision of sanitary facilities, housing and drainage, and community services such as libraries and playgrounds. Setting up programes such as labor camps, health initiatives for women and children and environmental conservation.

2.5.6. Support for Women

Women believe they have a responsibility to promote women's participation and improve the status of women generally. Many work actively to increase the numbers of women in this tier of government and to ensure that women's issues are kept high on the agenda.

Descriptions of what they had done included:

— *Running workshops for women interested in running for office and encouraging them to participate.* As a resource for these workshops, suggestions were made for an information kit which outlines what local government is about, the importance of women in local government, how to campaign and what a councillor does. This kit could be distributed to women's groups and to individual women.

— *Encouraging women to apply for positions in local government.* In line with research evidence, women in this part of the world stand for local government because they are encouraged to do so. Most of them were already heavily involved in their communities, knew a great deal about local issues, had already earned a public profile for the work they have done and now wanted to move on to more formal public participation where they could influence decision-making. They are involved in recruiting more women and increasing the number of women in consultative roles on various committee and programes.

— *Promoting women as political leaders and supporting them once elected or appointed.* This involves demystifying these positions, helping women feel more comfortable and helping them learn the ropes. Being prepared to be part of mentoring programes also assists other women. Supporting the promotion of women in decision-making positions in political, economic, cultural and social aspects at various levels. Offering solutions to increase female cadres in direction and management work and raise the percentage of female executive and the proportion of women participating in people's councils. There is some evidence that women stay in local government longer as a result of the satisfaction they get from the job.

— *Setting up and supporting services for women.* Setting up women's centre, negotiating contracts for women's services. The recognition that women are disadvantaged in many areas of their lives and poorly represented in all spheres of political activity has given many local government women a sense of responsibility to other women generally. Participating in formulating and carrying out specific policies to improve women's situation in society.

Promoting and supporting women's organisations, initiating economic empowerment programes and ensuring better access of women to services. A focus on improving the status of women has included encouraging women to provide information on issues of local governance and seeking justice for women who have been harassed.

— *Public speaking, participating in women's activities and running conferences for women in local government.* Being a guest speaker at meetings, seminars and conferences. Taking part in activities organised by federations of women, trade unions and other mass organisations to improve the quality of women's lives and providing financial support for women's activities. Mobilising demonstrations in support of a quota of women in local government and organising workshops for women on local governance. Taking part in radio and television programes promoting women's participation and lobbying for an increase in women's seats within the political parties. Organising forums to discuss women's issues, safeguard women's rights and help women with income earning activities.

2.6. Recommendations for Change

This comparative analysis shows very clearly the impact that women are having on the political environment, their cities and communities and on the status of women. It also shows that there are big differences between the levels of development throughout this whole region and this in itself raises different issues for women and means that different approaches need to be taken to ensure that women gain access to political decision-making positions in local government.

So what needs to happen? Achieving a significant increase in the number of women in local government is a priority. While it is clear that in all the 13 countries in this comparative analysis women have formal provisions that ensure their rights to participate and there is a great deal of political activity and initiative at NGO and community level that continues to work for change, there are still many barriers to be overcome. To overcome the barriers that remain there are several broad areas that need to be addressed. These are the systems within which local government operates, the attitudes towards women in local government and the strategies that need to be developed to enable a greater number of women to move into local government as elected representatives and as senior managers. There are also specific recommendations on training as this is an area that has received a lot of attention in the country reports. Some of the changes recommended are similar and relevant to the whole Asia and Pacific region and some are relevant to particular sub-regions. Common recommendations for the Asia-Pacific region are presented below. These are followed by recommendations presented in sub-regional format.

It is clear that a comprehensive country-level strategy that takes into account the specific issues related to the status of women in society, structures of government and the culture of governance, needs to be discussed and adopted in order to increase the representation and participation of women in local government.

The research suggests four key strategies for the Asia-Pacific region. These are:

1. *Changes to the systems within which local government operates:*
   a) A quota of reserved seats for women to be implemented in countries where few women have been elected. These reserved seats to be permanent, filled through direct and open elections and to have the same status as general seats
   b) Proportional representation systems of voting be implemented
   c) The number of elected positions at community level be maintained
   d) Wards systems for electing representatives be retained
   e) EEO programes to ensure more women are employed in local government and to enable more women to move into senior management positions
   f) Elected representatives to be paid at a level that will enable more women to participate
   g) Local government implement the policies outlined in Agenda 21 on good governance
   h) Consultation processes be established to ensure women participate

i) Funding allocated for gender and development that emphasises capacity building, networking and advocacy

j). Women's standing committees be established

k) Recruitment by political parties of women candidates

2. *Ways of changing attitudes towards women in local government:*

a) The culture of local government needs to change to ensure that women are treated fairly and equally and to make sure that discrimination against women is not acceptable

b) Gender awareness programes for men and women need to be developed

c) Local government needs to be more women friendly. Consensus style politics and meetings at times that fit into the other responsibilities that women have, will enhance the political environment

d) Opportunities need to be made available for women as soon as they are elected to learn about local government and their governance role and to provide them with support.

3. *Strategies to increase the number of women:*

a) Strategies need to be adopted to change policies and structures that perpetuate women's subordinate status

b) Policies on economic and social empowerment are needed to enable women to participate on an equal footing with men

c) Local government needs to work closely with NGOs, civil societies and women's groups to develop communities and services that take account of the needs of women

d) Women in local government need financial support, childcare, support systems and training opportunities

e) Women's associations to be established for women councilors and managers in local government to provide a voice for women's views and a base for networking

f) Women in local government need to encourage more women to participate

g) Funds to be established to assist women to run for election

h) Gender-disaggregated statistics need to be collected to increase the visibility of women.

4. *Training*:

a) Training programes to be established by NGOs, political parties, educational and political institutions to help women in local government develop skills and self confidence and to enable them to learn the functions and processes within this tier of government

b) Training to be provided for women candidates on the political system, local government functions and processes

c) Workshops be provided on gender awareness and development for both women and men in order to educate people on women's rights and the importance of women's equality

d) Girls and young women's education should include training on self reliance, self-confidence and their potential for decision-making positions.

More specific proposals for change in each sub-region are given belw:

2.6.1. South Asia

2.6.1.1. System

1. Legal provision be enacted for a quota of reserved seats for women representatives in all local governments in this sub-region. These quotas to be permanent.
2. Direct and open elections be held for these reserved seats.
3. Reserved seats to have the same status as general seats on local councils, ie. work responsibilities clearly gazetted for all decision-makers with equal access to funding and resources.
4. EEO programes be established to enable women employed in local government to move into senior management positions.
5. Local authorities to establish systems that ensure women are able to participate in and are consulted on issues in their communities.
6. Standing committees on women's issues be established on local authorities.
7. Political parties to actively recruit women candidates for local elections.

2.6.1.2. Attitudes

1. Local government needs to take a lead role in developing a culture that treats women equally and fairly. Women need to be on an equal footing to men in decision-making positions and in communities.
2. Local government has a responsibility to develop awareness of gender issues through programes for men and women.

2.6.1.3. Strategies

1. A common strategy needs to be adopted, informed by a common vision, in order to bring about changes in the policies and structures that perpetuate women's subordinate status.
2. Policies are needed on economic and social empowerment for women to enable them to ultimately participate on an equal footing with men.
3. Local government needs to work closely with NGOs, civil societies and other women's groups to develop communities and services that take into account the needs of women.
4. Women in local government need financial support and childcare.
5. Support systems and ongoing training opportunities need to be established for women in local government.
6. Statistics needs to be collected at regular intervals and research encouraged on women in representation and management roles in local government to increase the visibility of women. Gender-disaggregated data also needs to be collected for policy and service development in local communities.

2.6.1.4. Training

1. Gender awareness training programes be established and supported by government agencies, non-government organisations and political parties for men and women on the rights of women and their potential for leadership.
2. Training programes for women on political structures, processes and issues in local government and support for them to stand as candidates.

3. Training programes for women newly elected to local authorities on how the system works, how they can work effectively on the council and with their local communities to identify issues and develop initiatives.
4. Programes that enhance the self sufficiency of women be established by local authorities.
5. Awareness courses for women in communities on how to use local government to further their interest.

2.6.2. South-East Asia

2.6.2.1. System

1. To encourage more women to be employed in local government EEO programes need to be established in order to get women appointed to positions and to support them once there.
2. Local government implement the policies outlined in Agenda 21 on good governance and encouraging greater community participation of women in decision-making and capacity building processes.
3. Local government needs to comply with legislation that stipulates women's representation and allocate funding to ensure this occurs.
4. Both local and central government needs to allocate funding from ODA funds for gender and development for a comprehensive development fund that emphasis capacity building, networking and advocacy.

2.6.2.2. Attitudes

1. Local government needs to take a gender-balanced approach and ensure that women are in decision-making positions in governance and management roles, and women's issues are promoted in policy and service provision.
2. Opportunities for women to learn about local government and their role need to be available as soon as they have been elected in order to provide support and help with the adjustment to this governance role.

3. Promotion of women's status will help with building confidence and belief in their abilities.

2.6.2.3. Strategies

1. Women's associations are established for women councilors and managers in local government. These associations will provide a voice for women's views in local government. They will also provide a basc for networking between women in local government, NGOs and women at state and national of government.
2. Women in local government need to encourage more women to participate in local governance. This can be done by networking and by setting up formal organisations.
3. Organisations need to take responsibility to improve the opportunities of women to advance in politics by working together to ensure this happens.

2.6.2.4. Training

1. Training programes be established by NGOs, political parties and political institutions to help women in local government develop skills and self confidence to ensure they can be effective and can advance their careers. This will ensure a pool of capable women in local government who will work for balanced development.
2. Educational institutions need to conduct seminars for newly elected women.
3. Workshops are provided on gender awareness and development for both women and men. These should be promoted in order to educate people on women's rights and the importance of women's equality.

2.6.3. East Asia and the Pacific

2.6.3.1. System

1. The system of voting for local government elections should be changed to proportional representation.

2. The number of elected positions in local government needs to be maintained. Despite the greater focus today on participation, the democratic right to elect representatives needs to be ensured at community level.
3. The retention of the ward system for electing representatives also needs to be retained.
4. Quota systems are considered in some instances to increase the number of women in decision-making positions in local government, particularly where few women have been elected.
5. Mechanisms should be established to assist women employed in local government to move into higher management positions. These mechanisms should include: a review of current EEO policies to measure the level of women's participation at all senior levels in local government and the mechanisms currently being used by local authorities to comply with their EEO obligations; training opportunities established for women to enable them to develop skills and qualifications that will enable them to further their careers in local government; financial support for training; and mentoring support.
6. Elected representatives need to be paid more to enable them to participate, this payment covering quality dependent care and set at a rate that will attract younger women.
7. There also needs to be caps set on campaign expenditure.
8. Local governments adopt policies which promote gender equity.

2.6.3.2. Attitudes

1. Local government needs to become more women friendly. The culture of politics will be enhanced if there are more consensus style politics; meetings are held at times which fit within women's responsibilities; and workshops are held on gender sensitisation.
2. A political environment needs to be developed in local government in which discrimination against women is not acceptable

2.6.3.3. Strategies

1. In order to increase the number of women in local government a

comprehensive package needs to be developed and distributed nationally. This package to include information kits for women who are considering standing for election; workshop outlines and suggestions on how to support candidates; a media kit for use by women candidates; and a candidate database.

2. Funds are established to assist women to run for election.
3. Best practice models are developed on women and local government and all local government be encouraged to adopt them.
4. A mentoring programe be established to provide support, information, resources and assistance to women in local government
5. Women employed in local government are offered opportunities for career development.
6. Local government women's associations are established.
7. National databases are established on women in local government that provides resources and material for research on women and gender issues.
8. Guidelines need to be developed to measure the impact of all policies and programes on women and men.

2.6.3.4. Training

1. Citizen's awareness of gender, politics and human rights programes is established for men and women.
2. Training programes for women candidates on the political system, local government functions and processes and support for them to stand as candidates.
3. Training programes for elected women in local government functions and processes and in leadership skills.
4. Girls and young women's education should include training on self-reliance, self-confidence and their potential for decision-making positions.

2.7. Regional Support Mechanisms

It is clear that a regional structure needs to be considered as a pivotal part of changes put in place to ensure the numbers of women in local government increase, training and support networks are established and to assist with ensuring that the political environment become more women friendly and political agendas include women and development issues. While there are already regional networks in the Asia and Pacific area that focus on women's empowerment, particularly in politics and political activity, none of these focus primarily on women in local government.

It is also clear that regional and international contacts are beneficial in the drive for change. International initiatives on women's rights such as the Convention on the Elimination of All Forms of Discrimination against Women (CEDAW), the Beijing Declaration and Platform for Action of the Fourth World Conference on Women and Development and the Habitat Agenda of the Second United Nations Conference on Human Settlements (Habitat II), have established precedents for putting women's issues onto government agendas and forcing, in some cases, unprecedented changes. Both international and regional strategies, training opportunities, networking and conferences provide women with opportunities to share experiences develop new ideas and learn new ways in which they can initiate and work for changes which will ultimately lead to greater equity for women at both government and community levels. These contacts can also assist with access to funds for initiatives such as training at the country level.

Regional actions should focus on:

1. Establishing regional targets for increasing the number of women in local government within timeframes; monitoring progress achieved in meeting these targets and undertaking advocacy of gender mainstreaming and gender equality in local government as well as the transformative role than women play in local government.
2. Promoting exchange of experience and information as well as comparative research through networking among women in local government, governmental and non-governmental organisations, political parties and research and training institutes working on the issues of women and local government.

3. Promoting regional, sub-regional and country-based training programes on gender mainstreaming, training of women already in local government as well as training women aspiring for positions in local government through organising regional and sub-regional conferences and workshops for women in local government to share strategies, network, provide training and support.
4. Catalysing resource mobilisation at the country level to support training and campaigns of women candidates in local governments.

2.7.1. Regional Targets

The Asia-Pacific Gender Balance Declaration adopted by the conference on 50-50 by 2005: Get the Balance Right has established the target of achieving gender balance at all levels of government by 2005. The conference was organised by the Center for Legislative Development (CLD), the Center for Asia Pacific Women in Politics (CAPWIP), the United Nations Development Fund for Women (UNIFEM), the United Nations Economic and Social Commission for Asia and the Pacific (ESCAP) and the UNDP-Asia Pacific Gender Equality Network (APGEN). While the target itself is achievable, the proposed time-frame is rather optimistic. Even to achieve gender balance on paper would require passage of laws, constitutional amendments, development of administrative procedures and finally holding new elections under the amended legislation. The process is likely to take more than five years. Achieving real gender balance would require attitudinal, cultural and institutional change as well as capacity building of local government. A more feasible timeframe would be 10 to 15 years. It is recommended that the target of gender balance in local government be adopted for regional and country-level actions in promoting the number of women in local government to be achieved within 15 years time or by the end of the year 2016.

Based on this target annual reports on the State of Women in Local Government should be prepared and disseminated around the region. The first State of the Women in Urban Local Government Reports prepared by ESCAP in 14 countries of the region could be taken as the basis for preparing future reports. These reports would also assist in monitoring progress made in achieving the target of gender balance in local government by the year 2005.

2.7.2. Promoting Networks

Promoting exchange of experience and information among women already in local government, women aspiring for positions in local government, governmental and non-governmental organisations, political parties and research and training institutes working on the issues of women and local government, through out Asia and the Pacific through one regional network is neither possible or desirable. This is due to the fact that the vast majority of these women and organisations do not use English as their first language. Moreover, only those women who usually come from upper and higher middle income groups normally benefit from such regional exchanges. To reach the vast majority of women in local government a system of cascading networks would have to be used. Such a system would depend on the development of country level networks linked to a regional network. Thus information and experience sharing on outcomes of research, policies, best practices and advocacy campaigns could be translated into local languages by country level networks and shared among women in local government in those countries. Such cascading networks would be better able to undertake actions at the country level and to monitor progress in achieving gender balance in local government, while the regional network would be able to coordinate actions, share experiences and develop synergies among country level networks. With the advent of information and communication technologies such networking can be easily achieved through the Internet at relatively low costs.

2.7.3. Training and Research

Similar to networking, regional and sub-regional training programes that seek to provide training directly to women in local government will be able to reach a very limited number of women. In each country there are governmental and non-governmental organisations and research and training institutes that are already providing training to women in local government and in gender mainstreaming of local governments. On many instances the capacities of these organisations and institutions is limited. Regional support to training should concentrate on building capacities of these institutes. In this connection, ESCAP established the Network of Local Government Training and Research Institutes in Asia and the Pacific (LOGOTRI) in 1999. LOGOTRI now has its independent secretariat at the Urban Development Training Centre of the Local Development Training Academy of Nepal. LOGOTRI can become an important partner in promoting training of women in local government and in providing training for gender mainstreaming in local government.

Similarly networks such as the Regional Network of Local Authorities for the Management of Human Settlements (CityNet), Center for Asia Pacific Women in Politics (CAPWIP) and programes such as the UNDP-Asia-Pacific Gender Equality Network (APGEN), the UNDP-PARAGON Regional Governance Programe and the UNDP/UNOPS The Urban Governance Initiative (TUGI) can also play a pivotal role in promoting training and research at the country level.

2.7.4. Resource Mobilisation

International and regional organisations can also contribute to promoting gender balance in local government by assisting the country-level networks and organisations in mobilising monetary and human resources for training as well as for helping women candidates fund their election campaigns. This could be done through lobbying with political parties, private foundations and funds in developed countries and through developing linkages between political parties from developed countries and political parties in developing countries similar to the work done by the foundations of the German political parties.

References

Ashworth, Georgina, 1996, *Gendered Governance: An Agenda for Change, Gender* in Development Monograph Series, Number 3, UNDP, New York

Beall, Jo, 1996, *Urban Governance: Why Gender Matters, Gender* in Development Monograph Series, Number 1, UNDP, New York

Golandaz, H.M., 1996, *Human Resource Development for Better Cities with special reference to India*, Bombay, 1996

Haque, Syeda Obaida, 1996, *Urban Livelihood for Women*, Shakti Foundation, Bangladesh

Karmhus, (Mayor) Ingebjorg, 1996, *Municipal Planning on Women's Terms*, Experiences from the Project, Leksvik Municipality, Norway

Kumari, Ranjana and Anju Dubey, 1994, *Women Parliamentarians: A Study in the Indian Context*, Har-Anand Publications, New Delhi

Nuss, S.A., 1995, *List of Statistics on Women in Government, Public Sector Employment and Administration*, Judiciary United Nations Agencies and Conferences.

Siddiqui, Kamal, (ed.), 1992, *Local Government in South Asia: A Comparative Study*, University Press Limited, Dhaka, Bangladesh

Thomson, Suteera, 1995, *Women in Decision-Making Positions: Politics and Administration,* Gender and Development Institute, Bangkok, Thailand

3

Women in Political Decision-making

Two articles of the Convention on the Elimination of All Forms of Discrimination against Women (CEDAW) deal with women's participation in political and public life. Article 7 commits States parties to ensure equality between women and men in political and public life, including the right to vote, to be eligible for election, to participate in formulating government policy, to hold public office and to perform public functions. The Convention includes the right to participate in non-governmental organisations and other associations. Article 8 requires States parties to ensure that women have equal opportunities with men to represent their governments at the international level and to participate in the work of international organisations.

The Committee on the Elimination of Discrimination against Women provided additional guidance in the implementation of the Convention in 1997 in its General Recommendation 23, which highlighted the application of the Convention to all levels of government and to the activities of a range of organisations concerned with public and political life, including public boards, local councils, and the activities of political parties, trade unions and professional associations. General Recommendation 23 also stated that: "It is the Government's fundamental responsibility to encourage these initiatives to lead and guide public opinion and change attitudes that discriminate against women or discourage women's involvement in political and public life."

The Commission on the Status of Women continued to pay attention to the issue and adopted agreed conclusions on women and decision-making processes in 1997 and 2006.In its resolution 1325 on women, peace and security, the Security Council called on Member States to increase the representation of women in all institutions and mechanisms dealing with the prevention, management and resolution of conflict, including as special representatives and envoys of the Secretary-General and within the field operations as military observers, civilian police, human rights and humanitarian personnel.

The importance of the issue has been recognized within the framework of the Millennium Development Goals. One of the indicators for monitoring Millennium Development Goal 3 on gender equality is the proportion of seats held by women in national parliaments.

The 2005 World Summit Outcome reaffirmed the commitments to increased representation of women in government decision-making bodies, including opportunities to participate fully in the political process.

3.1. Progress at the National Level

Marked progress has been made since 1995 in the numbers of women elected to national parliaments.

Rwanda achieved 48.8 percent representation of women in the 2003 elections, a dramatic increase from the 17.1 percent representation in 1995 that illustrated the positive results of focused and coordinated efforts to address this issue in the period of post-conflict reconstruction. As noted by the Inter-Parliamentary Union, for countries in transition, "the process of establishing new constitutions and institutions and rewriting the rules of the political landscape provides a golden opportunity for women to influence the process and make their voices heard, especially in the drafting of electoral and political party laws."

It is also notable that, in addition to the post-conflict group, there is one other country in Sub-Saharan Africa and another four in Central and South America that have passed the 30 percent threshold and have considerably higher representation of women than a number of OECD countries with more resources and more established traditions of electoral politics, again demonstrating that the advancement of women is possible through political will and targeted action.

Almost all of the countries 20 countries included in table 1 have used some form of electoral quotas to ensure that women account for a certain number of percentage of candidates for office or officeholders, whether through a constitutional commitment, a provision of election legislation, voluntary action by political parties, or some combination of these.

Table 1. Women in national parliaments, 2006

Country	*% women*	*Last elections*	*Electoral system*	*If quota & type of quota*
Rwanda	48.8	2003	List PR	Yes – constitutional commitment, legislationestablishing 30% reserved seats (indirectly elected)
Sweden	45.3	2002	List PR	Yes – voluntary party quotas for candidates
Costa Rica	38.6	2006	List PR	Yes – legislated quota of 40% women candidates on party lists
Norway	37.9	2005	List PR	Yes – voluntary party quotas for candidates
Finland	37.5	2003	List PR	No
Denmark	36.9	2005	List PR	No – but did have at times in the past
Netherlands	36.7	2003	List PR	Yes – voluntary party quotas for candidates
Cuba	36.0	2003	Majority	No
Spain	36.0	2004	List PR	Yes – voluntary party quotas for candidates
Argentina	35.0	2005	List PR	Yes – constitutional commitment; legislated quota of 30% women on party lists; political party quotas for candidates
Mozambique	34.8	2004	List PR	Yes – voluntary party quotas for candidates
Belgium	34.7	2003	List PR	Yes – legislated quota of 33% women on party lists

Austria	33.9	2002	List PR	Yes – voluntary party quotas for candidates
Iceland	33.3	2003	List PR	Yes – voluntary party quotas for candidates
South Africa	32.8	2004	List PR	Yes – voluntary party quotas for candidates
New Zealand	32.2	2005	Mixed M & PR	No
Germany	31.8	2005	Mixed M & PR	Yes – voluntary party quotas for candidates
Guyana	30.8	2001	List PR	Yes – constitutional requirement for 33% quota for women on electoral lists
Burundi	30.5	2005	List PR	Yes – constitutional commitment, legislated quota of 30% women on party lists
Tanzania	30.4	2005	FPTP	Yes – constitutional quota, election law quota regulation (special seats)

Most countries have elected bodies at sub-national levels, some with state or provincial governments and most with elected local councils. Very little data is available for the intermediate (state or provincial level), but a database on women councilors and mayors is being developed by the organisation United Cities and Local Governments (UCLG) as part of their Global Programe on Women in Local Decision-Making. UCLG's conclusions from the preliminary and partial data available in 2005 were that 20 percent of councilors overall were women and that the participation of women in local politics was increasing steadily.

A number of countries have used constitutional or legislative quota systems to advance progress toward more equitable representation at the local level. The Global Database on Quotas for Women provides information on 30 countries with quotas at the sub-national level, mostly low and middle-income countries but also several in Europe – France, Greece, and Portugal. In some countries, an initiative to decentralize decision-making to more local levels have provided an opportunity to establish measures to ensure the participation of women. For example, India led the way before the

Fourth World Conference on Women in Beijing when its 1993 constitutional amendments to strengthen local governance included a measure to reserve one third of seats in panchayats (local governing councils) for women. Pakistan's Devolution of Power Plan of 2000 reserved one-third of seats for women at all sub-national levels.

The Indian experience with reserved seats for women has been much studied, and it has been cited as indicating the way women's presence and participation can change politics:

> "In India studies of women in panchayats attest to the myriad ways women's presence has changed local politics. There are reports that women have made the panchayats more responsive to community demands for infrastructure, housing, schools, and health. Women officials have improved implementation of various government programs, and their presence has made women citizens more likely to take advantage of state services and demand their rights. When women are the heads of panchayats, there is a greater likelihood that policies that are sensitive to women's needs will be implemented. Such effects take time to register, however. In the early stages of women's reservations, many women councilors seem merely to act as surrogates of their male relatives, but over time, they acquire the confidence and skills to act independently."

Other notable developments include the election of women heads of government and state in Chile, Germany, and Liberia in 2005 and 2006, joining a number of other women presidents and prime ministers (Bangladesh, Finland, Ireland, Jamaica, Latvia, Mozambique, New Zealand, the Philippines, Republic of Korea, and Sao Tomé and Principe). However, this number of 13 women heads of government or state barely marks an increase compared to 1995.

Several countries reported increased representation of women in the judiciary or appointments of women to key judicial positions (including, for example, Chile, Djibouti, Egypt, Nicaragua, Slovenia, and Spain). Four out of the nine judges on the Supreme Court of Canada, the country's final court of appeal, are women, including the Chief Justice. This is the result of considerable change throughout the Canadian judicial system in recent decades. In 2006, 29 percent of all federally-appointed judges were women, compared to 0.05 percent in 1969, the year that the Chief Justice began her career as a lawyer.

3.2. Gaps and Challenges

The developments noted above are promising and show what can be achieved. However, progress has been slow in all structures of power and types of decision-making.

3.2.1. Under-representation in National Parliaments

Women accounted for 11.6 percent on average of members of national parliaments in 1995, and this increased to only 17.3 percent by May 2007 despite the target of 30 percent that was to be reached by 1995 – a full decade earlier. There remain a number of countries with no representation of women in parliament (including one that has not yet extended the vote to women).

Evidence suggests that a major factor influencing progress is the nature of electoral systems and the practices of political parties. Proportional representation systems result in a higher proportion of women than those with plurality/majority or mixed proportional systems: overall, the former have an average of 16 percent women compared to 11 percent for the latter based on data for 174 countries in 2003. This is in large part because of the way the system interacts with the concerns and strategies of political parties: in plurality/majority systems the incentives to parties are to select the most "electable" candidate, whereas proportional systems allow for a greater number of candidates to be put forward. Even so, where women are placed on party lists also has a major influence on the likelihood of women obtaining a seat. Political parties thus play a key role in both types of system.

Even when elected, women are less likely than men to be in higher-level decision-making positions in national parliaments. The number of women serving as presiding officers in parliament decreased over the decade, down to 8% in 2005 from 10% in 1995. They are also continue to be under-represented in cabinet appointments. While Sweden and Spain had achieved a gender balance in cabinet appointments in 2005, their performance is the exception rather than the rule – globally, the proportion was 14.3 percent women as of January 2005.

3.2.2. Numbers and Effectiveness at the Local Level

Elections at the local level offer a greater number of opportunities for women simply because of the greater number of elected bodies and positions, and participation at the local level has served as a training ground for many politicians, both women and men. Great strides have been made through the use of quotas at the local level in several countries. For example, Bangladesh introduced reserved seats for women in local elections in 1997, which resulted in a total of 12,828 women elected to these reserved seats in some 4,400 locations, in addition to 110 women elected to general seats (of which there were over 39,000) and 20 women succeeding in the election as chairpersons (less than 1 percent). However, it remains a challenge for these women to function effectively because their participation is not yet well-accepted by their male colleagues and they face considerable resistance in carrying out functions and exercising authority. Many of the women elected to office come with limited experience in elected office and government structures. In Bangladesh and many other countries, the challenge of ensuring that local governments are effective and accountable to their citizens – both women and men – includes ensuring that male members have the capacity to work effectively with their female colleagues, and that the women members have the knowledge and skills to use the relevant procedures and address local issues. The trend toward decentralization of responsibilities to the local level increases the importance of addressing this challenge.

3.2.3. Share in Public and Private Sector Managerial Positions

Women's representation in decision-making positions in the civil service and public sector bodies are also concerns of the Platform for Action. The limited information available to assess progress illustrates the challenges in this area. The European Commission's database on women and men in decision-making is one of the few sources that focus specifically on senior public service positions. Considering the proportion of women in the highest-ranked civil service position under the Minister, only 5 of 31 countries passed the 30 percent threshold in 2006, although several others achieved this at the second highest level. Occupation data from labor force surveys on the census provides another source of data, although data about the public sector may be difficult to extract as labor force surveys generally combine information from the public and private sectors. The ILO has calculated that women's overall share of public and private sector managerial jobs (including posts as legislators, senior officials and managers) was between 20 and 40 percent in 48 of the 63 countries for which data could be obtained, a figure that remains considerably lower than women's overall share in employment.

Finally, considering the participation of women in strategic decision-making in the private sector, the "glass ceiling" – the barriers that limit the numbers of women reaching the top of the corporate hierarchy – is still evident. In the United States, a 2005 survey of women corporate officers found that Fortune 500 companies had on average 21.8 corporate officers, of which women held on average 3.6 positions. The study found that there had been little change over the previous decade and concluded that, with this rate of progress, "it could take 40 years for women to achieve parity with men in corporate officer positions." Another study by the same organisation found that the Fortune 500 companies with the highest percentages of women corporate officers, yielded higher returns than those with lower percentages of women. In Europe, a 2006 study found that among Europe's top corporations, the number with at least one woman on their board was higher in 2006 than in 2004, but that European corporations were lagging behind their American counterparts, except in Scandinavia, where proactive policies had been taken. The study also found that few of the women on boards held leadership position – less than 2 percent held positions as chair of the board or chief executive officer.

3.3. Measures in Support of Women

In addition to setting out government commitments, the Platform for Action urges a range of actors to take measures in support of women's participation in power structures and decision-making. These include political parties, the private sector, trade unions, the judiciary, employers' organisations, academic institutions and civil society, among others. However, governments have a lead role in encouraging and facilitating action by others, as well as in implementing measures in the management of public sector institutions. National governments can:

— Consider the potential for temporary special measures to accelerate progress toward gender balance in elected office, particularly in the context of electoral reform and decentralization;
— Develop or support programes that provide training to women candidates in the skills needed for effective campaigning, and to elected women in the skills in effectively carrying out their functions and supporting equality objectives;
— Facilitate linkages among various actors seeking to bring gender equality issues and women's views into the decision-making process;
— Establish specific time-bound targets and action plans for increasing women's representation in decision-making in the public sector;
— Establish mechanisms to facilitate consideration of women candidates in appointments to senior positions in government and public sector boards and agencies;
— Promote awareness and support for the goal of gender equality among decision-makers through public awareness campaigns; and
— Strengthen monitoring, reporting and knowledge about women's participation in decision-making through improved data collection, dissemination and analysis.

3.3.1. Influencing the Electoral Process.

Electoral quotas have been an important element in achieving progress in many countries, at both the national and local levels. However, quotas are only effective if they are appropriate to the particular electoral system of a country (or the level of government to which they apply). Proportional representation systems offer a broader range of options for quotas than plurality/majority systems. Even so, a quota initiative may require constitutional change or sanction, and the opportunity to introduce a quota system would therefore only arrive in the context of larger reform processes in which broad public support for them has been mobilized as has been the case in a number of post-conflict countries. Quotas can be useful measures, but the design and implementation must be strategically pursued.

If quotas are intended to be implemented by political parties, they must be designed so that evasion is difficult. However, as voluntary implementation is preferable to implementation under compulsion, it would seem desirable to seek to build broad public support at the stage of formulating such provisions in order to facilitate implementation. Quotas can also have a downside if the nature of the quota-based system results in women members who are seen as having less legitimacy as elected representatives than their male peers. Political parties play a key role in the electoral system. Some observers have suggested that not only are they the gatekeepers in women's access to politics, but that quotas have been most successful when they have been adopted on a voluntary basis by political parties who come to see this as being in their own interest.

Quota systems also need to be supplemented with other policies to enable women to be effective representatives. The importance of access to training and skills development was emphasised by the United Nations Expert Group on Equal Participation of Women and Men in Decision-making Processes:

> "Given that many women have had little experience with running for political office, it is of utmost importance that training be made readily available to allow women to develop and fine-tune their political skills. Once in office, women may also benefit from leadership training and mentoring to increase efficiency and ensure sustainability.

Training programes should also target men, to expose them to the complexities of gender discrimination and the necessity of and mechanisms for promoting women in public office."

3.3.2. Facilitating Linkages among Elected Women

Women elected to parliament at the national or local level remain in a minority, and many are relative newcomers to the process, so alliances among them and with other women's and equality advocates can be important to enabling women to be effective as parliamentarians and in advocacy for equality issues. The national women's machinery can play a role in facilitating the formation and work of such alliances. In Rwanda, for example, seminars during the constitutional process brought together the Forum of Women Parliamentarians, the Legal and Constitutional Committee, the Ministry of Gender Issues and representatives of civil society organisations. Through close collaboration among these actors, progress was made in a number of areas: mobilization of women to participate in the constitutional drafting and in the elections as voters and candidates; sensitization of the public on existing inequalities and women's rights; sensitization of decision-makers and planners on gender equality issues; development of a national gender equality policy; and joint work to review and advocate the repeal of discriminatory legislation.

In Uganda, a non-partisan Women's Caucus brought together members of the Constituent Assembly elected in 1994 and, with the assistance of the national women's machinery, organized seminars and skills-training workshops on advocacy, campaign management, constituency building, parliamentary procedures, etc. They also formed links with key organisations such as the Uganda Women Lawyers' Association, which assisted with the consideration of constitutional provisions, as well as with organisations that enabled the Women's Caucus to remain informed of the views of women at the grass-roots and to communicate with them. The experience gained through their effective interventions during the Constituent Assembly formed the basis for later work in building the capacity of women leaders at the local level and potential candidates for parliament, and in incorporating gender equality perspectives in legislation before parliament.

Many countries have established formal parliamentary bodies to consider issues related to the position of women and gender equality. These take a range of forms and many include men as well as women. An informative on-line database on the structures and mandates of such specialised bodies is maintained by the Inter-Parliamentary Union. It includes, for example: the Gender Caucus in Burkina Faso, the Network of Parliamentarians on Gender Issues in Niger, the Standing Committee on the Status of Women in Canada, and the Special Committee on Gender and Equality in Uruguay. These bodies provide forums for the discussion of gender equality issues among members and potentially a forum for exchanges with civil society organisations and advocates. This can be an important opportunity for another form of participation by women in decision-making by providing opportunities for women's organisations to participate in discussions of policy decisions that shape their societies and affect their lives. This is another area in which national women's machineries can play facilitating roles through, for example, bringing women's organisations to the attention of the parliamentary bodies, or enabling women's organisations to develop advocacy skills.

3.3.3. Making Information on Qualified Women

Ensuring that decision-makers have ready access to information about potential women candidates for senior appointments is a way of counter-balancing the more established networks that men with similar experience may have to bring their name to the attention of decision-makers. It is also a practical way to respond to the tendency of managers to assume that qualified candidates will have qualities similar to their own, or that there are no qualified women in the field assumptions that work against women as long as they are a small minority in decision-making positions.

The development of a directory or database of women in leadership positions is an approach reported by a number of countries. A more active approach has been taken by New Zealand, which has established an office that provides a service both to government decision-makers seeking to identify potential candidates and to women with the relevant interests and skills. This approach thus also addresses the information constraint often faced by women that appointments to senior positions may be made before information about the openings reaches women who may be qualified and interested.

Sector-specific strategies may also deliver good results. For example, women who could be qualified for appointments to the judiciary may also be less known to decision-makers than similarly qualified men. An approach taken by Canada to broaden the field of candidates for judicial appointments was to shift from a top-down selection system to one in which those interested in an appointment are required to submit an application, which is then reviewed by committees composed of judges, lawyers and citizens. The committees determine whether the candidates are qualified before the names enter a pool for possible appointments. This has brought into the system many women who may have been unnoticed in a strictly top-down system.

3.3. 4. Strengthening Analysis of Issues and Progress

There continues to be a need for better data to assess issues and progress. Data are lacking on many aspects of women's participation in leadership and decision-making positions. A United Nations review of data collection at the national level found that statistical agencies in many countries do not routinely collect and disseminate statistics on women in power and decision-making, due to a lack of capacity for collection and reporting and poorly developed methodologies for the use of existing data to examine gender equality issues in this area.

The best tracked level is the most clearly defined and visible – the number of women in national parliaments and key elected offices. The work of the Inter-Parliamentary Union has served to ensure reporting on these figures by national parliaments and the presentation of this information in an international database. Efforts are also being made by the organisation United Cities and Local Governments (UCLG), which has begun work on a database on women's participation in municipal and local governments, but this is a more complicated task because of the greater number and variety of levels and because limited data on these levels is gathered by national agencies.

Equally important is improved data on women's participation in other types of decision-making positions in the public sector, such as senior positions in the public service appointments to the judiciary, and positions on the boards of public agencies. Data on the proportion of women in managerial jobs in the public and private sectors together is not sufficiently specific to monitor the implementation of government commitments to the increased participation of women in decision-making positions over which the government itself has the power of promotion or appointment. Better data on women in such positions at the sub-national level is also important to the elaboration of policies at that level, and is particular urgent in those countries in which decentralisation processes increase the scope of responsibilities of local governments in policy development and service delivery.

3.4. Equal Opportunities Policy in European Union

With 52%, women make up the majority of the EU population. They are better educated than ever before and are becoming increasingly involved in working life. However, their equal participation in senior positions in society, industry and politics continues to be the exception. Only in Sweden are more than 50% of its government members female. On average in the EU only one in five members of a parliament or government is female. The national differences are also considerable. And this despite the fact that there are important framework conditions for the equal treatment of women: In the Treaties of Rome (1957) Article 119 stipulates "equal pay for equal work". This laid the foundation stone for the equal opportunities policy in the EU.

Since the mid-1970s the EU Council of Ministers has adopted directives to establish the principle of equal treatment for women and men in EU Member States (e.g. equal opportunities for access to employment and vocational training, social security, self-employment, and protection for pregnant women in the workplace). The European Court of Justice has developed legislation which makes direct and indirect gender discrimination unlawful in all the legal systems of Member States.

Since the beginning of the 1980s the European Commission has been organising action programes to promote equal opportunities. Whereas in the first two programes the emphasis was on equal opportunities at work, the 3rd Medium-Term Action Programe has recognised the importance of the active participation of women in political decision-making processes for equal opportunities policies. It has analysed and supported this through the Expert Network "Women in Decision-making". One of the main goals of the 4th Action Programe (1996-2000) is the balanced participation of women and men in decision-making. The follow-up programe announced in March 2000 will not change this weighting in any way.

Since the support from the structural funds failed to reach women in the EU, or if so only to a minor degree, the principle of equal opportunities for women and men in the labor market has been given are inforced bas is through the 1993 reform in the framework regulation for all three funds. By means of the NOW (New Opportunities for Women) scheme under the Community Initiative on EMPLOYMENT (1994-1999) financed by the European Social Fund, the only programe specifically for women has been created within the framework of the Community Initiatives. Its goals are model qualifications for occupations of the future, professional independence, better reconciliation of work and family and the encouragement of promotion into decision-making positions. In 1995 the equal opportunities group was set up. It includes five members of the European Commission and is chaired by the President. Its task is to make equal opportunities for women and men an integral part of all areas of policy (gender mainstreaming). In the Charter of Rome (1996) the EU Ministers for Women's Affairs call for a renewal of politics and society by means of an active equal opportunities policy: "The equal participation of women and men in decision-making processes is our major goal at European level". In its Recommendation of 2 December 1996 the Council of the European Union calls on the Member States to develop suitable measures and strategies to correct the under-representation of women in decision-making positions.

Forty years after the Treaties of Rome the EU Member States undertook in the Amsterdam Treaty (1997) to make equal opportunities an essential component of European and national policies. This makes equality between women and men a criterion against which all areas of policy must be measured. The Declaration of Paris (1999) carries on from the above commitment of the Commission and Member States in Athens (1992) and Rome (1996) and calls for a political pact between all the stakeholders. Gender mainstreaming was the tool with which equality could at last be guaranteed not only de jure but also de facto. The Declaration explicitly involves decision-makers in industry who should, in their own interests, tap female potential left fallow up to now in decision-making positions.

3.4.1. Gender Mainstreaming

Thanks to the efforts of the European Union the gender mainstreaming principle was laid down in the action platform of the Beijing World Women's Conference in 1995. Since then it has shaped the EU's equal opportunities policy. In essence, mainstreaming means the commitment by the European Commission to pursue an equal opportunities policy as a cross-sectional task. With the Amsterdam Treaty ratified in 1999 by the Member States, the strategy was developed further under the term Gender Mainstreaming. The term stands for the inclusion of equal opportunities for men and women in all areas of policy coupled with the continuation of positive activities (specific promotion of women) until equality has actually been achieved. Hence, equal opportunities is no longer a special subject but a fundamental component of all EU policies as a guiding principle of the actions of the Community bodies and a commitment of all EU Member States. In concrete terms this means that all proposals, plans, measures and programes must be examined prior to their adoption in order to determine what consequences they will have for equality between women and men. The same applies to the implementation of progress monitoring and evaluation.

The first effects can be se en in the Luxembourg Process, named after the Luxembourg Employment Summit (1997) at which the heads of state and government of the European Union adopted the European Employment Strategy (EPS). According to this strategy, the Council decides annually the employment policy guidelines which are then implemented by the Member States in National Action Plans (NAPs). Gender mainstreaming applies both to the EPS and to the most recent reform of the Structural Funds within the framework of the Agenda 2000.

The new ESF-funded Community Initiative E Q UA L (2000-2006) also incorporates the dual strategy of gender mainstreaming: inclusion of the equal opportunities for women and men dimension in all promoted measures and positive actions in the form of specific women's projects.

3.4.2. Women in European Commission

The European Commission was established in 1957 but more than three decades passed before women were appointed as Commissioners. Vasso Papandreou (Greece) and Christiane Scrivener (France) were the first two female Commissioners to come to Brussels in 1989. In the following period of office (1995-1999) there were already five female Commissioners; this corresponds to a share of 25%. In the new Commission (1999-2003) this share has not changed.

3.4.3. Women in European Council

The heads of state and government of EU Member States, represented on the European Council, no longer belong to a male-only club. At present, there is no female head of government in the EU but the Council has two members who are heads of state (Tarja Halonen/ Finland and Mary McAleese/Ireland) and three ministers of foreign affairs (Anna Lindh/ Sweden, Benita Maria Ferrero-Waldner/ Austria, Lydie Polfer/Luxembourg).

3.4.4. Women in European Parliament

Women account for 31.0% of the members of the European Parliament. In the "world rankings" of national parliaments it is in position 6 behind Iceland (34.9%) and Germany (31.2%), and in the EU in position 7 behind the Netherlands (36.7%) and the Federal Republic of Germany.

The French Nicole Fontaine was elected President by the European Parliament at the last European elections in 1999. Of her 14 deputies one is a woman. Women chair five of the 17 parliamentary committees (environment, health and consumer protection, legal affairs and internal market, economic and monetary affairs, budget control, women's rights). In committees like the environment, culture, foreign trade and petitions they reach the "critical mass" of 30% and more. As a rule they make up one in five committee members.

3.4.5. Women in Economic and Social Committee

The various interest groups from economic and social life in the EU are represented on the Economic and Social Committee. It is chaired by the Italian, Beatrice Rangoni-Machiavelli. There is roughly the same number of women in each of the three socially relevant groups – employers, employees and various interests. This amounts to a total share of 17.1% which is very low. Compared to the previous period of office, however, this number did increase by 2.1%.

3.4.6. Women in Committee of the Regions

222 delegates from local and regional politics in the EU Member States look after the interests of their regions in Brussels. In this political body, too, women are very much under-represented with a share of 14% (31 women). They are, however, far more active than their male colleagues. In the first period of office of this body (1994 - 1998) they prepared around 20% of the Committee drafts, twice as many as their percentage share in that body (9.9%). Luxembourg, the Netherlands and Portugal do not send any female delegates to the Committee of the Regions. Finland and Ireland have the highest proportion of women (both 44.4%).

3.4.7. Women in National Parliaments

One in four members of the national parliaments in the EU is a woman. However, this figure ignores the considerable national differences. Sweden with a proportion of women of 43.6% (1994: 40.4%) comes closest to parity-based representation. There are far fewer women in the parliaments of the Mediterranean region (aside from Spain) and in France, Belgium and Ireland. In five Member States women are parliamentary presidents (Finland, the Netherlands, Spain, Sweden and the United Kingdom). In almost all parliaments, women chair one or more parliamentary committees (with the exception of Ireland). The subjects are highly diverse and have long since moved beyond " soft" policy areas like social affairs, culture, youth or the family.

In almost all Member States women are also active in "hard" areas. They sit on budget and financial committees (exception: Ireland) but on a lower scale than their presence in parliament. All the same, in the Netherlands, Finland and the Federal Republic of Germany at least one in five members of the budget committee is female. In Sweden this committee is almost equally composed of women and men.

3.4.8. Women in Upper and Lower Chambers

In nine EU Member States the parliament is made up of two chambers. In the "upper chambers" (the name varies) women are represented on a lower scale than in the "lower chambers" (exceptions: Belgium,

Ireland). The EU average is 15.8%. Not all these chambers have elected members.

3.4.9. Women in the National Governments

The era of group photos without any women is over. In each government of the EU Member States there are at least two women. Besides Ireland, Finland now also has a female president. In the United Kingdom, the Netherlands and Denmark, queens are the highest representatives of state. The highest state office in female hands, however, is no guarantee for the balanced participation of women in government. In Portugal only seven women amongst 53 men have governmental responsibilities (11.7%).

There is a total of 77 female ministers and 62 female junior ministers in the EU. Almost one in four members of government is a woman (24.8%). The classical women's area, family policy, continues to be a female domain. In many countries it is located along with labor and social policy or youth and equal opportunities policy in one ministry. Women are becoming increasingly responsible for the so-called hard areas a total of 23 times as ministers or junior ministers of foreign affairs, justice, economic affairs, internal affairs and defence.

3.4.10. Women in Regional and Municipal Policy

In most countries the proportion of women in regional and local parliaments and governments is lower than on the national level.

Only 11 out of 15 EU Member States have elected regional parliaments. In almost all cases the proportion of women is below the critical mass of 30% in parliament and government (female ministers and female junior ministers). In Sweden, by contrast, women and men are almost equally represented in regional parliaments (47.2%). In three regions they have reached a share of more than 50%. In Styria/Austria and in Schleswig-Holstein/Germany women are at the top of regional government.

3.4.11. Strategies for Equal Participation

The proportion of women in executive poiitical positions has increased almost everywhere in the EU in the 1990s. The critical mass of 30% has still not been reached in most decision-making bodies. Only a long-term strategy can lead to the balanced participation of women and men in political decision-making processes. In the Scandinavian countries laws on equality between women and men introduced in the 1980s contain provisions for the balanced participation of women and men in public committees. The participation of women in political decision-making processes in these countries is a model for the EU.

Quota regulations are an important tool for giving women access to leading political positions.

Up to the spring of 2000 Belgium was the only EU Member State with a statutory quota regulation. It obliges all parties to give one-third of their list positions to women. After the elections in 1999, this led to a considerable increase of women in the national parliament from 13.3% to 23.3%. 1994 saw the establishment in France of the association "Demain la Parité." It organised campaigns for the equal representation of women and men in politics successfully. The public debate led to the adopting of a statutory regulation in the spring of 2000. The law stipulates that parties must present an equal number of women and men on their lists of candidates for local and European elections as well as the elections to the Senate conducted according the principle of proportional representation. National and regional elections are covered by the majority vote principle which does not allow quotas. Here, the law envisages financial sanctions for parties which deviate by 2% or more from the parity principle. They will lose part of their state subsidies. The law will be applied for the first time to the local elections in the year 2001.

In Italy there was a statutory quota regulation in 1993 for the local and provincial elections. It was rescinded in 1995 by the Italian Constitutional Court on the grounds that it contradicted the principle of equality. The proportion of women in the respective bodies more than doubled in the space of those two years from 6% to 13%. The Dutch government is pursuing a different path towards increasing the number of women in parliament. It offers the political parties financial support for strategies and activities aiming to increase the proportion of women in elected bodies. Aside from one small party, all organisations have accepted the subsidies and are developing strategies to promote women.

In most EU Member States the political parties have undertaken to increase the political participation of women by means of a quota system.

"1 in 2 a woman" was the undertaking of the Swedish Social Democrats in 1994. Since then Swedish women have not in fact been represented everywhere by 50%, but they are present in political office in far greater numbers than before.

In general the quotas have a positive effect on the nomination of female candidates. There is a higher representation of women in executive bodies of political parties with a quota regulation. Only in rare cases, however, are the quotas of the political parties reached in the national parliaments.

In Finland and Austria the Social Democrats have also reached their quota of 40% and 25% in their parliamentary factions.

In the Netherlands and the Federal Republic of Germany it is the small, left-wing parties which enforce their 50% quota in parliament, too. The position of female candidates on the lists is an important factor in their election. Some parties like the alliance of ecological parties in the Federal Republic of Germany, "B90/ Grüne", consistently use the "zipper" principle (men and women are placed alternately on the party list).

With this same principle the alliance of socialists (PS), left-wing radicals (PRDG) and citizens' movement (MDC) in France succeeded in increasing its proportion of female parliamentarians. The same holds for the French ecological alliance: from 29.4% to 45.5%; ecological party to 44.4%.

By means of awareness-raising campaigns non-governmental organisations in particular encourage male and female voters to vote for female candidates. This increases the pressure on parties to put forward more women. In the United Kingdom the "300 group" runs public campaigns. Its goal is to have 300 female MPs elected to parliament (at present they have a total of 121 or 18.4%). "Emily's list" provides financial support for the election campaign of female candidates irrespective of the political party they belong to. Prior to the elections for the European Parliament in 1999 the Commission published a brochure in 11 languages and a "campaign kit" which can be used in all EU Member States by governments and NGOs. The material distributed free of charge contains templates for ads and a TV spot. This is modelled on the campaign "Vote for Balance" organised in 1994 by the European Expert Network "Women in Decision-making".

The "*European Database – Women in Decision-making*" contains facts and figures on the political participation of women in the European Union and in Member States of the European Economic Area – Norway, Iceland and Liechtenstein. From 2000 onwards data will be recorded in the accession countries in central and eastern Europe.

The database can be accessed publicly via the Internet and is regularly updated (e.g. updates after elections).

The project is part of the Community's 4th Medium-Term Action Programe for Equal Opportunities for Women and Men. In the year 2000 the database will be extended to take in the banking and finance sector and the forward-oriented sector information and communications technologies.

The database is the basis for EU-wide analyses and studies. It contains a growing volume of information on progress in equal opportunities policies in the Member States and about women's paths into politics. It offers politicians, scientists, social partners and the media arguments and incentives for political actions with the goal of increasing the participation of women in decision-making positions. Together with supporters from everywhere in Europe the project team is endeavoring to guarantee the survival of the database beyond the support period of the 4th Action Programe.

3.4.12. Female Experts Network

The database draws on the work of the European Expert Network "Women in Decision-making" (1992-1996). Today, it co-operates with female experts from 18 EU and EEA Member States and is co-ordinated by the Frauen Computer ZentrumBerlin (FCZB – Women's Computer Centre Berlin). Another cooperation partner is the Center for the American Woman and Politics (CAW P), New Jersey/ USA which has been researching the political participation of women in the USA since 1971.

REFERENCES

Beckwith, Karen. 1992. "Comparative Research and Electoral Systems: Lessons from France and Italy." *Women and Politics* 12, no. 1: 1-33

Buckley, Mary and Malcolm Anderson, eds. 1988. *Women, Equality and Europe*. London: Macmillan

Davidson, Alastair. 1989. "The Italian women's movement and the Italian Communist Party." Pp. 156-187 in *Politics of the future*, ed. ?. South Melbourne: ?.

Gaspard, Françoise, ed. 1997. *Les femmes dans la prise de décision en France et en Europe* (Women in decision-making in France and Europe). Paris: L'Harmattan

Norris, Pippa and Joni Lovenduski. 1995. *Political Recruitment: Gender, Race, and Class in the British Parliament*. New York: Cambridge University Press.

United Nations. 1991. *Women in Decision-Making: Case-Study on Greece*. New York: United Nations.

Vallance, Elizabeth. 1981. "Women in the House of Commons." *Political Studies* 29, no. 3: 407-414.

4

Status of Women in Indian Politics

Despite the longstanding and vigorous women' movement, patriarchy remains deeply entrenched in India, influencing the structure of its political and social institutions and determining the opportunities open to women and men. The negotiation and conflict between patriarchy and the women' movement are central to the constitution of the nation-state. It is scarcely news that women are underrepresented in Indian politics. The issue has come sharply into focus for some years now, partly because of the thwarted moves towards providing one-third reservation for women in legislative bodies including Parli ament, along with the more successful moves to enforce such reservation in elections to rural panchayats.

What has emerged quite clearly in the current very long drawn out election process is how little has changed at one level since Independence. The candidates fielded by the various political parties are still dominantly male: women account for only five t o ten per cent of all candidates across parties and regions. This is the same broad pattern that has been observed in virtually the previous general elections in the country.

This is the case despite the hullabaloo made over the Constitution (84th Amendment) Bill relating to women's reservation even last year. The very parties that were most explicitly in favour of pushing for such reservation have put up the same proportion of women as always, and certainly not more than other parties that had opposed the Bill. The Congress party, led by a woman and supposedly pushing for reservation for women, has only 10 per cent of women among the candidates announced so far. For the BJP the proportion of women candidates is even lower at 7 per cent. Even in the case of the Communist Party of India (Marxist), only 7 per cent of the candidates are women.

What may be more significant in terms of political power than the proportion of women fighting the Lok Sabha polls is the importance of women in inner party structures. Here women are by and large even less represented, in all parties. Only in the All In dia Anna Dravida Munnetra Kazhagam (AIADMK) has there been a conscious move to bring many more women into decision-making levels and posts within the party.

In most parties, the women members are by and large thin on the ground if not invisible in the actual decision-making bodies and rarely influence the more significant party policies. Most often, indeed, they are relegated to the "women's wing" of the par ty, and made to concentrate on what are seen as specifically "women's issues" such as dowry and rape cases, and occasionally on more general concerns like price rise which are seen to affect especially "housewives".

Despite all this, only the foolhardy would suggest that women are unimportant in Indian politics today. In many ways, most of them qualitative, they have never been as important as they are today. This is most evident in the proliferation of women leader s and in the fact that, even though some of them may head parties that are relatively small in the national context, they simply cannot be ignored.

What is even more significant is that in many cases these women leaders have not emerged through the familiar South Asian paradigm of dynastic advantage. Sonia Gandhi, obviously, is a clear example of a dynastic leader, with an almost iconic relevance, b ut in fact in this respect she is in the minority among women leaders today. Thus, Jayalalitha and Mayawati may have originally based their rise in politics on their proximity to particular male leaders, but they are clearly now significant leaders in th eir own right, who can influence not only the decisions of their own parties but even the course of national politics. Mamata Banerjee, despite or indeed because of her controversial nature, is the leader of a party who can claim to have got where she is on her own, without male assistance in any of the more obvious ways.

Of course, one myth that is easily exploded by the role played by such women leaders is that political leadership by women is dramatically different from that by men. Nor is it necessarily more colourful, as some of the more extravagant male politicians like Laloo Prasad Yadav can establish.

Indeed, the truth is that most of our women political leaders are no better or worse than men, and in fact a bit of reflection would indicate that this is only to be expected. In fact, nor have women leaders been typically anxious to give greater represe ntation to other women within their own organisations or in the political process generally.

Recent reports in India indicating that many women politicians are finding it difficult to participate in politics, let alone equalise the gender gap that exists, point to an increasing need to analyse the role that women play in Indian politics. This has been supported by recent elections.

4.1. Women's Representation in Pollical Parties

India is a bicameral parliamentary democracy, with a strong multi-party political system. The lower house is called the Lok Sabha (Peoples' Assembly) and has 545 members. The upper house is called the Rajya Sabha (State Assembly) with 250 members. In 1991, women constituted 5.2 percent of the membership of the Lok Sabha and 9.8 percent of the membership of the Rajya Sabha. This was lower than the preceding 1989 parliament. The election results in 1996 showed a further decline in women's representation, but in the 1999 election, 8.8 percent of parliamentarians were women. This trend is worrying given the recent state-led initiatives to ensure women's representation in political institutions.

One of the reasons for the low representation may be the strength of the party system itself, which can lead to the marginalisation of issue-based politics, or to an expropriation of movements that are based on single issues. The women's movement in India has had to confront this issue. Indian political parties are, however, organisationally weak and dependent on local elites. This might be a second factor for the resistance to implementation of gender-sensitive political initiatives.

4.1.2. The Issue of Representation

The demand for greater representation of women in political institutions in India was not taken up in a systematic way until the setting up of the Committee on the Status of Women in India (CSWI) which published its report in 1976. Before this the focus of the growing women's movement had been on improving women's socio-economic position. The CSWI report suggested that women's representation in political institutions, especially at the grass-roots level, needed to be increased through a policy of reservation of seats for women. In 1988, the National Perspective Plan for Women suggested that a 30 percent quota for women be introduced at all levels of elective bodies. Women's groups insisted that reservation be restricted to the panchayat (village council) level to encourage grassroots participation in politics. The consensus around this demand resulted in the adoption of the 73rd and 74th amendments to the Indian Constitution in 1993.

In 1995, the question of quotas was raised again, but this time the focus was women in parliament. Initially, most political parties agreed to this proposition. But soon doubts surfaced. When the bill addressing this issue was introduced in the Eleventh Parliament in 1997, several parties and groups raised objections. The objections focused around two main issues: first, the issue of overlapping quotas for women in general and those for women of the lower castes; second, the issue of elitism. Most women's groups felt that the caste issue was a divisive one for women. Also, many felt uneasy about giving special privileges to elite women by ensuring seats for them in the parliament, while they had previously supported quotas for women at the grassroots level of the panchayats. To date, the amendment has not been passed by parliament. However, the current government of the Hindu nationalist Bharatiya Janata Party (BJP) has committed itself to introducing another quota bill for women in parliament.

4.2. Women in the Indian Parliament

The 39 women representatives in the 1991–1996 Indian Parliament were mostly middle-class, professional women, with little or no links to the women's movement. A significant number of them accessed politics through their families, some through student and civil rights movements and some as a result of state initiatives aimed at increasing representation from the lower castes.

The majority of women in the Indian Parliament are elite women. While their public role challenges some stereotypes, their class position often allows them a far greater range of options than are available to poorer women.

4.2.1. Gender and Caste in Parliament

Caste has been an important feature of Indian public and political life. Most of the women MPs in the Tenth Parliament were members of the higher castes. For example, there were six women from the Brahmin caste. This represents a sizeable 17.14 percent of the women MPs, while Brahmins comprise only 5.52 percent of the population. However, it is important to guard against making an easy correlation between caste and political representation. For example, of the six women who are Brahmins, two are MPs from the Communist Party of India. In both cases the caste factor is less important than their privileged class backgrounds. Further, both were products of political movements, the nationalist struggle and the anti-emergency movement.

The number of women who are able to avail of India's caste-based reservation system remains small. While 22 percent of the parliamentary seats were reserved for the Scheduled Castes, women occupied only 4.1 percent of the reserved seats. Two women MPs were from what are called the Scheduled Tribes. However, out of 39 women MPs in the Tenth Lok Sabha (representing seven percent of the total), 14 percent were from the Scheduled Castes. Two women MPs belonged to the "backward" castes and represented open constituencies. Caste, therefore, affects the profile, loyalties and work of representatives in the Indian Parliament.

4.2.2. Class, Social Position and Gender in Public Life

Out of the 39 women MPs in the 1991–1996 Lok Sabha, 32 had postgraduate qualifications; in the Rajya Sabha 14 out of the 17 women were graduates. The class position of these women is obviously more important to their educational levels than caste. Only one out of the seven lower caste women MPs was not a graduate and the one Scheduled Caste woman MP in the Rajya Sabha had postgraduate education. The levels of education are also reflected in the professional profiles of these women. Thirty percent of women MPs in the Rajya Sabha for example were lawyers and 25 percent in the Lok Sabha were either teachers or lecturers.

> The class from which most of the women MPs come is perhaps the most important factor in their successful inclusion into the political system.

Most of the women MPs (about 65 percent) were between their late 30s and 60s and therefore did not have the responsibility of bringing up a young family. Given the almost universal marriage pattern that exists in India, the figure for unmarried MPs is extraordinarily high and indicates the social pressures on women who join public life. For those who are married, the pressures of public life are eased a bit by their class situation. Most MPs are able to afford paid help in the home. In many cases the joint family system, or at least strong family support, also helps. However, the constraints of family life continue to be real concerns even for privileged women.

Women have different strategies to cope with these constraints. If the family has accepted a woman's career in politics, she can negotiate with her family. This is more likely if the family is an elite political family with more than one member participating in politics. If the woman was already active in political life before she married, she can face tremendous pressures from her husband's family to conform to a traditional role that allows little scope for pursuing an active political career. A woman politician's options in this case are either to conform to the expectations of the family and retreat from public life, or to leave the family in pursuit of an uncertain future in party politics. In the latter case, the lack of family support and the stigma of divorce are a clear disadvantage for a woman in politics.

Class also mediates the influence of religion. With only one woman Muslim MP in the Rajya Sabha and one in the Lok Sabha, Muslim women are significantly under-represented. Dr. Najma Heptullah, who was also the Deputy Speaker of the Rajya Sabha, is from an elite class and educational background and enjoys support for her work from both her natal and marital family. Margaret Alva, a

Christian, a former Minister of State and Founder Chair of the National Commission for Women of India, is from a similar background. In both cases the families were involved in the national movement, were influenced by liberal ideology and were highly educated.

Thus, the majority of women in the Indian Parliament are elite women. While their public role challenges some stereotypes, their class position often allows them far greater range of options than are available to poorer women.

4.2.3. Kinship

"Male equivalence" has been a dominant explanation for how women access political life. The assumption here is that women access political life with the support, backing and contacts of the family, in particular that of the husband. In the sample of 15 women surveyed 1/3 of the women MPs, for example, have "family support" in the background. However, in a well-argued critique of this theory, Carol Wolkowitz points out that "male equivalence" is an inadequate conceptual framework. First, because it is the public sphere (e.g. state institutions, press and political discourse) that has to be negotiated if the family decision to put forward a woman in politics is to succeed, it is not a private, but a public matter. Second, in many cases the husbands do not support the candidature of the wife at all. It is the pressure of party political bosses that forces the issue in many cases. The centralised system of distribution of seats in mass political parties helps in this context. A party's concern with levels of representation of certain groups within its ranks and consequences for legitimacy of the party among the under-represented groups might be the motive for including women.

4.2.4. Social and Political Movements

Together with "kinship link" and state initiatives, an important factor impacting on women's access to political life seems to be social and political movements. These movements have created windows of opportunity and some women have been able to take advantage of these opportunities to access political life.

For example, the national movement was an important mobiliser of women. Gandhi's contribution to bringing women into politics is well-documented; the left movement also mobilised women. Women's organisations were constituted under the umbrella and control of the party – the Mahila Congress and the All India Women's Federation (CPI). However, none of the women interviewed in this survey had strong links with the women's wing of their party prior to their entry into parliamentary politics.

The civil rights and anti-emergency movement led by Jaiprakash Narayan (JP) in 1975–1977 was an important political movement that brought students to the forefront of national politics. Many women, both on the right and on the left wing, joined this movement and continued on in politics. Finally, in the context of current politics in India, fundamentalist and communal parties are mobilising women. One of the most charismatic woman MPs is Uma Bharti, the product of the rise of Hindu militancy in Indian politics. She is the member of the Vishwa Hindu Parishad, a mobilisational wing of the BJP and a "preacher" of Hindu texts by profession. She was at the forefront of the movement that brought down the Babri Mosque in Ayodhyaya.

4.3. Political Leadership and Quotas

Quotas for women as a strategy for accessing the political arena has growing support among women MPs, despite the fact that very few have accessed the system through this route; most women are still firm believers in the meritocratic argument.

The influence of individual national leaders is also an important factor that militates against the "male equivalence" theory. While Indira Gandhi, for example, did little to promote women's representation in politics, Rajiv Gandhi accepted the principle of reservation of seats for women. He initiated measures that had a direct impact on the inclusion of women in politics, e.g., the 1993 provision for reservation of 33 percent of elected seats on village panchayats for women. The ability to take advantage of such reservations is mediated by class, ethnicity and caste. However, the support of the state and state/political leaders can be important to women who want to access the political system. Quotas for women as a strategy for accessing the political arena has growing support among women MPs, despite the fact that very few have accessed the system through that route and are firm believers in the meritocratic argument. Most women MPs have supported the 81st Amendment, which would ensure a 33 percent quota for women in parliament, even though party discipline has not allowed them to vote for this. This issue highlights the constraints that the party system poses for women politicians.

4.4. Gender and Public Power

Out of the 20 Congress women MPs in the 1991-1996 Lok Sabha, none was a Cabinet Minister; two were Ministers of State; and two were Deputy Ministers of State. In the Rajya Sabha, out of seven Congress women MPs, one is a Minister of State. The portfolios of these ministers included, human resource development, civil aviation and tourism, health and family welfare and personnel and public grievances. All these are generally regarded as "soft portfolios"; this does not, however, take away from the responsibility that these women ministers have. One Congress woman MP is the Deputy Chairperson of the Rajya Sabha. At the level of the party, one MP was on the disciplinary committee of the party and one was the President of the Mahila Congress. Among BJP women, the one Rajya Sabha member was the spokesperson on the economy and general political line of the party. Of the 10 members of the Lok Sabha, one was one of the vice-presidents of the party and two were on the National Executive Committee of their party.

Women's representation in the parliament, while important on the grounds of social justice and legitimacy of the political system, does not easily translate into improved representation of women's various interests.The system of institutional incentives and disincentives at the level of the party and parliament impact on the issues that women espouse in parliament. Most women MPs interviewed did not have women's issues high on their list of interests. Rather, they wanted to be on committees relating to economy, international relations and trade.

4.4.1. Accountability

One of the important issues for any discussion on gender and representation has to deal with the constituency that women represent.

As there are no "women's only" constituencies, women MPs are not accountable to women as women. And yet, when issues regarding women are raised in the parliament, these women are expected to and do participate in the debates. Issues such as the welfare of women and violence against women are particularly important in uniting women MPs. These issues are discussed in the "ladies room" in the parliament. However, as all the MPs questioned made clear, they are "party women first"; the party whip is rarely flouted.

Most women MPs interviewed did not have women's issues high on their list of interests. Rather, they wanted to be on the more influential committees relating to the economy, international relations and trade.

Some women MPs are also asked by the party leadership to get involved in the women's wing of the party. While the women MPs do not necessarily see this role as an enhancement of their status within the party, some have made a success of this role and as a result gained influence with the leadership of the party.

As "party women" with political ambitions, women MPs respond to the institutional incentives and disincentives that are placed on them. All these factors limit the potential of these women MPs for representing the interests of Indian women across a range of issues. As a result there seems to be little regular contact between women's groups and women MPs. The exception here is of course the women's wing of political parties that do liaise with women MPs. This does allow the possibility of women MPs becoming conduits between the party's leadership and its women members. They are also consulted from time to time by the party leadership on issues regarding the family and women's rights. But non-party women's groups do not seem to approach women MPs.

4.5. Women in Urban and Local Governments

India is a federal system of government with 25 states and 7 union territories. It has a population of about 1 billion out of which 26 percent live in urban areas. The per capita GDP of India is about US$ 370. Agriculture accounts for 31.1 percent of the economy, while industry and services account for 23 percent and 45.9 percent respectively, of the economy. The sex ratio of the population is 48.1 percent and is rather skewed in favor of males. The most favorable sex ratio in the country is in the state of Kerala at 50.9 percent, while the Union Territory of Lakshadweep has the worst sex ratio at 40 percent. Life expectancy at birth for women is 58.7 years and for men it is 57.7 percent. The overall literacy rate is 52.2 percent. Literacy among men is 64.1 percent and among women it is 39.3 percent. Women make up about 28 percent of the labor force. These overall figures show considerable disparities between men and women, which arise from traditional views of men being superior to women. Tables 1. provide overall demographic and socio-economic data for India. However, India is a diverse country and these figures vary from state to state.

Table 1. demographic and socio-economic data for India (Census Statistics 1971–91))

	Unit	1991	1981	1971
Population Density	(Mn.)	846 273	683 230	548 177
Persons per household	(No.)	5.52	5.55	5.46
Districts	(No.)	466	412	360
AUs & Towns	(No.)	3768	3378	2590
Villages (inhabited)	('000S)	627	579	576
Rural population	(Mn.)	629	524	439
Ur ban population	(Mn.)	218	159	109
Urban as % of total	(%)	25.7	23.3	19.9
Male population	(Mn.)	439	353	284
Female population	(Mn.)	407	330	264
Females per 1000 males	(No.)	927	934	930
Workers*	(Mn.)	306	242	181
Male	(Mn.)	219	179	145
Female	(Mn.)	87	63	36
Birth rate	(PER 1000)	32.5	37.2	41.2
Death rate	(PER 1000)	11.4	15.0	19.0
Expectation of life at birth	(%)	58.2	50.5	45.6
Male	(%)	57.7	50.9	46.4
Female	(%)	58.7	50.0	44.7
Literacy rate	(%)	52.2	43.6	34.5
Male	(%)	64.1	56.4	46.0
Female	(%)	39.3	29.8†	22.0

There still exists a significant gap in the education levels of men and women. The literacy level is a lowly 39.3% for women. Regional disparties are also quite significant, with Kerala having achieved cent percent literacy and Rajasthan having a dismal 20.4 percent literate women population.

Table 2. Levels ofWomen's education

FEMALE ADULT LITERACY		
Rate %	Index (1985-100)	As % of male rate
1997	1997	1997
39.4	134	59
FEMALE PRIMARY NET ENROLMENT		
Ratio (as %) of relevant age group)	Index (1985-100)	As % of male rate
1997	1997	1997
71.0	111	86
FEMALE SECONDARY NET ENROLMENT		
Ratio (as % of relevant age group)	Index (1985-100)	As % of male rate
1997	1997	1997
48.0	133	68
FEMALE TERTIARY STUDENTS		
Per 100,000 Women	Index (1985-100)	As % of male ratio
1996	1996	1996
481	134	61

Urban population increased 3.5 times from 62.4 million in 1951 to 217.6 million in 1991 with an average annual growth rate at 3.2 percent. In 1951 the urban population accounted for a mere 17.3 percent of the total Indian Population. In the next four decades this figure has gone up to 25.7 percent. This figure is expected to touch 33.16 percent by the year 2016. Similar to other statistics the rate of urbanisation varies considerably from state to state. For example in the period 1981-1991 the State of Kerala saw a growth of 61 percent, while the neighbouring state of Tamil Nadu grew the least at a mere 19.6 percent.

India has 23 cities with populations over 1 million. However, only about 33 percent of the urban population lives in these cities, including about 19 percent who live the top 5 urban centers.

Table 3. Urban agglomerations/cities with more than 1 million populations

Rank	*City*	*1981*		*1991*	
		Population	*Percentage to total urban population*	*Population*	*Percentage to total urban Population*
1	Greater Mumbai	8,243,405	5.17	12,596,243	5.79
2	Calcutta	9,194,018	5.77	11,021,918	5.06
3	Delhi	5,729,283	3.59	8,419,084	3.87
4	Chennai (Madras)	4,289,347	2.69	5,421,985	2.49
5	Hyderabad	2,545,836	1.60	4,344,437	2.00
6	Bangalore	2,921,751	1.83	4,130,288	1.90
7	Ahmedabad	2,548,057	1.60	3,312,216	1.52
8	Pune	1,686,109	1.06	2,493,987	1.15
9	Kanpur	1,639,064	1.03	2,029,889	0.93
10	Nagpur	1,302,066	0.82	1,664,006	0.76
11	Lucknow	1.007,604	0.63	1,669,204	0.77
12	Surat	913,8061,	0.57	1,518,950	0.70
13	Jaipur	1,015,160	0.64	1,518,235	0.70
14	Kochi	685,836	0.43	1,140,605	0.52
15	Coimbatore	920,355	0.58	1,100,746	0.51
16	Vadodara	744,881	0.47	1,126,824	0.52
17	Indore	829,327	0.52	1,109,056	0.51
18	Patna	918,903	0.58	1,099,647	0.51
19	Madurai	907,7 32	0.57	1,085,914	0.50
20	Bhopal	671,018	0.42	1,062,771	0.49
21	Visakhapatnam	603,630	0.38	1,057,118	0.49
22	Varanasi	797,162	0.50	1,030,863	0.47
23	Ludhiana	607,052	0.38	1,042,740	0.48
	Total	50,721,402	31.81	70,996,726	32.63

4.6. Politics and Governance

The political and administrative structure of the country is largely inherited from the British. The British introduced local democracy in India by constituting municipal councils and the municipal corporations in the last quarter of the nineteenth century. They also provided a federal structure to the country with the Government of India Act, 1935.

The country today has a quasi-federal structure. Apart from the Government of India in New Delhi, there are twenty-five States with their own state governments. The Seventh Schedule to the Constitution of India divides the subjects of State activity between the Union and state governments. The Union (Centre) as well as State governments in India both have a parliamentary form of government based on the Westminster pattern. The executive powers of the central government are vested in the Council of Ministers with the Prime Minister at its head. Similarly, the executive powers in the State governments are vested in its Council of Ministers with the Chief Minister at its head. However, following the Westminister pattern, the Head of the State is not the Prime Minister but an indirectly elected President, who broadly performs the role as the Head of State. India has a bicameral parliament, with the Lower House directly elected by the people on the lines of the House of Commons in the U.K. or the House of Representatives in the U.S.A. The Upper House is more like the U.S. Senate. It is a permanent house with one-third members retiring every two years. Like in the U.S.A. the Vice President of the country presides on the Upper House.

Although local government in India is a subject of the State governments, the seventy-third and the seventy-fourth amendments to the Constitution of India now make it obligatory for the State governments to organise local bodies, to hold regular elections to them and to give them appropriate finances.

The urban local bodies are of three grades; municipal corporations for cities with a population of more than (0.3 million), municipal councils for towns smaller than this population limit and nagar panchayats for villages in transition to becoming towns. These bodies are elected on a universal suffrage basis, with all citizens above the age of eighteen years of age having a right to vote.

The rural local bodies are organised in three tiers, the village panchayat at the village level, the block panchayat samiti for about 100 villages and a district council for a district comprising about 1000 villages. The rural local bodies do not have many resources of their own. They actually spend the state government funds as implementing agencies.

The civil service in India is a closed system, with a very limited scope for lateral entry at senior level. Most permanent officials join the service as a lifetime career through an entrance examination/ interview conducted by the Public Service Commission. The age of entry is usually 21 to 30 years and the age of retirement either 58 or 60 years of age.

The subject matter of the Government of India is divided between the Union Government and the State Governments. The respective governments recruit most of their employees independently. However, a unique feature of the Indian system is the existence of three All India Services, the Indian Administrative Service, the Indian Police Service and the Indian Forest Service. The Government of India recruits the members of these services although they work with the States where they are allotted (their cadres) for most of their career. However, the Government of India obtains the services of these officers at higher and middle management levels through deputation for a period of about five years. This enables a regular exchange of officers between the field and the central levels. Senior Indian Administrative Service Officers who have had their initial grounding in different States of India thus man the top secretariat posts in most ministries of the Government of India.

India is a democratic republic and full freedom of speech and religion is allowed to all its citizens. The Constitution of India guarantees the following Fundamental Rights to the citizens of India.

Right to Equality: This includes equality before law (Article 14), prohibition of discrimination on grounds of religion, race, caste, sex or place of birth (Article 15) and equality of opportunity in matters of employment (Article 16).

Right to Freedom: This includes protection of certain rights regarding freedom of speech etc. (Article 19), protection of life and personal liberty (Article 21) and protection against arrest and detention in certain cases (Article 22).

Right against Exploitation: This includes prohibition of traffic in human beings and forced labor (Article 23) and prohibition of employment of children in factories etc.

Right to Freedom of Religion: This includes freedom of conscience and free profession, practice and propagation of religion (Article 25), freedom to manage religious affairs (Article 26), freedom as to payment of taxes for promotion of any particular religion (Article 27) and freedom as to attendance at religious instruction or religious worship in certain educational institutions (Article 28).

Cultural and Educational Rights: These include protection of interests of minorities (Article 29) and the right of minorities to establish and administer educational institutions (Article 30).

The Constitution of India further guarantees the right to move to the Supreme Court for enforcement of the above rights.

India has a multitude of political parties; some organised on economic ideology, some on religious ideology while some on local and linguistic aspirations. However, only three or four parties really have a presence at the National level; the Congress Party that was the ruling party for more than forty years, the Bharatiya Janata Party (the present ruling party with its allies), the Janata Dal and the Communists. There are many religion-based parties like the Akali Dal (Sikhs in Punjab), the Muslim League etc. The regional parties like the DMK and AIADMK (Tamil Nadu), Shiv Sena (Maharashtra), Telugu Desam (Andhra Pradesh) and some parties in the smaller North-Eastern States have been contenders of powers in the State governments of their respective states. However, at the National level, only three parties have been able to provide the Prime Minister i.e. the Congress, the BJP and the Janata Party/Janata Dal i n alliance with smaller parties.

An independent body called the Election Commission of India conducts elections to the parliament and the state legislatures in India. The elections are based on a universal adult suffrage with voting rights to all citizens above eighteen years of age. The lower houses of the national and the state legislatures have a five-year term although elections are regularly held before this term expires.

The elections to the local bodies have been brought under the purview of a similarly constituted body called the State Election

Commission. These bodies also usually have a five-year term. It is statutorily not possible to supersede the local bodies for long periods or to keep them under Government-appointed Administrators. An age of more than twenty-one years is usually an eligibility condition for getting elected to an elective post in a local body. The eligibility for being a member of the Lower House of the National or state legislatures similarly prescribes the minimum age of twenty-five years. A minimum age-limit of thirty years is similarly a qualification for membership of the Upper Houses of the National and State legislatures. A minimum age-limit of thirty-five years is prescribed as a qualification for holding the post of the President or Vice-President of the Indian Republic.

The elections to both the urban and rural local bodies in India are ward based. The local area is divided into wards of more or less equal population. Each ward sends one representative to the concerned local body. After the Seventy-third and Seventy-fourth Amendments to the Constitution of India, one-third of the wards are reserved for women candidates and only women candidates can contest elections from these wards.

Table 4. Participation of women in national elections

Election Year	Voting % of men	Voting % of women	Total Seats contested by women	Seats won by women	% seats won of contested seats	Total Seats	% of Women Member
1952	53.00	37.10	51	23	45.09	499	4.40
1957	56.00	38.77	70	27	38.57	500	5.40
1962	62.10	46.63	68	35	51.47	503	6.70
1967	66.70	55.48	66	31	48.43	523	5.90
1971	69.70	49.15	86	22	27.50	521	4.20
1977	65.62	54.96	70	19	25.70	544	3.40
1980	57.69	51.22	142	28	19.70	544	5.14
1984	63.61	68.17	421	159	28.30	544	7.90
1989	70.90	43.90	189	28	14.80	525	5.30
1991	52.56	47.42	307	33	10.75	503	6.60

Political parties are allowed to take part in elections to all local bodies except the village panchayats in India. It is, however, not uncommon for locally influential politicians to form local fronts to contest and win elections to municipal councils and the smaller municipal corporations in the country.

India became independent in the year 1947. In all the elections held since independence, women had the voting rights. The pattern of participation by women in the national elections is provided in Table 4. The percentage of seats won against the seats contested is showing a declining trend only because the number of women contesting elections has increased sharply. However, it may be seen that voting for women in all tiers of Government has always been a feature of the Indian polity since 1947.

4.7. Women in Politics and Administration

4.7.1. Political Participation

Women play a dual role in politics – as voters and political representatives. On the voting front, though adult franchise was granted in 1937, it was the progressive spirit that pervaded the making of the constitution that made it a reality. The Constitution of India guarantees equal rights to men and women as voters and citizens.

Generally, in India, registration and participation of women as contestants is less than that of men. In recent past, records show that there has been an increase in the percentage of women who vote. Such participation is also contingent on the mobilisation efforts made by political parties, NGOs, Action Groups and the general awareness among the community of the importance of women exercising their franchise. Again, a note of caution is required, lest it be assumed that political participation always indicates political awareness on the part of the woman voter. Usually, however, countries that do hold regular elections show an improved recognition of women as a political constituency and parties and candidates tend to adopt pro-women stances and appeal specifically to women's votes, especially at the time of elections. This becomes very evident when we look at consecutive elections in the Indian context, wherein there is a growing consciouseness of the need to woo the woman voter and the need to pay attention to the needs and issues of women, in the election manifestos of political parties.

Since Independence, due to exercise of their franchise, Indian women have been exposed to the political processes and are showing increasing awareness about not only lack of rights but also their utility. A majority of illiterate rural women are also politically sensitive and aware of the various issues confronting them. Women get easily mobilised in the political processes by the political parties who approach women very often for party issues and for shor-term goals by winning elections, but not for long-term goals of bringing about social changes and gender equality in political power-sharing.

In all the elections held since independence, women had the voting rights. The percentage of seats won against the seats contested is showing a declining trend only because the number of women contesting elections has increased sharply. However, it may be seen that voting by women in all tiers of Government has always been a feature of the Indian Polity since 1947. Due to the parternalistic family and male dominated political structures which do not provide space for women in decision-making bodies, women constituted 3.1% of the total contestants in 1996 election and did not occupy more than 6.10% of the total seats in the state legislative assemblies and Parliament.

The number of women contestants in Parliamentary elections has not increased significantly over the years. Political parties are still reluctant to field women candidates at national level. In the early days of the Indian republic, the number of women representatives was a mere 22, which was a lowly 4.4% of the total seats in the Lok Sabha. The sixth Loksabha in the year 1977 saw an all time low of just 19 woman representatives. The twelfth Lok Sabha had 44 women i.e. 8.8% of the total.

Table 5. Increase in the share of women members of Parliament

	1996	1998
Total Constituencies	543	543
Total No. of women candidates	491	271
Total No. of women winners	40	43
Women voters	15,10,28,30	16,68,21679
Increase in women voters against 1996		5%

As analysed by the Prasad Leela Devi – Even as early as the 19th century Indian women had begun to appear on the national scene in public and political activity. Women were not only being accepted in public activity but were organising themselves to fight for their rights in different walks of life.

Though women constitute nearly half of the population of the country, it was only after Independence that efforts were made to promote women's participation in public life. Though the Constitution of India provides for the Government to make special provisions to safeguard the interests of women as detailed in Article 15 (3) and Article 39, it has not made any provision for reservation for women in respect of jobs and political offices. However the 73rd and 74th Constitional Amendment Act mandated reservation of one-third seats in the village, block, districts, municipal elected bodies in India. As a consequence, women had not advanced much politically and economically. From the records available of the past 50 years, since the independence, it is seen that the strength of women in the political field as reflected in State legislatures remained at an average of 3 % to 5% of those elected. At the level of Parlaiment, the position of women members has varied between 5 to 7%.

It is seen that women in large numbers have come out against atrocities on women, in defence of their traditional control over crucial resources, water, forests, and land, mass literacy drives and other issues. They are also coming out in large numbers over ecological degradation, price rise or protests against police repression, etc. While there is the increased participation in grass root political movements, it is not getting translated into a growing share of women in the formal political structure of the country.

Amongst the several reasons for such a situation is the growing money power and muscle power required to contest even the smallest of elections in India, the intimidation, violence and slander that a woman candidate has to face combined with the traditional male domination that seeks to keep her indoors. Narrow electoral arthmetic and the necessity of fielding a winning candidate makes most political parties shy away from fielding more than a token number of women candidates. And if they are fielded at all, kinship and affinity factors play a major role. It is very common to observe that the relatives of politicians are promoted and supported to emerge as politicians (FES).

Table 6. State-wise number of women candidates fielded in elections in 1998

State / Union Territory	No. of Women candidates	No. of Women who won
Uttar Pradesh	56	9
Madhya Pradesh	28	4
West Bengal	21	5
Bihar	21	4
Rajasthan	20	3
Maharashtra	20	2
Andhra Pradesh	18	2
Tamil Nadu	13	1
Delhi	10	2
Orissa	10	2
Kerala	10	1
Karnataka	10	0
Punjab	9	1
Gujarat	7	4
Haryana	6	1
Assam	3	1
Meghalaya	2	0
Chandigarh	2	0
Tripura	1	0
Goa	1	0
Jammu & Kashmir	1	0
Manipur	1	1
Daman & Diu	1	0
Arunachal Pradesh	0	0
Mizoram	0	0
Nagaland	0	0
Sikkim	0	0
Andaman & Nicobar Islands	0	0
Dadra and Nagar Haveli	0	0
Lakshadeep	0	0
Pondicherry	0	0
Himachal Pradesh	0	0

Table 7. Women in Government

At all levels (%)	At Ministerial levels (%)	At Sub – Ministerial levels (%)
5.8	6.2	3.2

Increasingly, women have stood for elections and got elected as members of State Legislative Assemblies and the Parliament. However, at the national level there is only one woman Cabinet Minister and 8 Ministers of State in a Cabinet of 70. There is only one woman Governor and one woman Chief Minister.

Table 8. Women representation in the Rajya Sabha (Upper House)

Year	*Total*	*No. of Women*	*Percentage*
1952	219	16	7.3
1957	237	18	7.6
1962	238	18	7.6
1967	240	20	8.3
1971	243	17	7.0
1977	244	25	10.2
1980	244	24	9.8
1985	244	28	11.4
1990	245	24	9.7
1991	245	38	15.5
1992	245	17	6.9
1994	245	20	8.1
1996	245	18	7.3
1997	245	18	7.3
1998	245	18	7.3

Some studies of Parliamentary participation indicate that women members participate more actively in 'women's issues' – health, welfare, atrocities against women, crimes like dowry and violations of human rights. This participation is confined to the more articulate women. In issues such as defence, finance, politics, etc. their participation is relatively limited. Table 9 shows women's representation in selected State Legislatures. The situation it appears has not improved much since the 1950s.

Table 9. Women's representation in selected state legislatures

State	*Year*	*Total*	*Women*
Assam	1996	122	6
Haryana	1999	90	4
J & K	1996	87	2
Himachal Pradesh	1998	68	6
Gujarat	1998	182	4
Kerala	1996	140	13
Meghalaya	1998	60	3
Punjab	1997	117	7
Pondicherry	1996	30	1
NCT Delhi	1998	70	9
Nagaland	1998	60	0
Madhya Pradesh	1998	320	26
Tamil Nadu	1996	234	9
Tripura	1998	60	2
Uttar Pradesh	1996	424	20
West Bengal	1996	294	20
Bihar	1999	324	19
Maharashtra	1995	288	11
Arunachal Pradesh	1995	60	1
Manipur	1999	60	1
Orissa	1999	147	13
Rajasthan	1998	200	14

Analysis of trends of womens' participation to contest elections to the State Legislatures indicate that there is a gender discrimination which is responsible for poor representation of women in India.

Women's role in decision making is one of the most important questions for consideration in the movement for their empowerment. The 73rd and 74th Amendments (1992) to the Indian Constitution have served as a major break through towards ensuring women's equal access and increased participation in political power structures. This Amendment provided for reservation of one third of seats for women at level of local governance in urban areas. There is also a one-third reservation for women for posts of chairpersons of these local bodies. This amendment has initiated a powerful strategy of affirmative action for providing the structural framework for women's participation in political decision-making and provided an opportunity to bring women to be forefront and centre of city development and develop new grass-root level leadership. There are about 1 million elected women representatives in Panchayats and Municipal Bodies in India. The following Table 10. indicates women in local governments in India.

Table 10. Number of urban local bodies and local elected representatives

State/Union Territory	*Municipal Corporation*	*Municipal Council*	*Nagar Panchayat*	*Total*
Andhra Pradesh	07 (395)	94 (2853)	15 (314)	116 (3542)
Assam	01	25 (353)	42 (204)	68 (557)
Bihar	06	70	93	169
Goa	-	13 (155)	-	13 (155)
Gujarat	06 (468)	86 (2745)	60 (1260)	152 (4473)
Haryana	01	20	32	53 (1359)
Himachal Pradesh	01 (25)	19 (183)	29 (221)	49 (429)
Karnataka	06 (410)	122 (3196)	89 (1355)	214 (4961)
Kerala	05 (298)	53 (1597)	-	58 (1895)
Madhya Pradesh	02 (1067)	106 (2527)	283 (4537)	409 (8131)
Maharashtra	15 (1417)	228 (4901)	-	243 (6318)
Manipur	-	07	20	27
Orissa	02 (70)	29 (560)	72 (1056)	103 (1686)
Punjab	03	97	34	134 (1699)
Rajasthan	03	11	169	183 (4412)
Tamil Nadu	06 (480)	102 (3494)	611 (9794)	719 (13768)
Tripura	-	01	12	13
Uttar Pradesh	11 (841)	226 (5970)	444 (5518)	681 (12329)
West Bengal	06	112	4	122 (2706)
A & N Islands	-	01	-	01
Chandigarh	01	-	-	01
Delhi	01	01	-	02 (134)
Pondicherry	-	05	-	05
Daman & Diu	-	02	-	02
Total	101	1430	2009	3540 (68554)

After 1993, women's participation in local governments increased quite radically, with the enactment of the legislation providing 33 percent reservation of seats for women in local bodies. The legislation and its implementation has added another level in political participation.

In Governments too, there has been limited representatives of women. A few eminent women have no doubt, occupied important administrative positions, such as Secretaries of Departments in the National Government as well as in State Governments. It is only 5.71% of the total number of persons in administrative services are women. It is noteworthy that within the premier civil services of India, the representation of women is not that encouraging.

Table 11. Women Selected in All India Services

Sr. No.	*Services*	*Year*	*Total*	*No. of Personnel in Position*		
1	Indian Administrative	1995	4284	*Males*	*Females*	% of
	Service	1992	4928	3973	311 430	Female
		1996	5047	4498	501 512	7.3
		1997	4991	4546		8.7
				4479		9.9
						10.3
2	Indian Police Service	1985	2343	2325	18	0.8
		1992	2825	2773	52	1.8
		1996	2947	2883	64	2.2
		1997	2964	2868	96	3.3
		1998	2985	2885	100	3.4
		1999	3115	3007	108	3.5
3	Indian Foreign Service	1985	535	485	50	9.3
		1992	721	658	83	8.7
		1995	547	481	66	12.1
		1996	567	501	66	11.6
		1997	586	519	67	11.4
		1998	587	520	67	11.4

Since relatively few women enter the civil services, several efforts have been made to improve the situation. The Department of Personnel and Administrative Reforms of the Government of India has also provided, wherever possible, women officers on the selection boards for posts and services.

4.8. Women's Participation in Local Government

The 74th Amendment to the Indian Constitution, 1992 has served as a major breakthrough towards ensuring women's equal access and increased participation in local government. The Constitution (74th Amendment) Act, 1992 aims at Constitutional guarantees to safeguard the interests of urban local self government to enable them to function as effective democratic and self governing institutions at the grass root level. This Amendment provides for reservation of 33 1/3 percent of elected seats for women at local government level in urban and rural areas. There is also a one-third reservation for women of posts of chairpersons of these local bodies. A very active role for women in local governance is envisaged as compared to governance at the state and national levels in India. These provisions have provided great opportunities and challenges to women in India, particularly in the local government field. This is of great significance, since this grass-root level participation has considerably broadened the base of women's participation in politics at city level.

Involvement of women in the political arena and in decision-making roles is an important tool for empowerment as well as monitoring standards of political performance at local level. However, in the present political process of entry into decision making political institutions, there is growing influence of money and muscle power, backroom dealings, communalisation and criminalisation. In many respects women and men elected representatives face similar problems on election to office. Above all there is a need to understand just how to be a good local politician. The role of political representatives at local level is demanding and all new 'recruits' need time to gain experience and to understand the rules, regulations and procedures governing the administrative bureaucracy with which they now have to work – often quite closely in the urban service delivery system.

Some of the major constraints that prevent women from effective participation at local level are as follows:

1. Lack of orientation / training in urban development issues and municipal administration.
2. No proper knowledge / orientation about municipal acts and rules and regulations.

3. No prior experience about dealing with multidimensional urban development issues / civic issues and its complexities.
4. Lack of knowledge about technical inputs related to urban service delivery system.
5. Lack of support from senior male / female colleagues in the party / municipal body.
6. Less co-operation from municipal officials understanding about various facets of the budget, such as allocation of budget at ward level (at central / ward level).
7. Lack of party support and poor organisational structure.
8. Lack of money and resources to sustain the electoral campaigns (inspite of code of conduct by election commission).
9. Discrimination in decision making at party level.
10. Specific notions towards politics and political atmosphere.
11. Fear and insecurity.
12. Lack of confidence in public speaking.
13. Criminalisation of politics and use of money power.
14. Family responsibilities.

4.8.1. Civil Society Initiatives

Political system in India works through political parties who contend for power by invoking popular support. Therefore it is necessary that if women want to share power they have to make a place for themselves within the political parties through which the Indian democratic system operates. The experience of the last 52 years show an inability to create 'this space' and recent studies show that there has been no significant change in either the nature of women's functioning or in the political parties' approach to women and women's issues. If we examine women's participation (prior to 1993) it is seen that the political parties have given less importance to women's issues in terms of ideology, either in priority in their party manifesto or in terms of the number and importance of the position that women occupied in individual political parties. Women are not seen as a vote bank to be approached, and once the men are mobilised, women will merely endorse their choice of party and candidate. Male candidates rarely have access to the female electorate and there are not enough women involved in political campaigns to be able to reach out to a large section of women even in big cities. As a result, the exposure of women to political debates and issues has always remained indirect. According to women from all parties the political environment was not conducive to women's participation in politics. The analysis made by Kumari and Kidwai stated that political parties have dominated the conservative 'cultural' perspective and no conscious attempt has been made to increase active participation of women.

Women in India today are agitating at the doors of Parliament, demanding reservation for 33 percent of the seats. The issue at stake here is more complex than it may seem. It is not only a question of a few more or a few less women in the corridors of Parliament and legislatures but also a response to the fact that a large section of society has historically been denied its legitimate share in the exercise of political power, power that ultimately determines its destiny. In this demand for reservation, women are also raising their voice against a system, which has consistently denied them space by harnessing the forces of tradition in order to marginalise and trivialise their role. Reservation of seats for women in Panchayats/Municipal bodies have shown that it has tremendous implications, not merely in terms of the number of women entering the public arena and holding public office, but also in terms of the social, economic and political impact that these reservations have had for the total system.

It is for these reasons that women are increasingly demanding political roles for themselves. They recognise that constitutional guarantees do not ensure effective participation and that these cannot ensure political equality. Hence the need to gain entry into political institutions and in the functioning of the state, and to share control over the power the state exercises. This alone would lead to a situation where women are able to reverse the existing situation, which has consistently been against their interests, and bring about the necessary changes in policy and the social structure so as to ensure a more equitable and humane order.

The role of women's participation in elected bodies should not be undervalued. Elections are after all a forum for self government and democracy, they are significant in drawing the attention of the nation to the problems and needs of disadvantaged sections; the manifestos, campaigns, promises made by individual candidates, track record and future course of action of political parties are indicative of national concerns as well as mandates for action. Proper selection of candidates in an election is vital if this representative democracy is to function in the interests of a majority of the population that is depressed and disadvantaged. Hence, opportunities for participation at this level are significant for the adoption of politics and measures for women's development.

Strong and dynamic women who would not dream of appropriating privilege are today talking of reservation because they have come to recognise that they will not give "easy entry" in the corridors of power without reservation. This hierarchy is so rigid that the natural processes of democracy and constitutional guarantees have not been able to make a dent in these fortresses of power. The demand for reservation should not therefore be seen as either a gift or a privilege that women are seeking. For most women it is the last straw and a desperate measure to ensure their coming into the political mainstream. Their participation becomes vital in the context of the adoption of development strategies that are negative and harmful to women. Today most of the political parties in India have initiated some initiatives to activate political participation of women and develop their capacities. However, most of the political parties have not yet developed any special programes to meet the special requirements of women in urban or rural areas, despite the fact that most of the women activists felt that if planned efforts were made, they could be easily mobilised. Different debates concerning struggles of women as well as various actions by women's groups and NGOs on local as well as national problems have forced the mainstream political parties to accept women's concerns in their political programes. The political parties started changing their attitude towards women which is reflected in their election manifestos, their attitudes towards women candidates, speeches and slogans.

Statistics on women's participation in the electoral process are not very encouraging. It is important not only to pressurise the political parties but also to make the leaders understand the significance of organising systematic training of women possessing leadership qualities, of carefully selecting women candidates and ensuring financial, technical and human resources for affirmative action.

The need to strengthen womens' participation and leadership is constantly emphasised by various institutions viz, All India Institute of Local Self Government, NIUA, HSMI, Rambhau Mhalaji Prabhodini, etc and several NGOs and Women's groups like SEWA, Working Womens' Forum, YUVA, Disha, Prayas, Astha, Winavani, SNDT University, Aalochana, Agni, FASDSP (Forum Against Sex-determination and Sex Preselection), Stree Mukti Sanghathana, etc.

Many NGOs / CBOs, Womens' groups have provided some training, however systematic training of women possessing leadership qualities is not enough and more concentrated efforts are required to facilitate the process of women's ascent to key positions in political field. It is essential that the women's groups and movement recognise the importance of women as a constitutency and ensure their participation and representation in policy formulation. The movement must provide a support system for women who enter political processes to win elections. As stated by Nath Kamale 'The women's movement has been a powerful agent of empowerment and has provided an alternative perspective for fundamental structural changes. The movement has created organisational strength of women, has focused on women's issues and mobilised them around these issues. The women in the movement, however, have shied away from active participation in politics.

The women's groups and women activists thus aim to bring about a change in the women's perceptions, but not necessarily in the structures which subordinate women. If we want to bring about change in the lives of women and transform mainstream politics, there is no other way than to get involved in politics and transform it.

The women's movement and groups have to recognise the importance of women as a constituency and ensure their participation and representation in policy formulation. This can be achieved through reorienting existing structures for entry into decision-making including the political party system and introduce quotas or reservation as a temporary means of women's representation. The movement should also provide a support system (women's groups) for women who enter political processes to win elections.

The women's groups working at the grassroots level are small and scattered and have diverse ways of empowering women. There are no infrastructural facilities of networking available that could bring them together and strengthen them while allowing autonomy in their functioning. It is important to create unity in diversity between women's groups, organisations and individuals involved with women's empowerment. They need to adopt a common strategy, informed by a common vision, to be able to bring about changes in the policies and structures that perpetuate their subordinate status.

4.8.2. Local Government Initiatives

Reservation for women in local government is not just a question of getting a certain number 'in'; it also develops their capacities to play their rightful roles in the development process and makes an important difference as the local governments deals mostly with the quality of life for citizens. Municipal responsibilities relate both to women's practical needs and their strategic needs. The better we meet women's strategic needs, the better they are able to contribute to good city governance. Good Local Governance, in turn, enables a better response to women's practical needs.

Most local governments have initiated orientation / training programes to encourage women to participate in local governance by organising city-specific induction or theme-based training programes, wherein intensive training is given in various subject areas, such as, municipal acts and its implementation, laws of meetings, municipal budgeting, budgeting at ward level, municipal taxation, mobilisation of resources, urban service delivery systems (solid waste management, water supply, sewerage, health care services, traffic and transportation), poverty alleviation schemes, community management, environment management, shelter programes, new reforms in municipal administration, functioning of ward committees, motivation techniques, communication skills, women and development, handling the media etc.

The Ministry of Urban Development, Government of India and Urban Development Department of State Governments organise a number of training programes, workshops, seminars for women elected representatives at local level through various training institutions. Many municipal bodies have initiated a series of in-house training in municipal administration and urban development, in collaboration with premier training institutions in India. State governments through their State Training Centres organise capacity building programes for women elected members from municipal bodies in their States. Special training / orientation programes are organised by Ministry of Urban Development and Poverty Alleviation, Government of India under the UNICEF assistance and government's funds in the area of poverty alleviation schemes and its implementation in urban areas (e.g. SJSRY, NSDP, etc.)

4.8.3. Gender Sensitising of Local Government

Local governments are using sex-desegregated data for policy and programe formulation. It is an obligatory duty of municipal governments in India to collect, compile and maintain vital statistics in their city limits. Sex-disaggregated data is in use in many cities of the States in India for policy programe formulation and implementation of some special programes and projects at local city level.

The Government of India regularly collects, analyses and disseminates quantitative and qualitative data on the number of women and men employed at various levels in government on an annual basis and many mechanisms have been set up within governmental structures for monitoring progress in this field.

The Department of Women and Child Development, Government of India is collecting and using gender-disaggregated data to evaluate development from a gender perspective. The Department is also developing a Gender Development Index (GDI) for the construction of EDI and Gender Empowerment Measure (GEM).

Bringing women to positions of political power in local government is just the first step in social transformation. Gender sensitisation of those in power, be they men or women, is of critical importance. Influencing the choices of those at decision – making levels and bringing gender issues to the political agenda are important factors. Over the years, this perspective has gained acceptance within organisations, action groups and political parties.

Government departments, other institutions, non-governmental organisations, and women's organisations have undertaken several programes to sensitise local governments about the issues and needs of women in their cities.

It is recognised that law enforcement is a critical factor for bringing about enduring changes in gender perceptions. Several initiatives have been taken by the Government of India and the voluntary sector to sensitise law enforcement personnel and policy makers. Gender sensitisation of police personnel and urban administrators in the National and State level training centres is now a regular programe. A National Centre for Gender Training and Research has set up in the National Academy of Administration in Mussourie with the objective of sensitising young administrators and policy makers on gender issues.

The Election Commission of India maintains updated information on women representatives in each Parliament, including categorised information on the number of scheduled castes women representatives. With the recent revolution in information technology, the entire information is available not only in print but also on the Internet in the Parliament and Election Commission websites. This increases outreach and access of this information to the general public.

The Ministry of Rural Development, Government of India maintains updated information on the representation of women in local self-government or Panchayati Raj. The Department of Women and Child Development, Government of India also has come out with publications like 'Women in India – A Statistical Profile' in 1997, which compiled information on all aspects related to women in India. The Planning Commission, which is mooting the process of collection of gender desegregated data by all concerned departments in various Ministers, has included information on women's representation in power and decision-making in its Ninth Five Year Plan Document.

Besides these, several independent organisations are carrying out their own research and surveys that provide updated information on the same. These are also widely used and are quoted in different public documents. Sensitising the leadership of people's movements in the country to gender issues need to be prioritised.

4.8.4. Legal and Political Initiatives

The number of women in politics at the local level had been very small, and their influence negligible. As stated by Kumari and Kidwai, "Prior to 1990, the women in local politics were generally either politicians who had lost membership of higher institutions, and those who were given such an opportunity to serve the purpose of publicity. In many cases, the motive was partially also to satisfy the aspirations of these few women, since they could be kept under virtual control and denied higher aspirations. The insignificant presence of women at these levels was an important indicator of two basic facts: one that women who are planted at the top often lacked the kind of training required for effective participation, secondly, the society was unable to accept women in politics, particularly at the grass-root level.

If we examine the reasons for low participation, as stated by Nath, Kamle, 'down the ages women have always been treated as subordinate to men in every aspect of life. Their place of work was confined to the domain of the household with household chores and rearing of children. Her identity was attached to that of her father, husband or son, i.e. she was given a status in accordance with that of her male partner. It is not that women in the past have not contributed substantially in politics, but because of their secondary status and low esteem, most of them were denied entry in political decision-making.

The 74th Amendment of the Indian Constitution in 1992 ushered in a new era in the democratic process of the country as it not only provided constitutional status to the municipal bodies but also provided an enabling environment for women to a direct part in the local self government and brought women to the forefront and centre of local development. Sharing power and responsibilities with immense control over resources for development and social change will be an empowering instrument for women.

Article 243 T (I) of Constitution Amendment (1992) states as follows: "Reservation of Seats:

1. Seats shall be reserved for the Scheduled Castes and the Scheduled Tribes in every Municipality and the number of seats so reserved shall bear, as nearly as may be, the same proportion to the total number of seats to be filled by direct election in that Municipality as the population of the Scheduled Castes in the Municipal area or of the Scheduled Tribes in the Municipal area bears to the total population of that area and such seats may be allotted by rotation to different constitutions in a Municipality.

2. Not less than one-third of the total number of seats reserved under clause (1) shall be reserved for women belonging to the Scheduled Castes or, as the case may be, the Scheduled Tribes.
3. Not less than one-third (including the number of seats reserved for women belonging to the Scheduled Castes and the Scheduled Tribes) of the total number of seats to be filled by direct election in every Municipality shall be reserved for women and such seats may be allotted by rotation to different constituencies in a Municipality.
4. The office of Chairpersons in the Municipalities shall be reserved for the Scheduled Castes, the Scheduled Tribes and common in such manner as the Legislature of a State may by law, provide.
5. The reservation of seats under clauses (1) and (2) and the reservation of office of Chairpersons (other than the reservation for women) under clause (4) shall cease to have effect on the expiration of the period specified in article 334.
6. Nothing in this Part shall prevent the Legislature of a State from making any provision for reservation of seats in any Municipality or office of Chairpersons in the Municipalities in favor of backward class of citizens."

Different political parties in India have shown great reluctance to field women candidates. Reservation of seats at Municipal level has put pressure on political parties to identify and field more women candidates.

4.8.5. Training and Support Mechanisms

Attention is being given to the training and capacity developing skills and capacities of all elected representatives in local government, including women. They are trained to acquire skills, knowledge and orientation needed to carry out the onerous responsibilities given to them. A time bound, systematic and comprehensive training programe has been drawn up which will be funded by the Central Government. The Indira Gandhi National Open University has been associated with the preparation of a syllabus on women and development. The Government of India is also committed to capacity building efforts by organising and funding training programes for women elected to municipal bodies in India. A large number of such kind of training programes for elected members are handled by All India Institute of Local Self Government which is a premier training institution in local government field (established in 1926) in India. Ministry of Urban Development (MUD) supports several such kind of training programes through Regional Centre for Urban and Environmental Studies (RCUES) which are functioning in all the regions of India.

Apart from this, some of the theme-based training programes are organised by State Training Institutions in several States for women elected members in municipal bodies.

Human Settlements Management Institute (HSMI) of HUDCO organises some specialised training for women elected representatives in India.

Some of the major training institutions in India offering orientation training to elected women representatives are:

1. State Womens' Commissions in all States in India (to deal with women and development issues)
2. All India Institute of Local Self Government branch offices at Mumbai, Ahmedabad, Vadodara, Bhubaneshwar, Bhopal, New Delhi, Panaji, Bangladesh.
3. Regional Centre for Urban and Environmental Studies (RCUES) of AIILSG, Mumbai.
4. Regional Centre for Urban and Environmental Studies (RCUES), Hyderabad.
5. Regional Centre for Urban and Environmental Studies (RCUES), Lucknow.
6. Indian Institute of Public Administration.
7. National Institute of Urban Affairs (NIUA), New Delhi.
8. Uttar Pradesh Academy of Administration (UPAA), Nainital / Lucknow.
9. Rajasthan State Institute of Public Administration (RIPA), Jaipur.
10. Kerala Institute of Local Administration (KILA), Trichur.
11. Administrative Training Institute (ATI), Guwahati.

12. Institute of Local Government and Urban Studies (ILGUS), Calcutta.
13. Centre for Urban and Environmental Studies, Trivandrum.
14. National Institute for Habitat Management (NIHM), Bhubaneshwar.
15. Tamil Nadu Institute of Urban Studies, Coimbatore.
16. Professional Development Centre (PDC), Maharashtra.
17. Housing and Area Development Authority (MHADA), Pune.
18. National Institute of Human Settlements, Bhopal.
19. Environmental Training Institute (ETI), Madras.
20. Training Institute of Housing Development Finance Corporation (HDFC), Lonavala, Maharashtra.
21. Indian Institute of Education, Pune.
22. Yashvantrao Chavan, Pratishthan, Mumbai.
23. Rambhau Mhalaji, Pratisthan, Mumbai.
24. P. V. Mandlik Trust, Maharashtra.
25. SNDT University, Mumbai.
26. Agni, Mumbai.
27. Society for Promotion of Area Resource Centres (SPARC).
28. YUVA, Mumbai.
29. Chitanya.
30. Law College Society, Pune.
31. Stree Aadhar Kendra, Pune.
32. Self Employed Women's Association, Ahemdabad.
33. Annapurna (Mumbai).
34. Working Women's Forum (Tamil Nadu).
35. Decan Development Society – an NGO in Andhra Pradesh.
36. Women's Feature Service, New Delhi.
37. Kriti, New Delhi.
38. Feminist Association for Social Action, Chennai,
39. Shramik Bharati, Kanpur,

40. Vasavvya Mahila Mandali – Andhra Pradesh.
41. Disha, Sharanpur,
42. Centre for Women's Development Studies, New Delhi.
43. MARG, New Delhi,
44. Women's Studies Development Centre, New Delhi,
45. Centre for Social Research, New Delhi.
46. Joint Women's Programe, New Delhi.
47. Indian Institute for Development Studies and Research, Allahabad.
48. Nirantar, New Delhi.
49. Working Women's Forum, Tamil Nadu,
50. Mahila Shikshan Kendra – Baroda, Uttar Pradesh
51. Aditi, Bihar
52. Hind Mazdoar Sabha
53. Sanchetna, Gujarat,
54. Chattis garh Women's Organisation, Madhya Pradesh.
55. Sanlaap, West Bengal.
56. Ahmedabad Women's Action Group (AWAG),
57. Jyoti Sangh, Ahmedabad.
58. Centre for Advocacy and Research Delhi, Lucknow, Ahmedabad, Maharashtra.

The examination indicates that women elected to local governments have not formed any formal associations, groups and forums. However, all women mayors meet during meetings organised by All India Council of Mayors (AICM), which is an association of mayors representing all cities in India. These meetings give women mayors an opportunity to interact with each other and with other male Mayors and exchange ideas, information about effective urban service delivery, good governance and also provide issue based support. Similarly, various seminars, workshops, training programes organised by Government of India, State Governments and National and Regional institutions provide wide opportunities for women elected members to meet and interact with elected women members from different municipal bodies in India. Similarly, events organised by political parties, women's groups, non-governmental organisations also provide an opportunity for women elected members for experience sharing, networking and sometimes lobbying for some specific purpose in urban development and good governance.

It is also observed that in many cities women elected members have close links with local NGOs, CBOs or Residents' Associations or action groups and through such networking women members support each other and initiate networking among themselves about governance at local level or any issues related to women and development.

4.8.5.1. Training Services

The following institutions undertake training of appointed officials:

1. Urban Development Department, Government of India and Urban Development Departments of various State Governments in India have initiated several capacity building or training initiatives to train women working at various levels of municipal administration.
2. National Academy of Administration in Mussourie is actively involved in training senior government officers from Indian Administrative Services in India. The Academy has set up a National Centre for Gender Training and Research to further issues related to women and development. Apart from this, several State Training Centre in various states organise training-cum orientation and workshops for women appointed in local government.

4.9. Women in Administrative Services

It is observed that women officers from the Indian Administrative Service (IAS), Police (IPS), and Foreign Services (IFS) have their associations in all the States of India. These associations organise periodic meetings and 'get together' which provide an opportunity for the women officials to interact with each other. The City Managers' Association of Gujarat State also provides opportunities for women officials in local government in Gujarat State. 'Metro Forum' an association of Municipal Commissioners of Metro Cities will also provide an opportunity for women municipal commissioners to meet and interact on issues related to civic governance and any other issues related to women and development. Similar efforts are underway to establish an association of women officials in all municipal bodies in India.

All India Institute of Local Self Government, through its various Centres in India imparts training in the field of municipal administration. Besides short-term specialised programes, it also organises full time diploma courses on various aspects of municipal administration for junior and middle level municipal personnel. These courses are attended by large number of women employed at junior and middle and senior levels in municipal bodies in India. The following main institutions also offer several need-based or tailor-made specialised programes for women working at different levels of municipal administration in India.

These Institutions are:

1. All India Institute of Local Self Government branch offices at Mumbai, Ahmedabad, Vadodara, Bhubaneshwar, Bhopal, New Delhi, Panaji, Bangladesh.
2. Regional Centre for Urban and Environmental Studies (RCUES) of All India Institute of Local Self Government, Mumbai.
3. Regional Centre for Urban and Environmental Studies (RCUES), Hyderabad.
4. Regional Centre for Urban and Environmental Studies (RCUES), Lucknow.
5. National Institute of Urban Affairs (NIUA), New Delhi.
6. Indian Institute of Public Administration.
7. Uttar Pradesh Academy of Administration (UPAA), Nainital / Lucknow.
8. Rajasthan State Institute of Public Administration (RIPA), Jaipur.
9. Kerala Institute of Local Administration (KILA), Trichur.
10. Administrative Training Institute (ATI), Guwahati.
11. Institute of Local Government and Urban Studies (ILGUS), Calcutta.

12. Centre for Urban and Environmental Studies, Trivandrum.
13. National Institute for Habitat Management (NIHM), Bhubaneshwar.
14. Tamil Nadu Institute of Urban Studies, Coimbatore.
15. Professional Development Centre (PDC), Maharashtra.
16. Housing and Area Development Authority (MHADA), Pune.
17. National Institute of Human Settlements, Bhopal.
18. Environmental Training Institute (ETI), Madras.
19. Training Institute of Housing Development Finance Corporation (HDFC), Lonavala, Maharashtra.
20. Indian Institute of Education, Pune.
21. Yashvantrao Chavan, Pratishthan, Mumbai.
22. Rambhau Mhalagi, Prabhodini Mumbai.
23. Institute of Social Sciences, New Delhi.
24. SNDT University, Mumbai.
25. State Training Institutes of various states Governments in India.

The main purpose of urban management training is to develop capacities of officials to deal with the complex urban problems in a holistic manner to achieve efficiently the aim of municipal bodies and of the urban sector as a whole.

These institutions cover the main areas for orientation / training or capacity building in urban development and municipal administration field.

1. Urban Development Management.
2. Municipal Administration.
3. 74th Amendment to Constitution (1992) & its implementation.
4. Information Technology and Application of Computers in Municipal Administration.
5. Project Planning and Management.
6. Urban Infrastructure Planning & Development.
7. Municipal Finance and Resource Mobilisation.
8. Urban Environment Management.

9. Housing and Slum Programes.
10. Urban Poverty, Poverty Alleviation Programes & Convergence
11. Traffic and Transportation,
12. Solid Waste Management,
13. Water and Waste Water Management,
14. Shelter Upgradation Programes,
15. Women and Development
16. Municipal Legislative Framework.
17. Laws of Meetings.
18. Motivation Techniques and Communication skills,
19. Disaster Management,
20. Public Health and Management of Healthcare programes in cities.
21. Management Information System in Municipal Administration.
22. Personnel Management,
23. GIS in Urban Development.
24. Human Resources Development.

4.9.1. Measures to Recruit Women in Civil Service

One of the variables that go into the Gender Empowerment Measure, as depicted in the Human Development Report, is the proportion of men and women at senior levels of government. In this context the study initiated in 1996 by the Department of Personnel and Training (DoPT), as part of a project 'Capacity Building for Civil Services', was a significant step. In order to crystallise the problems faced by women in Civil Services as well as to isolate areas which needed to be addressed through policy guidelines, a survey was carried out across a cross section of the services, among men and women officers, to ascertain the issues on which guidelines would have to focus. The survey questionnarie was formulated keeping in mind different areas of concern for women officers like Gender Image in workplace and in the family to stress factors.

Various government studies have been undertaken in the past on problems and issues related to the various individual services that constitute the Indian Administration. But this survey broke new ground in terms of coverage of services and levels of both women and men, as well as the range of related issues. Many issues, such as stress and motivation and sexual harassment, that persist across the services were touched upon for the first time. A national level Project Steering Committee was set up for carrying out the Capacity Building project, and a Focal Point was identified in the DoPT for examining the sphere of "Women's Issues in the Civil Service".

The Lal Bahadur Shastri National Academy of Administration (LBSNAA) was appointed as consultant for developing a curriculum for Gender Sensitisation Programes and ten Regional Seminars were conducted at nine State Administrative Training Institutes.

The Focal Point identified in the DoPT will begin work towards framing guidelines on women's issues by reviewing existing rules / regulations of various services. The task that has emerged for the Focal Point is as follows :

Review of existing rules and regulations for possible gender bias and discrimination against women and suggest corrective action.

Co-ordinate output flowing from various activities of the project related to the issues requiring policy formulation.

Table 12. Women at decision-making positions in the administrative service

STATE/UNION TERRITORY	*DECISION – MAKING POSITIONS*			
	I.A.S. (As on 1 May 2000)		*I.P.S. (As on 1 April 2000)*	
	Women	*Men*	*Women*	*Men*
INDIA	535 (10.4%)	4624	110 (3.3%)	3191
STATES				
Andhra Pradesh	33	281	11	179
Arunachal Pradesh	38	194	9	147
Assam	10	216	2	134
Bihar	33	360	14	233
Goa	X	X	X	X
Gujarat	23	225	3	133
Haryana	32	180	4	100

Himachal Pradesh	17	109	1	73
Jammu & Kashmir	3	109	1	80
Karnataka	35	213	4	167
Kerala	21	157	2	114
Madhya Pradesh	54	342	9	273
Maharashtra	40	311	6	201
Manipur	5	193	3	98
Meghalaya	xx	xx	xx	xx
Mizoram	x	x	x	x
Nagaland	1	63	1	39
Orissa	17	185	7	129
Punjab	28	165	6	144
Rajasthan	29	231	6	141
Sikkim	5	45	Nil	24
Tamil Nadu	37	288	7	176
Tripura	xxx	xxx	xxx	xxx
Uttar Pradesh	51	484	10	381
West Bengal Union Territories :	23	273	4	255
Andaman & Nicobar Islands	x	x	x	x
Chandigarh	x	x	x	x
Dadra & Nagar Haveli	x	x	x	x
Daman & Diu	x	x	x	x
Delhi	x	x	x	x
Lakshadweep	x	x	x	x
Pondicheery	x	x	x	x

In the Civil Services, the overall percentage of women in 1997 was 7.5%, the highest being 12.3% in the Indian Foreign Service. Women are increasing their presence in other sectors such as the Revenue Services, the Railway Management Cadres, Telecommunication etc. On the whole, women in 1997 represented 13.8% of the employee strength in the public sector, as against only 8.6% in 1971.

Women's Organisation or other civil society organisation have taken some initiatives in some states of India to encourage women to stand in local government elections, however, these groups or organisations are small and scattered and have diverse ways of empowering women. There are no infrastructural facilities of networking that could bring them together and strengthen them while allowing autonomy in their functioning. It is important to create unity in diversity between women's groups and civil society organisations involved with women's empowerment.

Political participation would make a significant different if it came from those who are at the helm of affairs of political parties, and if women are there wielding power, the situation can improve to a great extent and political participation would give every woman a sense of dignity as a individual.

Nath analysed that the women's movement and groups have to recognise the importance of women as a constituency and ensure their participation and representation in policy formulation. This can be achieved through reorienting existing structures for entry into decision-making including the political party system and introduce quotas or reservation as a temporary means of women's representation. The movement should also provide a support system (women's groups) for women who enter political processes to win elections.

The women's groups working at the grassroots level are small and scattered and have diverse ways of empowering women. There are no infrastructural facilities of networking available that could bring them together and strengthen them while allowing autonomy in their functioning. It is important to create unity in diversity between women's groups, organisations and individuals involved with women's empowerment. They need to adopt a common strategy, informed by a common vision, to be able to bring about changes in the policies and structures that perpetuate their subordinate status.

Non-partisan women's groups should provide necessary moral and advisory support to women candidates to increase their chances of being elected to political offices. They should work towards enhancing the capacity of women candidates to win the elections by providing them with a forum whereby they could exchange ideas and experiences and learn from experts on electoral laws and politics and evolve issues and strategies to win elections.

4.10. Initiatives to Encourage Women in Local Elections

The 33 percent for women in municipal bodies has brought into focus the fact that there is a need to bring more and more women into the party. But the problem is that many women are often not equipped to become members of the political parties, as the party expects a certain level of consciousness for membership not everybody can become a member. Also, women have difficulty in attending party meetings, study circles or demonstrations because of their timings and the pressure of housework. Most of the parties have not yet developed any special tailor made programe to meet the special requirements of women in urban areas, despite the fact that most women activists felt that if such an effort was made, they could easily be mobilised.

As analysed by Kumari and Kidwai at one level, the party's ideology itself may be discriminatory, on the other hand its ambiguity in a traditional society may leave adequate space for discrimination. Party workers at times exhibit a sense of lack of gender equality because they carry with them their traditional value systems which are often feudal and patriarchal, into the party. Much of the discrimination against women in the party is because of the attitudes of these individuals. But at the same time women assert that the party does not try to change the attitude of both men and women who come to the party or make them more gender sensitive.

The nature of electoral politics in India also marginalises women and women's issues from the political agenda. Many women feel that electoral politics, at times limits the kind of support women politicians would like to extend to members of their own sex, since they realise that they cannot win elections on women's issues alone. Most of them are still hesitant to identify themselves with women's issues, claiming that women form only one section of their constituency and till recently not the determining section. Also, elections are largely conducted by men and with men's support. Electoral expediency requires women participants to compromise to survive in the man's world of politics.

All parties recognise the need to win women's votes, but often seem unsure of the best way to gain support among women.

The type of leadership required is of transformational type. Women's entry into processes of governance should create change in the very institutions of governance. In order to effect such change, leaders have to emerge which can occur only through participatory processes. The participation allows empowerment, which then generates leadership. It is only through their leadership, and their implied changes in the hierarchy of party and power that they may provide that they can justifiably participate in governance as representing something 'different'. This leadership can emerge only through active participation. Therein lies the role of the political parties in creating an enabling environment for active leadership generating participation. Prior to 1992, political parties have not been initiating any special initiatives or programes to encourage women to stand in local government elections. The number of women in politics at the local level has been very small, and their influence negligible. After 1993, women's participation in local governments increased quite radically with the enactment of the legislation providing one-third reservation of seats for women in local bodies. The effective implementation of this legislation has added another level in political participation. According to women from all parties the one third reservation for women in local governments has brought into focus the fact that there is a need to bring more and more women into the local government field and develop their capacities.

This particular 74th Amendment of the Indian Constitution ushered in a new era in the democratic process in India as it not only provided constitutional status to the municipal bodies but also provided an enabling environment for women to take direct part in the process of local self government and brought women to the forefront of city development.

The 74th Amendment mandated reservation of one – third seats in municipal bodies for women. There is also one third reservations for women in position of chairpersons of these local bodies in India.

A very active role for women in local governance is envisaged as compared to governance at the state and national levels in India. These provisions have provided great opportunities and challenges to women in India.

The challenge now is to transfer this large presence of women at local government level supported by the real delegation of power and responsibilities.

Women's role in decision making is one of the most important questions for consideration in the movement for their empowerment. Reservation of seats for women in local bodies has shown that it has tremendous implications, not merely in terms of the number of women entering the public arena and holding public office, but also in terms of the social, economic and political impact that these reservations have had for the total system.

Recognising various constraints such as present day politics, elements of criminatisation, corruption, muscle power, violence, lack of awareness of political participation, preparation to fulfil the role and responsibilities as elected representative, etc, the Government, NGOs, Womens Groups and activist's have been actively involved in providing necessary inputs to women. Women have been mobilised to participate in elections as candidates and voters, and to be vigilant citizens where elections are held. Communities have received gender sensitisation to facilitate acceptance of the new roles assigned to women. Leadership and organisational training of women has been conducted to enable them to be dynamic change agents. Networks have been interacting, to influence mass based political structures to prove more space to women.

References

Afshar, Haleh. ed. 1987. *Women, State and Ideology.* Studies from Africa and Asia. London and New York: Routledge.

Agnihotri, I. and V. Mazumdar. July 22, 1995. "Changing Terms of Political Discourse: Women's Movement in India, 1970s–1990s" *Economic and Political Weekly*, Vol. xxx, No. 29. pp. 1869–1878.

Bjorkman, James W. 1987. "India: Party, Personality and Dynasty", in Alan Ware. ed. *Political Parties*. Oxford: Blackwell.

Hoskyns, C. and S. Rai. 1996. "Gender, Class and Representation: India and the European Union", Paper presented at the 1996 Political Studies Association Conference. Glasgow, 10 April.

Phillips, A. 1991. *Engendering Democracy.* Cambridge: Polity.

Rai, S. M. 1995. "Women Negotiating Boundaries: Gender, Law and the Indian State". *Social and Legal Studies*, Vol. 4, No. 3, September.

Sarkar, T. and U. Butalia. eds. 1995. *Women and Right-Wing Movements: Indian Experiences.* London: Zed Press.

5

Women's Participation Budget Process

The budget is the most important economic policy tool of a government and provides a comprehensive statement of the priorities of a nation. As the representative institutions of the people, it falls to national legislatures to ensure that the budget optimally matches a nation's needs with available resources. Effective legislative participation in the budget process establishes checks and balances that are crucial for transparent and accountable government and ensuring efficient delivery of public services.

An important component of legislative scrutiny is to ensure that the budget addresses the needs of women and men equitably, and that it is supportive of particularly vulnerable groups in society including poor girls and boys, people with disabilities, minorities and the aged. The legislature ratifies international conventions relating to human rights. These conventions represent the State's obligations to undertake measures at national level.

Governments are large and complex institutions, and this is reflected in their budgets. Measured in terms of revenues and numbers of employees, some national governments are among the biggest organisations in the world. Budget documents can comprise thousands of pages, the format of the budget is not always easily understandable, and thorough analysis can take considerable time. For such reasons, budget scrutiny can be a daunting challenge facing legislators when they are asked to consider the annual revenue and expenditure proposals of the government.

Over the longer term, the influence of national legislatures on budget policy has declined in many industrialised countries. Several developments help to explain this trend. The emergence of disciplined political parties in the 19th century has curbed legislative independence. In many cases decentralisation of spending, and to a lesser extent of revenues, to regional or local levels of government has chipped away at the comprehensive control of public funds by national legislatures. In addition, the expansion of welfare spending in the 20th century has pre-committed large sections of the budget and thus reduced flexibility to reallocate spending from one year to the next. Over time, executive budget proposals gradually became the standard against which legislative action was measured.

It now appears, however, that many legislatures are rethinking their role in the budget process and reasserting themselves as more active players. Two reasons for this are the spread of democracy and a wave of constitutional reform, which have opened the way for increased participation by both legislatures and civil society. In addition, in many of the world's poorer nations, greater attention is being paid to the role of the budget in poverty reduction and eradication, and legislatures are reclaiming a voice in development debates.

New partnerships are emerging that can help to broaden participation in budgeting, and to foster consensus about some of the difficult choices and trade-offs that have to be made in this process. In many parts of the world, women's organisations are analysing budgets for their likely differential impacts on women and men of different social and economic categories. These organisations have formed partnerships with legislators to hold governments accountable on their commitments to gender equality.

5.1. Issues in Budgeting

Budgets are perhaps the most important documents that governments produce. Given the size of national budgets, they are powerful tools in influencing economic and social development. They also determine to a large extent whether there is equitable access to services by different groups of the population, such as women and men. By allocating money, spending plans reveal the priorities of the government in concrete terms, and they lay the foundation for sound operational management at the departmental or ministerial level.

The word 'budget' appears to have been first used in the early 19th century, and its legal definition can be traced back to a French law of 1862. Broadly speaking, the budget contains the financial plans of the government for an upcoming period. It is drafted at regular intervals by the executive and tabled in the legislature for approval, normally on an annual basis. Budgets that cover a period of two years at a time are less common. The budget serves the purposes of macroeconomic stabilisation, redistribution of income, and the allocation of financial resources to various government functions.

The budget has two main components, income and expenditures. Sources of income vary substantially between countries. They usually include direct taxes, such as those on personal and corporate income, and indirect taxes such as sales taxes. Other sources of income might consist of user charges for certain services, foreign aid, and income from commercial activities.

In considering its tax options, the government has to weigh advantages and disadvantages, including the likely impacts on different groups of women and men. For example, boosting reliance on sales taxes makes taxation more regressive. This means that a poor person will pay as much tax as a rich person when purchasing an item of clothing or food, as it does not take account of income differentials. Such taxes have gendered implications especially if they apply to the most essential commodities consumed by the poor, in part because women are often responsible for buying household consumables.

On the other hand, income taxes are progressive when they apply higher rates to individuals with a higher level of income. But if the formal economy is small, excessive taxation of a few individuals with high incomes can undercut investment, which hampers growth and employment creation. Over time, this might erode the tax base and reduce the ability of government to raise revenues. Taxation policies can have direct impacts on gender relations especially within the paradigm of a male breadwinner that puts female headed households at a disadvantage. Similarly, income taxes affect female labor force participation especially in light of women's responsibilities within the house-hold. For example, while many working women spend part of their income on day-care facilities for their children, these expenditures may not be deductable from taxable income. Raising an adequate amount of revenues, while at the same time preserving equity and stimulating economic growth, can be a difficult balancing act.

On the expenditure side of the budget, government allocates funds to various functions such as health care, education, agriculture, justice, defence and so on. The share of total expenditures allocated to each sector is a key indicator of spending priorities for a given year and of shifts in priorities over a period of time.

In economic terms, a distinction can be made between current and capital expenditures. Current expenditures are on goods and services that are consumed immediately, for example wages of civil servants or supplies of educational materials for schools. Capital expenditures comprise money spent on the purchase of goods that can be used to produce other goods, for example machinery or infrastructure. The balance between current and capital spending is important. When a clinic is built and equipped to service a community (a capital expenditure), then government has to make sure that it sets aside sufficient funds to run the clinic on a day-to-day basis, which requires budgeting for wages, medicines and the like (current expenditures)

When government spends more money than the available revenues, it can either raise taxes or budget for a deficit and cover the shortfall with borrowed money. There is a wide range of alternate deficit measures, but the size of the conventional deficit is widely quoted as the central indicator of fiscal health. This deficit is measured as the excess of government's total expenditure over total revenue. There is no absolute figure that can indicate whether the deficit is too large - this depends on the size of the economy. For this reason, the deficit to Gross Domestic Product (GDP) ratio is used to indicate the share of national income that will have to be used to finance the deficit. Although the appropriate size of the deficit depends on a variety of factors that determine sustainability on a case-by-case basis, one rough but widely accepted benchmark was set in the European Union's Maastricht Treaty with a figure of three percent of GDP. However, some go further and demand 'balanced budgets' where revenues are equal to expenditures.

Changes in the deficit do not have to be the result of a shift in fiscal policy, but can also be a reflection of the business cycle, for instance. Consistently growing deficits, however, give cause for concern:

— First, government borrowing can put upward pressure on interest rates so as to 'crowd out' private sector investment. In other words, when government uses most of the capital available on the borrowing market, less is available for the private sector to borrow in order to expand its activities. This can dampen economic growth.

— Second, deficit spending is expensive. Because government will have to put aside a proportion of funds to service its stock of debt, there will be less money for service delivery. Reductions in service delivery programes often affect women more than men. For example a decision to service debt and to reduce child-care or health services would most likely increase women's unpaid labor since they are the primary family caregivers.

— Third, it is unfair if extensive borrowing forces future generations to make sacrifices so that they effectively pay for spending that we enjoy today. This problem is exacerbated when borrowed funds are not invested productively.

— A fourth problem associated with excessive deficits is high inflation. Some governments have resorted to 'printing money' in order to meet debt servicing obligations. However, this strategy is difficult to pursue when the central bank enjoys entrenched independence from the government both legally and in practice.

Maintaining a certain size of deficit should not be seen as an end in itself but rather as a means of improving the standard of living of citizens. Sometimes, there can be a trade-off between the objective of reducing the budget deficit and that of achieving long-term equitable and broad-based growth.

Meanwhile, it is important to point out that budgets and macroeconomic policies are tools for achieving both economic and social development goals. While some assume that economic development automatically results in social and human development, evidence shows that the trickle down effect will not happen unless policies are formulated to intentionally ensure the equitable distribution of benefits of economic growth for all, especially poor men and women, minority groups, children and people with disabilities.

5.2. Budgets and Poverty Reduction Strategies

Countries formulate national development plans and sectoral strategies relating to the needs of diverse groups of people, in order to pursue a particular vision of society. Many developing countries are investing effort in addressing poverty on the basis of comprehensive development strategies. This trend is now supported in a number of developing countries by international financial institutions, which require countries to compile Poverty Reduction Strategy Papers (PRSPs) to qualify for debt relief, concessional loans and bilateral assistance.

Ideally, PRSPs are elaborated through country-owned participatory processes where poor women and men, civil society organisations and other stakeholders are involved, in some way, in defining poverty reduction goals and identifying poverty policy priorities. They include plans with clear targets and indicators for monitoring and evaluating the impact of policies through outcomes that benefit the poor. Where the strategy is in place, the budget is the most important tool for implementing a PRSP. Money should be allocated in line with the policy priorities in the strategy. Sector-wide strategies, development plans and MTEFs are used together with the annual budget in implementing a PRSP.

PRSPs and other types of development strategies are therefore useful yardsticks for assessing and monitoring budgets, and parliamentarians in particular can assess the budget against the commitments made to different groups of poor women and men and other vulnerable groups in these strategies when they consider the government's annual revenue and spending proposals. In addition, parliament should participate in the elaboration of PRSPs given that it involves making important decisions about the direction of a nation's development policy. In fact, legislatures have an important role to play not only in ensuring that sufficient funds are allocated and disbursed to the priority expenditure areas, but also that the money is spent efficiently. Otherwise, the goals contained in PRSPs and other development plans are unlikely to be attained.

Although the formulation of PRSPs is supposed to be guided by the voices of the poor, critics of PRSPs say that the poverty priority policies contained in them are not different from the old structural adjustment programes (SAPs). They reflect the orthodox economic thinking of the World Bank and the International Monetary Fund (IMF) and do not include gender as a variable in macroeconomic analysis. Policies such as trade liberalisation, privatisation and tight fiscal, monetary and exchange rate policies recognise market-oriented work and ignore non-market work. In many developing countries, most of this work is the unpaid subsistence, reproductive and care work poor women do in households.

Translation of the policy aspirations of poor women and men into policy priorities is led by ministries of finance and planning. But turning people's aspirations into policies is a political function. Politicians consult their constituents to develop their political platforms and work with experts to translate the platforms into appropriate policies. By failing to adequately involve legislatures in PRSP processes, the exercises have been denied some measure of political legitimacy and national ownership. Much as some civil society organisations have been able to influence aspects of PRSPs, they can never replace the role of elected parliaments in determining policy priorities for the people. Parliaments have the constitutional mandate to oversee government and if well facilitated and empowered legally, can act more independently vis-à-vis the executive branch than donor-dependent non-governmental organisations (NGOs).

Gender equality advocates introduce a shift from the growth-based focus of PRSPs to a human rights approach. They argue that budgets are not just about figures in dollars and cents but reflect a country's priorities and values. Budgets are the main instruments through which governments can fulfil people's social and economic rights. It is argued, therefore, that a PRSP, through its budgets, should make full use of the maximum available resources for progressive realisation of poor women and men's human rights, which countries have ratified in international and regional agreements such as the Universal Declaration of Human Rights (UDHR), the Convention on the Elimination of All Forms of Discrimination against Women (CEDAW), and the Convention on the Rights of the Child (CRC).

PRSPs focus on prioritising domestic policies to reduce poverty and channelling resources to those priorities. But critics point out that the poor are adversely affected by external factors as well. The most important of these are the World Trade Organisation (WTO) rules and other trade agreements. It is estimated that to export to the rich countries, developing countries face trade barriers four times higher than those faced by rich countries. The annual cost is about US$100 billion, twice as much as they receive in development assistance. Promoting market access for developing country products will achieve rapid reductions in poverty. PRSPs have included policies such as privatisation of basic services while the WTO rules have committed poor countries to open up to large international corporations. This may in future mean that governments cannot provide basic services, for example, to reduce the domestic workload of poor women without being in breach of WTO rules. These are issues that are external but which have a bearing on domestic policies and on poor women's lives. They should be discussed in the PRSP processes and in particular, by legislatures.

5.3. The Budget Process

Understanding the way budgets are assembled is a crucial first step in influencing decision making. The budget is the result of a process. The priorities and choices it embodies reflect the power of various actors in this process. Those who are effective in influencing the budget succeed in having their choices and priorities included.

5.3.1. Actors in the Budget Process

Within the executive, the role of a finance ministry or treasury is to coordinate and drive the budget process in accordance with a schedule. The finance ministry has the economic expertise to prepare macroeconomic projections. These are important in order to assess the amount of money that will be available for spending. The finance ministry also plays a crucial role in guiding the drafting of the budget, and later in monitoring budget implementation. Various spending departments and agencies also participate in the drafting process, and they are ultimately responsible for expenditures within their jurisdiction. They will often try to extract as many resources as possible, whereas the role of the finance ministry or treasury is that of the guardian of the public purse.

Democratic constitutions require taxation and public spending to be approved by parliament. Therefore, the role of the legislature is to scrutinise and authorise revenues and expenditures,.and to ensure the budget is properly implemented. The nature and effect of legislative engagement vary. Some legislatures write the budget; others approve executive budget proposals without changes. In some legislatures most of the debate around the budget takes place on the floor of the House; elsewhere the emphasis is on discussion in committees. Some legislatures fragment decision-making power in the budget process across various committees; others have a single financial committee that dominates the process. Ultimately, the final vote takes place in the chamber. However, where committees play a strong role, the House tends to be guided by committee reports in approving financial legislation. As representatives of the people, legislators should engage in consultations with their constituencies in order to ensure that their priorities and needs are reflected in the approved budget.

Independent supreme audit institutions carry out an audit of government accounts in order to determine whether government did in fact implement that budget as passed by the legislature, and whether it did so efficiently and effectively. While this basic task is similar across different systems, there are differences in the institutional design of supreme audit institutions. For instance, some are directly linked to the legislature, while others have judicial independence. There are also differences with regard to capacity resources, and types of audit conducted.

The potential contribution to the budget process of civil society organisations, covering the full spectrum from think tanks to community based organisations, is only slowly being fully appreciated. Civil society organisations can provide independent research from a perspective that is not covered by conventional analyses. One example is the work on the impact of the budget on vulnerable groups such as women or children that civil society groups have pioneered, sometimes in collaboration with the legislature. In some countries where the legislature has limited research capacity, civil society input has proven crucial in enhancing legislative engagement with the budget. Civil society has also contributed to raising awareness of budget issues, for instance through the publication of accessible analyses and budget guides targeted at a popular audience, and through training activities. Civil society input to the legislature is promoted when committee and chamber debates are open to the public, legislative information is freely available, and committees conduct hearings and receive submissions on legislation and budgets. In many countries, legislative reforms increasingly enable civil society involvement.

International financial institutions and donor agencies play a powerful role in the budget process of poor countries with particularly high levels of foreign debt. When international financial institutions and donors attach stringent conditions to loans, the legislature's role may be limited to rubberstamping budgets that reflect prior agreements between lenders and the executive. To be supportive of sound budget practices, donor funding needs to be transparent and predictable, and full information on such funding should be given in the budget.

Increasingly, the negotiations around debt and new financing which used to take place annually in Paris under a cloud of secrecy (Paris Club meetings) have been shifted to national capitals and involve a wider range of State and non-State actors. Consultative Group Meetings, as they are called, have become important opportunities for the private sector and civil society groups to make their voices heard by governments and donors on economic policy and budget issues. In some countries, parliamentarians participate in these meetings on an individual basis and by invitation. For a legislature to make an effective input, however, an institutionalised approach to its participation has to be adopted. For example, a parliament may authorise its budget or finance committee to coordinate its input by liaising with other committees and having some or all of its members attend the Consultative Group Meetings. Some Brazilian legislators recently formed a caucus to monitor government-donor relations.

5.4. Gender Perspective on Budget

In tandem with increasing calls for greater parliamentary oversight of the budget and more involvement of the parliament in the process, the concept of gender-responsive budgeting has gained ground and various tools have been proposed to put it into practice.

There is often confusion between the two terms sex and gender. While sex is used to refer to the basic biological differences between men and women, gender has taken on a more complex meaning. As a concept, it refers to socio-cultural characteristics which vary and evolve depending on religion, education, socio-cultural values or economic variables and determine the role and place of men and women in society.

In all countries, developed and developing, gender roles and relationships change slowly over time. They are determined by society and transmitted through cultural traditions, beliefs and norms. Gender identities and relationships are ascribed to people by the societies they live in. Moreover, the varying roles of women and men in their communities generate different needs and concerns.

It is often assumed that a national budget is gender-neutral; that in its functions, a budget will benefit women and men, girls and boys equally. In fact, by failing to take account of the different roles, capabilities and needs of women and men, budgets can reinforce existing inequalities.

As a group, women are as diverse as men, differentiated by class, race, ethnicity, age, education and so on. There are consequently competing claims from social groups on how the analysis of budgetary implications and impacts should be performed, and these claims vary according to their importance in different national contexts. The purpose of bringing a gender perspective to the budget is to ensure that budgets and economic policies address the needs of women and men, girls and boys of different backgrounds equitably, and attempt to close any social and economic gaps that exist between them.

At the apex of the pyramid is the visible, formal economy. It consists of paid activities done in the private and public sectors and is accounted for in government calculations of the size of the economy. In most developing countries, fewer women than men work in the formal sector and those women who do are concentrated in lower-paying jobs. The informal sector consists of many micro and small-scale enterprises that rely heavily on the unpaid labor of family members, especially women. In the less developed economies, the informal sector can be much larger than the formal one while in the industrialised countries it tends to be smaller.

The goods and services of the subsistence economy are produced and consumed in households. For many poor rural communities, subsistence farming is the main activity that falls within this sector. Since 1993, estimates of subsistence work done by households are included in standard national accounts but the sector is not yet fully integrated. At the base of the pyramid is the care economy that consists of all the tasks involved in producing and caring for people and building safe, peaceful and cohesive communities where they can live and work. Child-care, cooking, cleaning, laundry, fetching water and fuel wood, caring for the sick, elderly and disabled and voluntary work in neighbourhoods, are all part of this labor-intensive and unpaid sector on which all the other sectors of the economy depend. Although men and boys participate in it, the care sector depends almost exclusively on women's unpaid labor.

Failure to take into account the linkages between care work and the paid economy can result in less effective policies and inefficient allocations of the budget. On the other hand, expenditures on water, domestic fuels, child-care, education, health, unemployment benefits and pensions can reduce the burden of household work on women and free their time to engage in paid work. This can result in a synergic effect of policy objectives, such as increased family incomes, an increased rate of economic growth, higher levels of women's empowerment and increased mothers' investments in their children's health, nutrition and education. To achieve economic efficiency budgets and the policies they finance should recognise the dependence of the paid economy on the unpaid care sector and plan for both of them appropriately. While economic efficiency is a compelling reason for budgets to be gender-responsive, the goal of equity is equally important. Importantly, gender-sensitive budgets do not mean separate budgets for women.

National constitutions usually state that all citizens are equal under the law and prohibit discrimination against women. By signing international human rights agreements such as the Universal Declaration of Human Rights (UDHR), the UN Covenant on

Economic, Social and Cultural Rights (CESCR), the UN Convention on the Elimination of All forms of Discrimination against Women (CEDAW), and the Beijing Platform For Action (BPFA), governments have committed to working progressively towards equality and equity between women and men, girls and boys. At the UN Millennium Summit in 2000, governments of the world endorsed the Millennium Development Goals (MDG) to be achieved by the year 2015. Gender equality and women's empowerment is the third MDG. It is also recognised that it will be difficult to achieve the other MDGs without the attainment of gender equality. Governments therefore have a moral and legal obligation to achieve this goal.

Parliaments can monitor government commitments fulfilled through the allocation of resources to bridge existing gender gaps in capabilities, opportunities and decision-making power. In addition, tracking expenditures against gender and development commitments improves accountability and transparency of the budgetary process and the effectiveness of budget policies.

In many traditional communities, men are expected to build and repair houses and herd animals while women cook, look after children, clean the home and care for the sick and elderly. In most Sub-Saharan African countries for example, boys inherit land and property while girls do not. And in many parts of the world, a man is considered the head of his household and takes most of the decisions that affect his family. A woman is expected to obey her husband. In the industrialised countries, women have entered paid work in large numbers but they still spend more time than men doing household work, as an Australian time use study shows.

Table 1. Average minutes spent daily on activities of Australian women and men in 1992

Activity	Women	Men	Average
Labor force	425	516	482
Domestic, child care and shopping	301	175	242
Personal	628	621	624
Education	325	384	354
Community participation	99	125	110
Social and leisure	345	351	348

Because, in the past, women and men have not enjoyed the same rights and access to key resources such as education, land, credit and decision-making power, women and girls lag behind men and boys in many ways. For example, globally there are more illiterate women than men. Less than 5 percent of women worldwide own land. More teenage girls than boys are infected with HIV/AIDS. Unequal rights and access to resources limit women's ability to make decisions in their homes, communities or at the national level. Globally, more men than women hold government positions. Furthermore, on average, women occupy just over 15 percent of seats in parliaments worldwide. While men and boys are discriminated against or disadvantaged by systems of gendered social relations, it is mostly women who suffer from gender inequality.

Gender is a social category like class or race or ethnicity or any other group that defines the rights and opportunities that are available for the individuals who make up that group. Gender analysis is an approach that is used to plan for all people, women and men, girls and boys. There are many ways that experts have adopted to measure gender relations and monitor progress towards equality. One framework that has been adopted by the UN Millennium Development Goals (MDG) Task Force on Education and Gender Equality defines the following three levels of equality between women and men.

National governments and international organisations collect data that typifies gender roles and relations in all these three dimensions. For example, the Inter-Parliamentary Union (IPU) collects data on women's participation in parliaments worldwide and the United Nations Development Programe (UNDP) publishes annual data on women and men's human capabilities. There are also new indicators that have been developed by experts to measure the causes and effects of gender inequalities. Using an analytical framework and gender disaggregated data, it is possible to make development plans that address the different needs of both sexes.

5.5. Gender Analysis of Budgets

Several tools have been developed for use in gender analysis of expenditures and revenues. A commonly used tool is the Gender-Aware Budget Statement, which can be applied to the whole budget or to a number of sectors. Expenditures and revenues are analysed, using various tools, for their likely impacts on different groups of women and men, girls and boys.

5.5.1. Analysis of Expenditures

Step 1: Situation gender analysis of a sector:

This analysis begins with studying key documents and data on gender issues in the country and identifying their underlying causes and effects, both immediate and long-term. Very often, parliamentarians and civil society organisations have a fair idea about the social and economic situation of women and men, girls and boys in their constituencies. Data can be found in the line ministries, statistical departments and international reports.

Step 2: Gender analysis of sector policy:

In the second stage, sector policy and programe documents are examined to see whether they address the gender issues previously identified. Does the policy reduce gender inequalities, leave them as they are or increase them?

Step 3: Gender analysis of budget allocations

The third stage analyses the extent to which any policy commitments to addressing gender concerns are matched by allocations from the budget. Does the government do what it says it is going to do? An assessment is also made of whether the allocations address the gender issues identified in step one.

There are other tools that can be used to bring a gender perspective at the stage of monitoring budget implementation. For example a sex-disaggregated public expenditure incidence analysis can be done to estimate the unit cost of providing a service and the level of utilisation by different groups of women and men. Some surveys done using this tool have revealed that a public service intended for poor women actually benefited richer women more. Sex-disaggregated beneficiary assessments are used to find out the extent to which a service addresses the needs of poor women and men. It is a measure of how poor people, themselves, value a particular service. Parliamentarians can enhance their oversight role and better reflect their constituents' interests through the use of these analytical tools.

5.5.2. Analysis of Revenues

Gender studies of revenues are not as well-developed as analysis of expenditures, but some examples exist from South Africa, the UK and a few other countries. Gender analysis of revenues is important because expenditures are determined after the questions of the size of the budget and the sources of revenues have been answered. In developing countries external funds form a large part of total revenues and direct taxes affect mainly the middle and richer classes. But changes in taxes and benefits are widely felt in the developed countries because of the wider revenue bases and the social welfare systems.

Revenues can be divided into three categories as follows:

— Taxation, direct and indirect

— Donor funds in the form of loans or grants

— Other revenues, such as from user fees and asset sales

It may be possible to examine how much women and men contribute to personal income tax if the data is sex-disaggregated. Men will usually pay more of this tax than women because they work more in the paid economy and occupy the better-paying jobs. In poor countries, this tax makes up a very small percentage of revenues because the majority of people are not required to pay it. Because households, rather than individuals, sometimes pay income tax, the gender impact of taxation can be difficult to study. Other types of analyses consider how particular taxes affect women and men because of the sector they work in, the types of jobs they do or their levels of income.

Donor funds may be tied to particular programes and policies that have a gendered impact. User fees in the education, health care, water and electricity services can put such services out of the reach of poor households. Parents may withdraw girls from schools if they cannot raise fees for all the children and women's work burdens may increase if they have to switch from piped water and electricity and cover long distances to collect water and fuel wood.

There are several key issues to be kept in mind when conducting a gender analysis of revenues:

— *The unpaid care economy:* Where women have been the unpaid primary careers of their household, tax and benefit implications arise. For example, where governments decide to save money by reducing the number of available hospital beds, it is women, as unpaid primary careers, who take on the extra responsibility of caring for sick relatives. This responsibility consequently limits women's ability to generate any potential revenue.

— *Gender differences in household decision-making:* Research shows that women tend to spend a higher proportion of income under their control than men do on basic goods such as food, education, healthcare and the general well-being of their children. Where the prices of these items are raised, due to indirect taxation, women can be affected in two ways. First, time commitments can change if women subsequently become responsible for taking on extra duties or commitments to compensate for the price increase. Women, for example, may have to stay home with the children rather than sending them to a child-care centre. Second, consumption patterns can change. Women may be forced to purchase cheaper, less nutritional substitutes, or may decide to spend more time at home processing food rather than paying someone else to do it.

— *Gender differences in property rights*: In a number of developing countries it is customary to restrict women's ability to own or inherit property and reduce their capacity to manage risk successfully. Although women may not be currently taxed as property owners, increasing development and gender equality in property rights will eventually see women as an important part of the tax net.

5.6. Gender Budgeting Initiatives

Gender budgeting initiatives have been developed in over fifty countries. Some were one-off activities and others have lost momentum while others are on-going. UNIFEM's 2003 mid-term review of its Gender Responsive Budgets Program identified twenty countries with ongoing gender budgeting activities, namely : India, Nepal, Brazil, Chile, Kenya, Peru, Ecuador, Bolivia, the Philippines, Nigeria, Tanzania, Uganda, Sri Lanka, Guatemala, Morocco, Egypt, Mexico, Belize, Senegal and Mozambique.

Different constituencies have found the tools of gender budgeting useful for different purposes. Gender equality advocates use the techniques to call for equity in resource allocations and to promote women's rights by asking governments to allocate resources towards the fulfilment of international commitments contained in human rights instruments such as the Convention on the Elimination of all Forms of Discrimination against Women and the Convention on the Rights of the Child. They can enhance efficiency, effectiveness, accountability and transparency in public spending. The interest of governments, legislatures, civil society organisations and development agencies in gender-responsive budgeting has grown for these varied reasons.

International agencies, notably the IPU, UNIFEM, UNDP and the Commonwealth Secretariat, have provided support for gender budgeting initiatives to governments, civil society groups and to partnerships with parliamentarians. The Commonwealth Secretariat for example, has been engaged in an international advocacy campaign to promote gender-responsive budgeting among its member States. It has been involved in the production of tools, methodology and capacity-building materials. UNIFEM has played similar roles of advocate or provider of technical and financial assistance, as well as catalysing and leveraging funds for new and innovative initiatives.

Progress continues to be made on various fronts. For example, the Latin America and Caribbean region is leading in innovations in the area of tool development, while the Andean initiatives are strong at local level budgetary analysis and participatory exercises. In East Africa, a knowledge network has been established. It is strong in policy advocacy, training and awareness-raising among policy-makers, NGOs and researchers. South Asia and Central America have strong research and capacity-building tools while other regions such as the Arab States, South East Asia and West Africa are working with donor agencies to integrate a gender perspective in PRSPs, MTEFs and performance-based budgeting techniques.

5.6.1. Factors Affecting Gender Budgeting

Various challenges remain in implementing gender budgeting and accepting the analysis generated by these processes, including:

Collection of sex-disaggregated data: In most countries there is some sex-disaggregated data within and outside government which can be useful. However, there is a need to generate more information in order to shed more light on the differences between women and men, girls and boys, particularly in access to resources, opportunities and security. Without accurate and relevant data, it is not possible to integrate a gender perspective in the budget process. For legislators, information to enable a gender analysis of the budget should be timely and brief enough to be utilised during the period of budget debate.

Assessing priority areas: There may be budgetary constraints or 'trade-offs' which make it difficult to prioritise outcomes suggested by gender-responsive budgeting. A gender disaggregated beneficiary incidence analysis may identify the different needs and interests of women and men with respect to a particular service but how does that information translate into priority changes in policy and expenditure patterns? How, for example, does an analyst compare differential spending on healthcare for men and women, since they have different healthcare needs and issues? There is a need to develop appropriate frameworks to assist in determining priority gender issues within and across sectors in the context of the whole budget. This is particularly important where country-wide poverty reduction strategies are being implemented.

From analysis to changes in policy and budgets: Currently, most of the gender budgeting initiatives worldwide are at the stage of analysis and there is limited evidence connecting analysis with policy and budget changes. This is not surprising given the rigidity of government decision-making processes and the tendency of public officials to avoid experimentation such as that involved in gender-sensitive budgeting. A few initiatives, such as that of the Tanzania Gender Networking programe have moved beyond analysis to mainstreaming gender into the budget. There is no prescribed formula or recipe for achieving a gender-responsive budget. Introducing a gender perspective to budgeting is a political process influenced by the broader political context in a country as well as the economic, social and cultural situation. However, partnerships of legislators, civil society groups, researchers and government budget planners can increase and sustain pressure for the introduction of policy changes, and changes to expenditure patterns to support gender equality goals. Broad coalitions can also help to spread a range of skills, such as advocacy, research techniques, budget literacy and analysis, to budget stakeholders and government planners. Gender budget work is fairly new and still evolving but it is important that it moves from the conceptual and theoretical phase to practice. Identifying, documenting and sharing information about initiatives which have progressed from the analytical stage to the stage of integrating gender in budget formulation is important.

Limitations on legislative intervention: Legislatures, in partnership with gender experts and civil society groups, have sometimes played an important advocacy role, for instance in South Africa, Uganda and Scotland. However, there are limits to parliamentary interventions. The role of legislatures in the budget process is often confined to budgetary approval and oversight, while budget formulation and execution are more commonly functions of the executive. To integrate a gender perspective in a budget requires gender mainstreaming of policies and programes behind the budget. An active and gender-aware legislature can use the enactment stage to question budget priorities and call for allocations to promote equality.

Institutionalising gender budgeting tools: Gender budgeting requires political will, adequate resources and capacity, and a high level of budget literacy' amongst civil society partners and within women's policy-making machinery (women's bureaucracies and parliamentarians). Gender-responsive budgeting is a political tool to call for accountability on issues of gender equality. It is a powerful factor for change and its success depends on whether political will can be generated within government to support a process of transforming the traditional budget-making and policy processes by removing long-standing, in-built biases which disadvantage women and girls.

Challenging the traditional and dominant economic thinking of powerful bureaucrats in ministries of finance and international financial institutions requires technical skills and ideological persuasion. Civil society organisations and reformist parliamentarians committed to a vision of social change, as well as women's policy-making machineries need to build economic literacy skills to meaningfully engage in economic policy debates. Moreover, there is need to build specialised capacity and tools for gender analysis of budgets. Coalitions and networks of civil society, gender researchers, parliamentarians and government officials have been useful for spreading skills among various actors in the budget process.

Utilisation of gender budget tools requires resources, particularly those that focus on ex ante monitoring and evaluation of the budget. There has been support both within and outside the gender budget circles for improved, innovative and less costly tools to gather relevant and timely information. There is a need for continued support especially in countries where resources and capacity are scarce. Although there is currently great enthusiasm for gender responsive budgeting among donors, there is a possibility that such interest may wane. It is therefore important to have a realistic perspective about the objectives, progress and limits of gender budgeting to avoid future claims of failure.

5.7. Strengthening Legislative Participation

Too often legislatures find their capacity constrained, and are unable to participate effectively in the budget process. A number of obstacles can prevent legislatures from playing an active role in the budget process, for instance:

— When the executive commands a disciplined majority in the legislature, there may be less opportunity for legislative engagement than in cases where governments rely on the support of an uncertain coalition of parties.

— Legal frameworks may not be conducive to legislative participation.

— The committee system may be too weak to make a meaningful contribution to budgetary debates.

— The legislature may have insufficient time or lack the research capacity to properly assess budgets.

Nonetheless, there is an emerging trend in legislatures to strengthen their budgetary role. All over the world, political processes are opening up to citizens for greater engagement. As more women and representatives of other previously excluded groups take their place in legislatures, they seek not only to influence policies and budgets but also to transform the processes and culture of legislative decision-making. This presents challenges of developing the necessary attitudes and skills to embrace new issues and approaches. Looking at budgets from a gender perspective is one such challenge.

5.7.1. Reviewing Legislative Powers

Legal frameworks need to provide sufficient opportunity for meaningful legislative engagement. The budgetary powers of legislatures need not be set in stone. Even if they are entrenched in a constitution, change may not be impossible. For instance, amendment powers can be reformed as part of a constitutional review process. But budget amendment powers are not always enshrined in the constitution. Sometimes they are contained in legislative rules, or based merely on tradition and conventions. There are thus different levels of entrenchment. This is important in considering the possibility of reform efforts aimed at broadening the legislature's ability to engage with budgets.

5.7.2. Enabling Legislative Input

An exclusive focus on amendment powers is probably not sufficient, and perhaps not desirable. Budgets are increasingly based on a medium-term perspective. In addition, the potential impact of incremental year-by-year changes on budget policy is limited, as many aspects of the budget are too inflexible for short-term shifts. For instance, strategies to cut personnel spending have to be implemented over the medium term in order not to threaten service delivery.

The legislature's annual review of the budget proposal, therefore, needs to be anchored in a firm understanding of the medium-term direction of budget policy. For this reason, it is desirable that legislatures also debate and scrutinise medium-term budget policies, as well as the annual budget. To achieve this, a medium-term budget policy statement could be tabled and debated by the legislature ahead of the presentation of the annual budget. If the legislature is effective in making its voice heard in the determination of medium-term budget policy, the need for amendments to the annual budget may diminish. The opportunity to consider the budget strategy over a longer period of time may also enable the introduction of more far-reaching changes such as the use of gender analysis tools.

5.7.3. Establishing Independent Budget Research Capacity

Parliamentarians have to be empowered to independently analyse the budget if they are to play a meaningful role in the process. Even when the legislature has legal powers and the political space to shape budgets, analytical capacity is necessary to make sound budgetary choices. The ability to understand the budget and to make informed changes depends on detailed scrutiny that is only possible with sound analysis. It is important, therefore, for the legislature to have access to independent information and analysis on the budget preferably through its own research service. This can be complemented with analyses by independent think tanks, private sector economists and academics.

Table 2. Some options for establishing budget research capacity

Structure	Example
Large and fully fledged budget office	United States
Specialised budget office on a smaller scale	Uganda
Budget unit as part of a general legislative research service	Poland
General research service with limited budget skills	United Kingdom

Some of the more active legislatures, in budgetary terms, have their own substantial budget research capacity. For instance, the Congressional Budget Office (CBO) of the United States has almost 250 highly trained staff, and there are almost 50 employees in the Congressional Planning and Budget Office (CPBO) of the Philippines. Uganda's Parliament recently established a Budget Office with 13 economists. Some legislatures have smaller research units that specialise in budget analysis, for example in Poland, and yet others have general research units that can deliver budget analysis when needed, such as the Research Service of the House of Commons Library in the United Kingdom. However, in many legislatures, budget research capacity is negligible or non-existent. Building such capacity should be an important component of efforts to strengthen the role of the legislature in budgeting.

On their own, parliamentarians cannot conduct an independent gender analysis of the budget. They need professional staff with reasonable knowledge of the subject who can provide brief, accurate, and timely information to use in budget debates. Budget offices or the staff responsible for supporting budget oversight committees can establish links with institutions that can carry out gender analysis of budgets such as universities and research-based civil society groups, and with sources of data such as statistical departments. As part of their advocacy strategies, some women's organisations and other civil society groups provide parliamentarians with well-researched information on issues of concern. Activists sometimes undertake training programes for legislators to raise awareness of gender issues and introduce new skills and tools for integrating a gender perspective into legislation and budgets.

5.7.4. Enhancing Capacities of Parliamentarians

To make the best use of information on the budget, parliamentarians need to build their own knowledge of economic policy, budgets and gender issues. Many civil society groups and research institutes provide training in these fields. For example, the Centre for Legislative Development in Manila and PARAGON/UNDP provide various capacity enhancement programes for legislators and their staff in a number of Asian and Pacific countries. The Southern African Development Community (SADC) Parliamentary Forum based in Windhoek, Namibia provides training and exchanges between parliamentarians and parliamentary staff for the thirteen SADC countries. The Canadian Parliamentary Centre has capacity building programes for staff and parliamentarians in many countries. Similarly, the International Budget Project (IBP) in Washington D.C. provides support specifically aimed at building budget analysis skills. The Inter-Parliamentary Union has organised a series of regional and national capacity-building seminars for parliamentarians and parliamentary staff on the parliament's role in the budget process, including from a gender perspective. Without a basic understanding of economic and budget issues and a minimum level of gender awareness among legislators, budget research and analysis will remain under-utilised.

5.7.5. Broadening Access to Information

Legislative decision-making needs to be based on comprehensive, accurate, appropriate and timely information supplied by the executive. The amount of supporting documentation that accompanies the budget figures is crucial. In many countries, the budget document itself contains little narrative that outlines the policies underlying tax and spending proposals. Often the only source of narrative information is the budget speech. This makes it difficult for parliamentarians and their staff to understand the policy basis of the budget, and to evaluate whether the budget adequately reflects stated government policy.

In many developing countries, the comprehensiveness of information on donor funding needs to be strengthened. Donor funding should be included in the budget, and legislatures should receive detailed information on any funding agreements and attached conditions.

Also needed is in-year actual spending information. This can help the legislature to control unauthorised expenditures and variance between approved and actual figures in a timely fashion. Budgetary decisions should be made in the knowledge of actual spending information, rather than on the basis of budgeted figures that might be little more than fiction. Apart from good in-year reporting, this also requires effective interaction between the legislature and the audit body, for instance through regular liaison mechanisms. Another frequently-occurring reform challenge is to narrow the gap between the end of the fiscal year and the finalisation of audit findings, to ensure that the usefulness of this information is maximised.

Many budgets do not sufficiently relate expenditures to budget objectives and this limits the possibility of examining the likely gender impacts. If this is the case, it becomes necessary to encourage a government to change its budget format so that it integrates relevant output and outcome information.

5.7.6. Expanding the Role of Committees

Legislatures need strong committees to be effective. Legislative committees are the 'engine room' of the legislature. It is here that in-depth and more technical debate can take place, away from the political grandstanding that often characterises proceedings on the floor of the House. Where the committee stage is underdeveloped, and discussion takes place mainly on the floor of the House, the budgetary role of the legislature is weak. Useful reforms might entail:

— Establishing a comprehensive system of financial committees,
— Introducing public hearings on the budget,
— Boosting the numbers of support staff, and
— Expanding the time for committee consideration of the draft budget in order to facilitate more in-depth scrutiny.

Introducing a gender perspective requires that parliament allows itself sufficient time to scrutinise the budget in-depth and make alternative proposals, preferably through the committee system. Rules of procedure should enable sufficient committee scrutiny of sector budgets and public engagement, because without inputs from civil society advocacy groups through public hearings, parliaments alone are not likely to initiate and sustain pressure to integrate gender analysis into the budgeting process.

5.7.7. Reassessing the Timing of the Budget Process

Legislatures require both sufficient time and a properly timed budget process to facilitate meaningful decision-making. International experience suggests that a minimum of three to four months is required for the approval of the budget by the legislature on the basis of meaningful analysis and scrutiny. However, sufficient time is not enough in itself. The budget should also be tabled sufficiently in advance of the fiscal year to which it relates in order to enable the legislature to make decisions that matter, when they matter. Reforms to the budget process strengthen the legislature when they address both issues.

5.7.8. Institutionalising a Gender Perspective on the Budget

Every new idea needs a champion. Within a parliament, a committee concerned with gender issues or the budget committee can assume the responsibility for planning and institutionalising a gender perspective on the budget. Alternatively, a less formal structure such as a women's caucus can take up the challenge and work with budget oversight committees. In South Africa, a sub-committee of the powerful Finance Committee led the process of integrating gender into the committee's work. In Uganda, members of the Special Interest Groups (SIG) Caucus, through their respective parliamentary oversight committees, began this process. Two new formal structures, the Budget Office and the Committee for Equal Opportunities, have taken over the roles of facilitating integration of gender issues in the budget and gender mainstreaming respectively. The appropriate institutional mechanism for introducing a gender perspective on the budget will be determined by the political and legislative system in place. Without such a mechanism, however, the momentum for such a transformative process can be difficult to sustain.

References

Debbie Budlender & UNIFEM. 2004. *Budgeting to Fulfil International Gender and Human Rights Commitments*, Frontline Electronic Publishing Ltd, Harare.

Folasade Ayorinde. 2005*Local Government Budget & Gender, A Guide Analysis of Kuje Area Council Budget, Abuja, Case Study of the Education & Health sectors*, Nigeria Gender Budget Network.

Okojie C.E & Amadi S.I (Eds). 2008*Gender Responsive Budgeting and Parliament: A Handbook for Nigerian Legislators*, a publication of the Centre for Democracy and Development (CDD) and Henrich Boll Foundation (HBF).

Ramkumar V. 2008. *Our Money, Our Responsibility, A Citizens' Guide to MonitoringGovernment Expenditures,* The International Budget Project.

Okojie C.E & Amadi S.I (Eds). 2008*Gender Responsive Budgeting and Parliament: A Handbook for Nigerian Legislators*, a publication of the Centre for Democracy and Development (CDD) and Henrich Boll Foundation (HBF).

6

Women-Men Partnership in Democracy

Aacording to the Inter-Parliamentary Union (IPU) " The achievement of democracy presupposes a genuine partnership between men and women in the conduct if the affairs of society in which they work in equality and complementarity, drawing mutual enrichment from their differences." These few lines from the Universal Declaration on Democracy concisely define the philosophy which has inspired the Inter-Parliamentary Union (IPU) in its work to promote the status of women in the last twenty years. While it seeks to examine all aspects of women's status in society, IPU focuses particularly on women's contribution to and impact on the political and parliamentary process a relatively unexplored field prior to the mid-1980s and one in which IPU felt decisive progress needed to be made if democracy and sustained development were to be achieved.

Twenty to 30 years ago, the gender imbalance in politics anywhere in the world was even more flagrant than it is today. Anxious to find ways to redress the situation, the IPU decided first to take detailed stock of it, in its historical and cultural diversity. In this regard, it undertook what appeared to be a straightforward exercise but was in fact a complex and difficult process: collecting information on the dates on which women were granted the right to vote around the world and data on women's presence in national parliaments since the creation of the first sovereign national parliamentary assembly.

The findings cast a harsh spotlight on reality. What young generations of women and men in well-established democracies may consider an obvious part of their political rights, and may even view with a certain negligence, was not a right that women had less than a century ago. In fact, these rights still remain elusive for women, hopefully not for long, in at least two countries with a national legislature (Kuwait and the United Arab Emirates).

The world chronology of women's suffrage reveals that it took women almost a whole century to gain recognition of their right to vote and their right to stand for elections. The chronology also reveals that for many countries women's political emancipation came hand-in-hand with emancipation from colonial rule, and that it has not been uncommon for women in the South to obtain the franchise before women in the North. In many cases, the rights to vote and to stand for election were granted in stages. In some isolated cases women were given the right to stand for elections before they were considered able to express their own electoral choice; for example, women in the U.S. were given the right to stand for elections in 1788, but were not given the right to vote until 1920.

In many countries, the right to vote for women was coupled with certain conditions. These conditions were meant to highlight that, in the view of those in power, only certain women could share in what was still considered a highly elitist right: that of ruling others. IPU's surveys revealed that, in addition to the usual requirements of citizenship, age and residence, the restrictions (now abolished) imposed on women's suffrage included that a woman: be a wife or a widow; be the mother of a member of the armed forces; be literate or have reached a certain degree of education; have a certain level of income or social standing; or belong to a given racial group. Such conditions would have been inconceivable for men. The surveys reveal that a long time often elapsed between women being granted the right to vote and actually getting elected. There were also long delays between the formal recognition of women's right to stand for elections and the time when either women dared to run or parties dared to select them as candidates; and further delays until the time that electors actually placed their confidence in women and elected them as their representatives.

IPU's surveys, which have since diversified and expanded beyond just the collection of statistical and historical data, show that these issues need to be analysed in the light of historical, political, cultural and sociological developments throughout the world. They also highlight the fact that for men to accept women as equal partners in the paid labor force and as equal contributors to society's well-being and development, beyond their roles at home, still involve a major shift in values. This process is far from complete anywhere in the world, even in countries where a war or a struggle for independence has upset, at least temporarily, the traditional division of labor between men and women. Whatever a country's historical experience and the degree to which attitudes have evolved, the fact remains that men are reluctant to accept women as political partners. This only reinforces the fact that a great deal of awareness-raising still needs to be done.

6.1. Changing Attitudes

Since the 1980s a strong network for women, IPU's Meeting of Women Parliamentarians, had developed within the organisation. This group was able to convince a male dominated IPU that it should organise a special event to discuss women's participation in the political and parliamentary decision-making process. Despite the reluctance of some feminist hard-liners, it was agreed that since politics was very much in the hands of men, no viable solutions could be found and applied unless men embarked with women on assessing the problem and were also involved in the search for solutions. In reality, it was not easy for the IPU to convince member parliaments to send male MPs to a meeting called upon to discuss women's political integration. While not always daring to confess this, many men felt that this was not their business or feared that they would be put on trial for holding onto the political decision-making process in contravention to democratic principles. In the end, 16 percent of the men invited, mostly from the developing countries and some from very conservative cultural backgrounds, attended the meeting in Geneva in November 1989. Their very presence generated a unique and fresh debate, especially as it had been decided that preprepared speeches and country statements would not be allowed.

A vision, not just of politics but of society at large, emerged from the session. Although in practice politics was still a "no-woman's land", participants agreed that its conduct and outcome affected the lives of women as much as that of men and that it was the concern of both genders. They agreed that the more women are involved in the political decision-making process in parties, elected bodies, governments and international bodies - both in numbers that reflect the percentage of the population which they constitute and as active players in the process, the more the concept of democracy would assume true and tangible expression. Internationally, this was the first time that an equation between democracy and women's involvement was established in a straightforward manner by both men and women together. Although many possible solutions had been discussed and some action identified, an overall strategy still needed to be devised to change a reality that contradicted the equation.

6.2. Men and Women in Partnership

In April 1992, the overwhelmingly male plenary policy-making body of the IPU, the Inter-Parliamentary Council, confirmed that "the concept of democracy will only assume true and dynamic significance when political policies and national legislation are decided upon jointly by men and women with equitable regard for the interests and aptitudes of both halves of the population". This opened the way to setting up a group of six men and six women, representing the six main regions and the various political systems and cultural backgrounds of the world, to work on a full-fledged Plan of Action to Correct Present Imbalances in the Participation of Men and Women in Political Life. The project was seen as a contribution to the Fourth World Conference on Women (FWCW) in Beijing in September 1995 and was to place special emphasis on women's participation in political life.

To define pragmatic strategies which states and, more importantly, political parties and organisations could use as guidelines, the IPU decided not only to set up a parity group (this process alone took several months due to the reluctance of some regional groupings, particularly the Europeans), but also to carry out an in-depth consultation process with parliaments which would take into account the relevance of any proposed strategies vis-à-vis national diversity. The undertaking lasted almost two years: a first draft, based on the results of the consultation, was sent to all parliaments for analysis and amendment; in March 1994 the IPU reached a consensus on a Plan of Action that fits into its larger project of promoting representative democracy. This plan was one of the sources of inspiration for the Beijing governmental Declaration and Platform for Action.

The key feature of the Plan of Action was that for the first time it defined gender partnership as being the bedrock of democracy and the path to sustained development. The Plan is particularly popular and practical for political actors because:

— It addresses the basic issues without disregarding the cultural, religious, social, political and institutional diversity of the different countries;

— It offers practical solutions to problems common to all countries while proposing a broad spectrum of options to meet the specific situations in different countries and regions;

— It tackles women's participation in politics while taking into account other indicators, such as the enjoyment of civil, economic, social and cultural rights;

— It interprets the interests and skills of women without causing a backlash from men, who had long held centrestage on the political scene.

6.3. Making a Political Commitment

Given the role of parliaments in states' affairs, it was natural to ensure that they were closely involved in the preparatory process for the Beijing Conference and in its decisions which, even if they were taken by governments alone, incur the responsibility of the state. The IPU thus urged parliaments to make arrangements for a number of their members to take part, both in the government conference and in the parallel non-governmental organisations (NGOs) forum. It also organised a Parliamentarians' Day which was hosted by the Chinese National People's Congress, chaired by the President of the FWCW and gathered some 500 MPs, both men and women, from 102 countries.

Noble principles and the best guidelines enunciated in internationally agreed documents after days and months of arduous negotiations can gather dust on a shelf if the political will, and the adequate budgetary appropriations, are not there to translate them into national legislation and programes. For this reason, the Parliamentarians' Day concluded with the adoption by consensus of the Beijing Parliamentary Declaration, a text later endorsed by IPU's plenary governing body, which stated the commitment of parliaments and their members to take their share of the follow-up process of the FWCW and "to ensure that the necessary resources are made available for carrying out any measure" adopted in that context. The Declaration once more reiterated that "no country can any longer afford to overlook any portion of its human resources" and that "active partnership of both elements of society is indeed one of the surest, most lasting foundations of democracy and development, and urgently needed establishing through structural and legislative measures aimed at the equal participation of women and men in the political decision-making process".

6.3.1. A New Social Contract

In addition to suggestions aimed at governments, parliaments, political parties and organisations, non-governmental organisations and the media regarding ways to correct the gender imbalance in the daily running of public affairs, the Plan of Action provided for the continuation of IPU's world surveys and comparative studies on women's issues, for structural changes within the IPU itself to render it consistent with this vision of democracy, and for a periodical review of achievements, nationally and internationally. It also provided for the holding of another meeting around the concept of gender partnership in politics. Thus, as part of the follow-up process of the Beijing FWCW, an international specialised conference was organised by the IPU in February 1997 on the theme Towards Partnership Between Men and Women in Politics.

Hosted by the Indian Parliament, the event gathered, perhaps for the first time on the international scene, an equal number of men and women. During four days, participants departed from the usual ritual of international conferences, refrained from making pre-prepared speeches, and instead carried out a dynamic and creative brain-storming session on ways to correct the current democratic deficit. Their discussions covered the link between democracy and gender partnership, practical ways to further women's political and electoral training, the controversial technique of quotas, and ways to ensure the adequate funding of women's electoral campaigns. The programe of events also included a second stimulating round table with the media on the image of women politicians in the media (the first one had been held in Geneva). To facilitate participants' reflections and comments, the IPU had produced a world comparative study based on a survey carried out with all existing national parliaments and covering the various aspects of women's participation in political parties, their involvement in the electoral process both as electors and as candidates, and their presence, role and functions in parliament. Accompanied with a poster presenting the situation on a world map, the study contained both statistical and substantial data and was entitled, Men and Women in Politics: Democracy Still in the Making.

The New Delhi Declaration and the publication, Towards Partnership Between Men and Women in Politics, convey the creative spirit that inspired the discussion. Speaking from their personal experience, men and women participants identified concrete measures likely to generate a change. They concluded that "what is basically at stake is democracy itself". They asserted that "what has to be developed, in modern democratic societies, is nothing less than a new social contract in which men and women work in equality and complementarity, enriching each other mutually from their differences". They felt that "to address the current deficit, a major shift in the mind-set of both men and women is needed", stressing that "this would generate a positive change of attitudes towards women and lead to a new balance in society at large and in politics in particular".

In analysing the outcome of the conference two months later, the IPU Council urged governments, parliaments and political parties to take inspiration from the concrete suggestions made by the New Delhi Conference "so that politics may better reflect and interpret the national population in its dual composition and is carried out in a spirit of partnership, a consolidating factor of democracy". Further, it decided to establish within the IPU a Gender Partnership Group aimed at securing the implementation of the principle advocated at large.

6.4. Women's Political Input and Impact

This is the current "state of the art" at the IPU on the issue of women's political participation. Having started its work on the basis of numbers some 20 years ago, it has since gone beyond numbers to analyse the root-causes of the problem and its various forms and consequences, and to design remedies.

At a time when many tend to deny that women's emergence on the political scene has had any positive impact, IPU is initiating work to collect direct testimonies of women parliamentarians on their input and impact on daily politics. This survey should enable the international community to assess to what extent women's participation has affected both the work of political parties and the running and political outcome of parliamentary work. Like previous IPU world comparative surveys, it may reveal unexpected realities, dispel prejudices, generate a re-adjustment of men's and women's visions of their respective input in politics, help developing self-confidence among women and, hopefully, demonstrate that democracy is gaining in strength.

6.4.1. Strategies to Enhance Women's Political Impact

6.4.1.1. Women's Political and Electoral Training

Training targeting:

(i) The exercise of citizenship so that participation in political life is not reduced merely to depositing a vote in a ballot box at more or less regular intervals and is perceived as a lasting commitment and contribution to the building of a more just society;

(ii) The ability to stand for election and to conduct an electoral campaign, which implies gaining the necessary self-confidence, putting together the requisite moral, material and logistical support in the political party and informal support networks and, lastly, winning the voters' trust; and

(iii) The use of parliamentary procedures so as to be able to fulfil electoral commitments. Trainers drawn from either sex. Training focusing on the working of government, the building of democracy and problems tied to social relations between men and women, and pertaining to such topics as communications, campaign organisation, work with volunteers, media and non-governmental organisations (NGOs), and the role of political parties. Training which involves learning how to examine the national budget so as to understand its different components and determine the extent to which it takes into account the needs of women. Establishing a directory of institutions worldwide that are able to provide political training for women.

6.4.1.2. Financing of Women's Electoral Campaigns

Reduce the costs of campaigns by placing a ceiling on spending, by shortening the time for campaigning and by introducing reduced rates for the use of media time in campaigns. Have appropriate legislation to regulate funding from all sources, whether public, business, foundations or private. Compensate the scarcity of funding for women's campaigns in the following manners:

(i) Political parties putting forward, as a matter of principle, at least one-third women candidates and allocating to them one-third of their campaign resources;

(ii) Political parties, foundations and international financial institutions such as the World Bank establishing special funds offering cash contributions or interest-free loans to women candidates or to reimburse their campaign expenses;

(iii) The generation of at least partial public funding of campaigns. Wherever public funding of political parties is possible, link the amount of funding or refunding of election campaign expenses to the percentage of women candidates put forward by each party and/or elected to parliament. In those countries where funding is provided to parliamentary political groups, foresee an additional premium linked to the proportion of women MPs.

6.4.1.3. Media

Media personnel at all levels, from editor to reporter, from publisher to columnist, should be made aware of the fact that "stories" that sell or pretend to do so often perpetuate gender patterns which are adverse to the strengthening of democracy. Make women candidates aware of the fact that commitment, active ongoing presence, and conviction can make up for insufficient resources, including financial means, and that good media coverage does as much to win an election as large sums of money. Assist women politicians to learn how to get their message across through training on how to conduct media interviews and press conferences, make presentations, prepare press kits and communiqués, etc. Assist women to become more assertive in presenting their ideas and achievements as in fact, irrespective of sex, the media tend to come to people who stand tall and believe in their cause. Encourage the media to treat women politicians as political protagonists and to cover and interview them as much as men politicians. Encourage governments to restructure their communications policy so as to make them more gender sensitive and also to promote a fairer image of women politicians.

References

Barry, Trudie, Sneha Palnitkar . 1996. *Women and Local Politics in Mumbai and London : The quota Innovation*' Third IIAS International Conference (International Institute of Administrative Sciences) – Beijing, China 8 – 11, October, 1996.

Chattopadhyaya, Kamaladevi. 1983. *Indian Women's Battle for Freedom*. New Delhi: Abhinav Press.

CWDS. 1995. *Towards Beijing: A Perspective from the Indian Women's Movement*. New Delhi.

Desai, Neera. 1991. 'Indian March Towards Equity – A Review of a Decade and half of Action and Policy on Women, *Janata : A Journal of Democratic Socialism*, Vol. 45, Nos. 36 - 40, Jan 6, 1991, pg.9 – 16.

Joshi, P. 1989. *Gandhi on Women*. New Delhi: Navjivan Press.

Liddle, J. and R. Joshi. 1986. *Daughters of Independence*. New Delhi: Kali for Women.

Patel, Vibhuti. 1986. *Getting a foothold in Politics, Reading in Women's Studies Series* : RCUES, SNDT, Bombay.

7

Women in Politics and Good Governance

Recently the terms "governance" and "good governance" are being increasingly used in development literature. Bad governance is being increasingly regarded as one of the root causes of all evil within our societies. Major donors and international financial institutions are increasingly basing their aid and loans on the condition that reforms that ensure "good governance" are undertaken.

The concept of "governance" is not new. It is as old as human civilization. Simply put "governance" means: the process of decision-making and the process by which decisions are implemented (or not implemented). Governance can be used in several contexts such as corporate governance, international governance, national governance and local governance.

Since governance is the process of decision-making and the process by which decisions are implemented, an analysis of governance focuses on the formal and informal actors involved in decision-making and implementing the decisions made and the formal and informal structures that have been set in place to arrive at and implement the decision.

Government is one of the actors in governance. Other actors involved in governance vary depending on the level of government that is under discussion. In rural areas, for example, other actors may include influential land lords, associations of peasant farmers, cooperatives, NGOs, research institutes, religious leaders, finance institutions political parties, the military etc. The situation in urban areas is much more complex.

At the national level, in addition to the above actors, media, lobbyists, international donors, multinational corporations, etc. may play a role in decision-making or in influencing the decision-making process. All actors other than government and the military are grouped together as part of the "civil society." In some countries in addition to the civil society, organized crime syndicates also influence decision-making, particularly in urban areas and at the national level.

Similarly formal government structures are one means by which decisions are arrived at and implemented. At the national level, informal decision-making structures, such as "kitchen cabinets" or informal advisors may exist. In urban areas, organized crime syndicates such as the "land Mafia" may influence decision-making. In some rural areas locally powerful families may make or influence decision-making. Such, informal decision-making is often the result of corrupt practices or leads to corrupt practices.

7.1. Characteristics of Good Governance

Good governance has 8 major characteristics. It is participatory, consensus oriented, accountable, transparent, responsive, effective and efficient, equitable and inclusive and follows the rule of law. It assures that corruption is minimized, the views of minorities are taken into account and that the voices of the most vulnerable in society are heard in decision-making. It is also responsive to the present and future needs of society.

7.1.1. Participation

Participation by both men and women is a key cornerstone of good governance. Participation could be either direct or through legitimate intermediate institutions or representatives. It is important to point out that representative democracy does not necessarily mean that the concerns of the most vulnerable in society would be taken into consideration in decision making. Participation needs to be informed and organized. This means freedom of association and expression on the one hand and an organized civil society on the other hand.

7.1.2. Rule of Law

Good governance requires fair legal frameworks that are enforced impartially. It also requires full protection of human rights, particularly those of minorities. Impartial enforcement of laws requires an independent judiciary and an impartial and incorruptible police force.

7.1.3. Transparency

Transparency means that decisions taken and their enforcement are done in a manner that follows rules and regulations. It also means that information is freely available and directly accessible to those who will be affected by such decisions and their enforcement. It also means that enough information is provided and that it is provided in easily understandable forms and media.

7.1.4. Responsiveness

Good governance requires that institutions and processes try to serve all stakeholders within a reasonable timeframe.

7.1.5. Consensus Oriented

There are several actors and as many view points in a given society. Good governance requires mediation of the different interests in society to reach a broad consensus in society on what is in the best interest of the whole community and how this can be achieved. It also requires a broad and long-term perspective on what is needed for sustainable human development and how to achieve the goals of such development. This can only result from an understanding of the historical, cultural and social contexts of a given society or community.

7.1.6. Equity and Inclusiveness

A society's well being depends on ensuring that all its members feel that they have a stake in it and do not feel excluded from the mainstream of society. This requires all groups, but particularly the most vulnerable, have opportunities to improve or maintain their well being.

7.1.7. Effectiveness and Efficiency

Good governance means that processes and institutions produce results that meet the needs of society while making the best use of resources at their disposal. The concept of efficiency in the context of good governance also covers the sustainable use of natural resources and the protection of the environment.

7.1.8. Accountability

Accountability is a key requirement of good governance. Not only governmental institutions but also the private sector and civil society organizations must be accountable to the public and to their institutional stakeholders. Who is accountable to whom varies depending on whether decisions or actions taken are internal or external to an organization or institution. In general an organization or an institution is accountable to those who will be affected by its decisions or actions. Accountability cannot be enforced without transparency and the rule of law.

From the above discussion it should be clear that good governance is an ideal which is difficult to achieve in its totality. Very few countries and societies have come close to achieving good governance in its totality. However, to ensure sustainable human development, actions must be taken to work towards this ideal with the aim of making it a reality.

7.2. Women's Struggle for Equality

If we hurtle into modern times, we find that two years before the French Revolution of 1789, Condorcet, author of the Progress of the Human Mind, proposed that women be declared eligible for election to governing bodies. Again, the idea was not a terribly radical departure from a number of practices throughout Western Europe. Women of property had often voted in local councils; many women over many centuries had wielded power behind the throne; a good number had ruled whole nations, whether as regents or in their own right. France now stood— albeit very briefly—on the edge of democracy.

Condorcet was a nobleman, a marquis as well as a mathematician, philosopher and passionate advocate for universal education. But a self-educated butcher's daughter, Olympe de Gouges, led women of all classes in presenting a women's reform agenda to the National Assembly in October 1789. Shortly thereafter, she proclaimed that the new French Declaration on the Rights of Man negated the principle of natural equality because it excluded people from ciitizenship on the basis of gender and race. Even before her middle-class English contemporary, Mary Wollstonecraft, had published her Vindication of the Rights of Women in 1792, Gouges had written and issued a Declaration on the Rights of Women. She continued to organise her female compatriots in packing the galleries of successive French legislative bodies during the Revolution. In 1793, as the ostensibly democratic Committee on Public Security unleashed what came to be known as the "Reign of Terror", it beheaded Gouges and outlawed women's political associations.

With parallel developments earlier in the new United States of America and later in Great Britain, the rebirth of democracy in the modern West went hand in hand with the disenfranchisement of women. For more than a century after the French Revolution, western women went on losing the few political rights that their privileged sisters had held before. Only in 1893 did any western democracy—New Zealand—grant women the right to vote.

Although the world-wide movement for women's equality took new impetus from the birth of the United Nations and the promulgation of the 1948 Universal Declaration of Human Rights, it was not until the preparations for the First World Conference on Women, which took place in Mexico City in 1975, that the international community took systematic stock of the inequities that continued to render women second-class citizens in every country, including the industrialised democracies of the western world. In 1979, for the first time in history, women's rights took codified form in an international human rights instrument. The Convention on the Elimination of All Forms of Discrimination Against Women (CEDAW) has been in force only since 1981. Currently, 139 countries—more than two thirds of the Member States of the United Nations— are parties to the treaty. Another 44 have acceded to the treaty with reservations on certain provisions of the text. Women's participation in governance, however, still lags far behind that of men. Structures, these often do not have significant impact elsewhere in governance. Nor have these targets, even when achieved, endured. Moreover, statistical data and analysis on decision-making in the private sector and in local government is incomplete. Finally, as most of the current statistics come from developed countries, the strategies recommended for increasing women's political participation are often focused on models from these polities that do not meet the needs of developing nations.

Earlier research carried out by the UN Research Institute on Social Development (UNRISD) with funding from UNDP is summed up in Technical Co-operation and Women's Lives: Integrating Gender into Development Policy. It reviewed the experiences of development institutions in addressing development policies and programes in seven countries and highlighted the need to engender macroeconomic policies and to bring together different national actors that influence these policies. It also recognised that the men elected to the executive and legislative branches of government, who hold the key to decision-making for development priorities, planning and expenditure, are largely unaware of household needs and the ways in which these relate to socio-economic development at the community, local, provincial and national levels.

Considerable progress has taken place in women's political participation, particularly towards the end of this century. Despite this progress, however, the 21st century begins with enormous unfinished business in this realm.

7.2.1. Achievements

Twenty five years after the First World Conference on Women in Mexico City, more than 20 after CEDAW, and five after the Fourth World Conference in Beijing, gender equality has finally been inscribed on the political agenda of most of the world. For example, the Beijing Platform for Action set the goal of 30 percent for women in national decision-making positions, as a milestone toward the ultimate objective of 50 percent. Five years after Beijing, the level of women in parliaments in the world has increased from 10 percent to 12 percent. However, regional variations are significant. They range from 37.6 percent in the Nordic countries to 15.5 percent in the Americas, 13.4 percent in Asia, 12.5 percent in Europe excluding the Nordic countries, 11.6 percent in Sub-Saharan Africa, 8.3 percent in the

Pacific and 3.3 percent in the Arab states. Since Beijing, women speakers of parliament have been named for the first time in six countries: Ethiopia (1995), Latvia (1995), Peru (1995), Jamaica (1996), Malta (1996) and Poland (1997).

With regard to ministerial and sub-ministerial positions, two countries have reached over 30 percent representation for women (Sweden and the Bahamas). At the other end of the spectrum, there are 15 countries in which there is no presence of women in these posts (Afghanistan, Bahrain, Djibouti, Lebanon, Monaco, Myanmar, Nauru, Nepal, Saudi Arabia, the Solomon Islands, Somalia, United Arab Emirates and Yemen). Six women are currently presidents or prime ministers: Bangladesh (Prime Minister), Guyana (President), Ireland (President), New Zealand (Prime Minister) and Sri Lanka (President and Prime Minister),

At the local level, the International Association of Local Authorities (IULA) has set the goal of not more than 60 percent of either gender represented in local assemblies. It also points out that information on the current situation in local assemblies is incomplete. Estimates on woman as local counsellors are 23 percent in the United States, 20 percent for Europe (ranging from 40 percent in Sweden to 4 percent in Greece), 18 percent in Canada, less than 5 percent in Africa and 3.8 percent in Latin America. No estimate is available for Asia.

Differences by sector are significant in all countries. For example, Sweden has the highest percentage of women in parliament (44 percent), but less than 10 percent of women in senior academic positions, while in Egypt women constitute less than 2 percent of Parliament, but over 40 percent of senior academic staff.

Women want to influence the decisions that affect their lives and the lives of their families, the political economy and destiny of their communities and nations, as well as the structure of international relations. Political participation and representation is essential for the achievement of these ends. This will allow women and men of all ages and races the full exercise of their human rights. It is also the avenue for influencing equitable resource allocations for development that shape the lives of girls and boys, as well as women and men.

There is growing recognition that economic participation and political participation cannot be separated. Institutional transformations are needed to create the enabling environment for the economic and political empowerment of women. A more profound understanding of the barriers in labor markets and remuneration processes is also necessary as a precondition for their transformation. This is particularly important since women's economic independence is critical for their exercise of influence on decisions that affect their lives and their families.

There are strong linkages between processes that lead to poverty and those that result in gender disparities. Efforts at poverty reduction therefore need to be informed by a gender analysis. Transforming and increasing the accountability of institutions to women's interests, and especially the interests of poor women, is necessary for poverty reduction and good governance.

The feminisation of poverty manifests itself differently in different contexts. In many contexts, the poor in general and other disadvantaged groups share many of the conditions and needs represented by the women's movement for equity, inclusion, participation and representation. In many instances at present, they also suffer disproportionately from the impact of globalisation on their livelihoods. For example, with liberalisation of the economy in India, multinational corporations have entered into the production of goods earlier made by the poor, women in particular, and have pushed poor women out of their traditional livelihood niches.

Greater levels of transparency and accountability, including rapid responsiveness to citizen demands, are necessary to strengthen good governance. They also constitute the conditions necessary for advances in gender equity. Uganda, for instance, has experimented with transparency measures for making government disbursement information available to the public: with a push from its Women's Caucus, the Ugandan Parliament made it mandatory that funds allocated for communities must be made public. Indeed, as a recent World Bank study indicates, a decrease in corruption in government may be linked to an increase in women's political participation.

Politics and participation range from the home through the locality to the national level. Women need to participate at the micro level of the home, the meso level of community organisations and local government, and at the macro level of national party, parliamentary and governmental politics. Decentralisation, with its devolution of power and resources, appears to be opening more scenarios for the meaningful participation and representation of women.

7.3. Women in Governance

In Development as Freedom, the Nobel Laureate Amartya Sen recalls Mary Wollenstonecraft's 1792 classic Vindication of the Rights of Woman to illustrate the distinction between women as beneficiaries of the development process whose well-being it enhances—the "welfare" approach to enhancing women's status—and women as agents of development, as movers and shapers of change that benefits men and children as well—the "agency" approach. Sen looks back even further than the revolution Wollstonecraft was advocating as an exile in Paris while the French Revolution swirled about her, excluding women from the political changes sweeping Europe at that time. He recalls the medieval idea of agent and patient:

> "... the role of a person as an 'agent' is fundamentally distinct from (though not independent of) the role of the same person as a 'patient'. The fact that the agent may have to see herself as a patient as well does not alter the additional modalities and responsibilities that are inescapably associated with the agency of a person.... not only are we well or ill, but we also act or refuse to act, and can choose to act one way rather than another. And thus we—women and men—must take responsibility for doing things or not doing them. It makes a difference...."

In most countries, the "less-than-equal" status of women to men still prevails, prompting a welfarist approach to the advancement of women—even in efforts to "mainstream" gender issues by governments, civil society, bilateral and multilateral development agencies. This tendency belies and even denies the idea that women are responsible persons, not only capable of making choices, but necessary to this process in any democratic society. This concept is the perspective within which we must appraise every effort to meet the 21st century challenges to women's political participation.

As Sen, among others, points out, such factors as literacy, education, earning power, an economic role outside the family and access to property rights have contributed to women's assuming independent voice and agency, particularly in the family. The enormous literature on women's education and employment in their empowerment and emancipation is still growing. Numerous studies have also demonstrated the improvement of nutritional intake in the household as a result of women's independent income. Research in India has shown a correlation between women's education and economic independence and increased child survival rates and, as UNFPA analysis over the years has illustrated, increasing educational attainment among women correlates closely with lower fertility rates and their impact on population growth.

Women's participation in politics cannot be isolated from their overall socio-economic status, the following factors in particular: Women usually do not have equal access with men to the means for participation, such as the enabling skills acquired through education and training or controlling the means of production or access to the information media, including the new communications technologies. They often do not have decision-making power within the household to translate into the public sphere; in many developing countries, their possessions, including land and other collateral, are legally the property of their husbands, fathers or sons. For this very reason, they have not been able to overcome gender biases and other barriers that obstruct their access to political decision-making. Further, because of increasing trends in most countries, including the industrialised nations, to the feminisation of poverty, women's needs remain largely invisible. Despite 20th century progress, women have not been able to make their material needs, as well as the household needs that they recognise better than most men, known to policy-makers— nor, certainly, to influence those who make law to reduce and eventually eradicate gender biases. Against these odds, many women after Wollstonecraft will be remembered for extending the rights of well over half the human race. They rallied in the streets and brought other organised pressures to bear for universal adult franchise under their respective constitutions in most countries and used their hard-won political rights on behalf of other population sectors. Twentieth century women served as presidents, prime ministers,

The demand for women's equality has gone forward from changing the laws to insisting that they be implemented for women's equality with men. Individually and collectively, women have enlarged their advocacy efforts beyond their local, national, and regional boundaries to the international forums. At no time in history have women organised themselves into such forceful non-governmental pressure groups and networks as in the last decade of the 20th century.

7.3.1. Early Indications

Recent indicators of women's agency range from raising consciousness of women's issues to changing institutional structures and processes and influencing the governance discourse in itself. Although there are expectations on women politicians to advance the gender agenda while in office, they do not necessarily do so. They usually cannot. In most cases, their numbers have not yet reached the necessary critical mass. Even when critical mass has been attained, critical alliances must be sought and cemented. The Ugandan experience showed that women politicians had more impact working in teams rather than individually, and in parliamentary committees rather than in plenary.

7.4. Transforming the Political Agenda

In Bhopal, India, the last of four women rulers introduced compulsory education for girls throughout their kingdom. This contributed to Bhopal having universal education for girls to this date. Nationwide, the presence of a chairwoman on the Indian University Grants Commission was critical in a marked increase in women's accessing grants. In addition, India is also one of the few countries in which women parliamentarians have succeeded in persuading their fellow parliamentarians during the budgetary hearings to set a target of 30 percent for women in the earmarking of total development funds.

In Uganda, the Women's Caucus in Parliament succeeded in increasing the government's budget allocations for nutrition and for childhood development projects. Similarly, in the Philippines, committed women parliamentarians introduced the very principle of targeted budget allocations for women and achieved an initial rate of 5 percent. In 1998, their efforts also led to the adoption of a bill on rape.

7.4.1. Legislation Meaningful to Women's Lives

Again in Uganda, women introduced the issue of women's equity into the overall land reform bill. Kenyan women have repeatedly striven, inside and outside Parliament, to persuade the government to give women title to land and to establish bank accounts in their own name without the approval of their fathers or husbands.

The interpretation of law is equally important. Most observers credit the new force of sexual harassment law throughout the USA to the presence of two women Justices on the nine-member Supreme Court, who mobilised their colleagues into considering a case, even in a primary school. In that country, legislation on sexual harassment is an issue left to the each of the 50 states (as is capital punishment and most education and health matters).

7.4.2. Women's Impact on Corruption

A recent World Bank study indicates a close correlation between women's representation in parliaments and a decrease in the incidence of corruption. If the findings of this initial 1999 inquiry, "Are Women Really the 'Fairer' Sex", is borne out by further study, the implications are immense for women's entry into politics, as well as for government efficiency.

7.4.3. Women's Networking for Co-operation

From the 1992 Earth Summit on, women caucused formally or informally at all the major UN conferences of the 1990s. Many took this experience back to the national level in structures ranging from parliaments through municipal assemblies—Uganda being only one example, which has had its own ripple effect throughout Sub-Saharan Africa. Similarly women's regional and international networks disseminated knowledge of the South African Women's Budget. This initiative is being replicated as far from that country as Barbados.

7.4.4. Changing Institutional Structures and Processes

Again in South Africa, women parliamentarians— together with civil society representatives and committed individuals—changed that country's electoral college system (including its competency requirements) to broaden the access of women to electoral posts. Similar movements are underway in countries as different as Botswana and Uruguay.

7.4.5. Influencing the Discourse of Governance

The word "empowerment" in contemporary political parlance is very closely associated with the international women's movement. The impact of feminist language—including gender-neutral terminology—is also increasingly evident in the media and in legislation at all levels, including the international.

7.5. Key Challenges of Women's Political Participation

Despite all these remarkable advances, the 21st century opens with over one hundred million women missing in the world's population—as Sen himself pointed out in 1990. We do not know how many thousands were aborted before birth, especially in South and East Asia, as a result of medical progress in identifying the sex of the foetus. This single ominous development of recent years points to the ferocity of preference for males that has dominated human history.

We can hardly estimate the number of girls killed at birth or in childhood because of preferential nutrition and general care for their brothers over the millennia, let alone the 20th century denial of inoculation to girls against the major child-killers and other crippling or fatal diseases. The successive economic upheavals of the 20th century have accelerated the feminisation of poverty in many countries, both developed and developing, in particular the unprecedented pace of globalisation during the last decade. In addition, war and civil strife now victimise civilian populations—with their majority of women—as never before. Beyond the industrialisation of war introduced by mass bombing in the First and Second World Wars, "ethnic cleansing", with gender-based atrocities, has become a military strategy and tool practiced from Bosnia to Rwanda to the guerrilla battlefields of Latin America. Nonetheless, none of these phenomena is essentially new. Women's political participation is.

7.5.1. Mainstreaming Debate

Paradoxically, a major question of women's agency in governance has arisen around the issue of mainstreaming—whether to join traditional political and other institutions or to change them by remaining outside their structures and the manifold relationships of those structures. This matter of choice—the free exercise of agency— has become almost an ideological divide in a number of countries and cultures.

The late Bella Abzug was quoted as stating that "mainstreaming is not about joining the polluted stream, but rather finding fresh new streams." During the 20th century, women the world over have often viewed mainstream politics as polluted— mired in corruption, hopelessly divided by class and ethnic interests, and frequently criminalised. In addition, many women have found that engaging in the political process requires money, muscle, exposure to hostile media and the adoption of male norms of behavior, both aggressive and adversarial. In this connection, it is interesting to note that a 1999 World Bank study states that in a number of countries, a correlation exists between increasing women's representation in parliaments and decreasing incidence of corruption.

During India's long struggle for Independence, Mohandas Gandhi's call upon Indians to address themselves to society rather than the state may well have increased the number of his followers among women. Despite his plea for their direct governmental participation once independence had been won, most politically active women in India had rooted their leadership in civil society roles rather than vying for seats in Parliament and other state positions. Worldwide, women's historic exclusion from the hierarchical structures of the state may have directed them to exercising their agency in spheres of influence rather than in public political arenas.

Yet in India, too, it is women's political participation in local government structures that has led to perceiving women's political leadership as different from that of men. As the Indian feminist Devaki Jain recently remarked about the 1994 Panchayati raj (PRI) "revolution":

> "Some of the ways in which women, through PRI, are changing governance are evident in the issues they choose to tackle: water,

alcohol abuse, education, health, and domestic violence. Women also express different values. Women value proximity, whether it be to a drinking water source, a fuel source, a creche, a health centre, a court of justice or an office of administration. The enormous expansion of women in decentralised governance structures has highlighted the advantage of proximity, namely the redress of grievance and (most important of all, the ability to mobilise struggle at a local level where it is most meaningful ..."

7.5.2. Attaining Critical Mass

Whatever one's views on Jain's statement, the almost million women now in Indian local government assemblies were swept into public political life by an affirmative action measure. Again, the concept of critical mass—30 percent or more—emerges as central to women's agency in governance. The "mainstreaming" and "outsider" approaches do not really exclude each other. In practice, they are mutually supportive. One example is the transformation of work practices in the United States during the 1990s, women having established themselves well beyond critical mass in the mainstream (paid) labor force. Only then did the conflicting demands of home and work obligations push the private sector to begin introducing "family-friendly" policies—such as paternal leave, tele-commuting and flexitime— to keep highly trained and educated women in both the professions and other paid occupations that demand high levels of specialised skill. We will have to continue looking at numbers time and again in appraising gains in women's agency, particularly in governance.

7.5.3. Misperceptions

Because most efforts to increase women's participation in politics have concentrated on enabling gender equality throughout society as a whole, this issue still tends to be perceived as a women's question rather than as an essential human concern—moreover, a matter vital to the survival of democracy. Consequently, one must look at a great number of factors that contribute to building women's agency in politics, whether or not they initially appear to constitute governance issues. The approaches listed below are by no means exhaustive, but provide a framework for concomitant strategies to achieve gender balance early in the 21st century.

7.6. Suggested Strategies for Women's Agency

A time frame for achieving gender balance in political representation by 2010 must be formulated. Without time-bound goals, governments, political parties, lobbyists and women's groups cannot be held accountable.

7.6.1. Affirmative Action in Legislative Bodies

Justice delayed is justice denied. Ironically, this American legal adage has long been accepted for individuals indicted on criminal charges, but not for the female half of any country's population. Affirmative action in the political realm is a temporary measure required to attain long-belated justice to women economically and socially in the private as well as public realms. The general minimum target of 30 to 33 1/3 percent is no more than critical mass. This is far from equality. It is arguable even as equity.

In respect of affirmative action, it is worth noting the careful language of the 1979 Convention on the Elimination of All Forms of Discrimination against Women:

> "Adoption by States Parties of temporary measures aimed at accelerating de facto equality between men and women shall not be considered discrimination, but shall in no way entail as a consequence the maintenance of unequal or separate standards; these measures shall be discontinued when the objectives of equality of opportunity and treatment have been achieved"

7.6.2. Political Party and Electoral System Reform

The party system, so long a beneficiary of women's work from the ward level upwards, has long been an impediment to women's political leadership. In addition to affirmative action at the legislative level, political parties should honour commitments to equality and ensure that women constitute fifty percent of party membership, leadership, committee officers and candidates.

For the moment, in Jamaica, where the Secretary-General of the ruling party is a woman, women also serve as Speaker of the House, President of the Senate, Leader of Government Business and Majority

Whip. It is also true that women slightly outnumber men in Jamaica. But this is the case in many other countries as well—and in most, no woman occupies any party or political post of any significance.

Party and electoral system reform have proved an effective tool for increasing women's agency in countries with widely different cultures. In South Africa, after changes to the law concerning party lists, women constituted 27 percent of Parliament. In India, three parties headed by women— including the Congress Party that for so long dominated the country—have adopted a quota of one third for the nomination of women candidates. Across the globe in Chile, the Democracy Party, with a woman Vice-President, has adopted a rule whereby neither gender can have more than 60 percent representation. And in Yemen, an emerging democracy, a constitutional amendment provides for a list system by which parties must nominate women candidates. Although only two of the 301 Yemeni MPs are currently women, this represents a step forward. The number of women judges in that country has now reached 44. Out with regard to groups concerned with issues such as environment, agriculture, health and water worldwide—women's organisations can overcome a number of the bureaucratic and other hierarchical conditions that hamper policy-makers in traditional institutions.

7.6.3. Development of Training Strategies

It is important to developing training strategies for increasing women's political participation in the following areas:

— Advocacy in gender awareness in politics

— Capacity-building through networking

— Negotiation skills;

— Management;

— Constituency-building;

— Budget analysis;

— Gender mainstreaming skills;

— Use of mass media;

— Political and voter education;

— Mass mobilisation;
— Long-term strategies for engaging younger generations.

7.6.4. Establishment of Alliances

Experiences in India, South Africa and Uganda, as well as a number of industrialised countries, point to the importance of building alliances between the various actors in local government, national government, the private sector and civil society to improve women's political participation. The alliance-building process requires partners to operate together on different issues in different spheres of governance. The role of the state is to enhance policies, such as affirmative action, for reaching gender balance in governmental structures. Civil society's strength lies in providing measures that will improve the quality of women's political participation such as training, lobby and outreach. And both influence the private sector—in which women appear poised to enter corporate senior management. Perhaps more important, women worldwide are establishing more and more small and medium-size enterprises, especially in the retail and service trades, where start-up costs are lower than in manufacturing and other businesses and where e-commerce offers particular advantages.

In almost all countries there is also a need to create more positive relations between politicians and civil society and an exchange between women in different substantive spheres to shape complementary strategies. In addition, engagement with religious groups is required to address gender inequities debates with religious hierarchies, particularly where sacred texts are interpreted to inhibit women's potential participation.

All in all, alliance building serves as an effective mechanism for:

— Exchanging information on women's experience in identifying the conditions necessary to create sustainable linkages among different governance actors;
— Dialogue among all these actors to increase the impact of women's political participation; and
— Establishing accountability towards women in different constituencies.

7.6.5. Role Models

Special collaborative, alliance-building efforts are needed to change perceptions concerning women's leadership, particularly by validating women's leadership to the women-in-the-street (and on the small farmstead) as credible, effective, and better than men's on a variety of issues. The average woman needs to know that women leaders, like themselves, have to juggle responsibilities and priorities in the public and private worlds— that the leader is also a parent and homemaker like the woman who operates a market stall or factory sewing machine. The human person, female or male, plays different roles at different times. Women still tend to appreciate their contribution in their private and unpaid roles more than men do, in aspects relating to social maintenance.

The role of the mass news media is particularly crucial. Proactive and continuous dialogue between women leaders and women's lobbies with the news media is needed not only for highlighting women's leadership, but for the coverage of issues particularly important to redressing gender inequities. These range from areas as diverse as early marriage and health research allocations. To take another example, the increasing news attention to national and international drug trafficking should feature not only the negative impacts of these illegal trades on women and their agency (as distinct from welfare), but their diversion of funding from vital development concerns.

7.6.6. Targeting Young Women

Most development and political participation activities still target adult women. Yet in attempting to leapfrog a gender bias heritage of millennia, one cannot forget the primacy of early conditioning and training. "The child is father to the man," remarked the English poet William Wordsworth. "Give me the child until the age of six," said the Jesuit educator Ignatius Loyola, "and I shall show you the man." Both injunctions apply equally to girls. Unless their political education, and agency, starts before women are encumbered by their other roles—care-giving in the home and economic activity, paid or unpaid, inside or outside the home—the transformation of political systems will take perhaps another century, if not another millennium.

7.7. Beijing + 5: Women in Power and Decision-Making

On the eve of the 21st century, more than a hundred years after women finally attained the franchise in New Zealand, the first of all countries to recognise this inalienable right, the question of women's political participation has become permanently inscribed on the international agenda and permeates many regional and national plans of action. In 1995, when the Fourth World Conference on Women adopted the Beijing Platform for Action, 10 percent of the members of national legislative bodies worldwide were women. Today, the percentage has gone up to 12 percent. An increase of 2 percent over a period of five years may appear infinitesimal. But when climbing a steep precipice, arriving at higher plateau is no small achievement.

Whether political, social, economic or cultural, the rights women have achieved over the last 100 years and more have hardly been given, but hard-fought and hard-won. Even when men presided over the ultimate authority and decision-making structures, it was women who expressed, formulated, lobbied, and sometimes simply protested their rights into place.

Alluding to Virginia Wolf in A Room of One's Own, Alida Brill states that the mirror women have so long held up to men—a mirror that exaggerates and flatters male attributes—has increasingly projected a more realistic image since women's entry into public life. However, she cautions, many men resent these newer projections and therefore fight against them. Some argue that in many cases, women politicians have become "just like other men" in their attitudes— usually meaning aggressive, manipulative, unfair or any of a number of pejorative adjectives. Others contend that many women in public life have studiously avoided taking up issues particularly (but by no means only) relevant to women's welfare or interests. Brill therefore asks again: "Is there a woman's voice in politics which is unique? Does it really make a difference that women have achieved political office? Would it be just as good if there were more men in politics worldwide who were sympathetic to the women's agenda?"

She answers by insisting "... without our own voices being heard inside the government arena and halls of public policy and debate, we are without the right of accountability a basic entitlement of those who are governed". She subsequently argues, like many others, that women's presence in the political arena has changed the nature of the political agenda itself. Questions concerning reproductive health and choice, nutrition, equality in education and in employment opportunities and circumstances, child care and related 'family-friendly' aspects, and environment are only a few the areas that women have either brought into public debate or highlighted with significant substantive victories at both national and international levels.

Nelson and Chowdhury, among others, take this point further by specifying two dimensions that are crucial to considerations of any international endeavour:

— In addition to the issues mentioned above— many of them erroneously perceived as women-specific—women actually consider all broader social and political concerns within their political interests and mandate; and

— Many commonalties exist between concerns considered crucial by women, regardless of their geo-political and socio-economic situations. Nelson and Chowdhury cite violence against women and economic participation in particular.

This latter dimension is significant because it indicates that all societies share difficulties in achieving comprehensive gender-fair changes. It also underlines the power of women as a "mobilising force".

Two other important features of women's entry into politics are highlighted Nelson and Chowdhury, as well as the United Nations Development Programe (UNDP) Human Development Report 1995: Gender and Development:

7.7.1. Beijing Platform for Action

> ...[W]omen's equal participation in political life plays a pivotal role in the general process of the advancement of women. Women's equal participation in decision-making is not only a demand for simple justice or democracy but can also be seen as a necessary condition for women's interests to be taken into account. Without the active participation of women and the incorporation of women's perspectives at all levels of decision-making, the goals of equality, development and peace cannot be achieved."

Thus begins the Platform's section on Women in Power and Decision-Making.

In no society do women enjoy the same opportunities as men; and some of the recommendations of the Platform can be summarised as follows:

— Setting a firm timetable to end all manner of legal discrimination against women (along the lines of CEDAW), as well as establishing a framework to promote legal equality;

— Initiating specific measures targeted to acquiring a short-term threshold of 30 percent for women in national decision-making positions, with a long-term aim of 50 percent;

— Mobilising national and international efforts to facilitate for everyone—and for women in particular—greater access to economic and political opportunities.

The Beijing Platform for Action advocates institutional mechanisms in the form of national machinery to focus on mainstreaming (integrating at all levels) gender concerns within national policy, creating the conditions for gender equality at all levels, and allocating specific national and international resources towards these ends. The Platform embodies two strategic objectives:

— Ensuring women's equal access to and full participation in power structures and decision-making; and

— Increasing women's capacity to participate in decision-making and leadership.

The recommendations are thus specifically directed to governments, political parties, the United Nations (UN), and civil society.

The United Nations is one of the organisations in which much hope is invested and which has consistently been the motor for ensuring the gender issue is on the global agenda in a number of ways. However, the Organisation has had to struggle with problems of credibility and efficiency, particularly in implementing its recommendations.

This underlines the importance of working in partnership with a wide array, not only of institutions, but also of objectives and visions—the more so in this era of economic globalisation, in which so much power has moved from governments into the marketplace.

It is important to note that equality and enhancement are not necessarily one and the same goal. In many countries, the vast majority of men lack significant social, economic, and political powers. Thus far, priority does go to gender-equality policies: this enterprise is difficult enough. However, we should not concentrate on equality in numbers at the expense of more strategic objectives, such as *enhancing* the performance of those women already in decision-making positions. This is not to say that women's performance should be monitored more closely than men's or those expectations of women should be higher. Nor does it negate the target of 30 percent. But it must be remembered that the political sphere has usually slighted roles traditionally assigned to women, notably family and household management and has therefore ignored the need of most women in politics to balance time between their new responsibilities and those dictated by the vast majority of cultures. Geared to a context of male lifestyles, political arenas provide their lessons within it—at the simplest level, excluding women from bars and any number of clubs and other spaces that serve as caucuses. Even where such barriers have dropped, women are relatively late entrants to politics and could benefit immensely from systematised methods of exchanging experiences with veterans, both male and female. This is probably as critical to political impact as the 30 percent threshold. In addition, the time has now come to also look at *how* women are making an impact, what their needs are—from local councils to the office of national president or prime minister— and what mechanisms already in use, have been shown to be powerful, effective and different.

7.8. Women's Participation in Politics since 1995

The number of women heads of state or government (excluding queens) now totals six, four of whom came to power after 1995—in Bangladesh (Prime Minister since June 1996), Guyana (President since 1997), Ireland (President since 1997) and Sri Lanka, where a mother and daughter are, respectively, President and Prime Minister. According to the Inter-Parliamentary Union (IPU) statistics, from 1945 to 1995 the percentage of women MPs worldwide has increased fourfold. Their latest statistics indicate that, in 1998, the world average of women in parliaments (both houses combined) is 12.7 percent, with the highest in the Nordic countries (37.6 percent), followed by the Americas (15.5 percent), Asia (13.4 percent), Europe OSCE member countries (excluding the Nordic countries) (12.5 percent), sub-Saharan Africa (11.6 percent) the Pacific (8.3 percent) and, last, the Arab states (3.3 percent). In addition, since 1995, six countries elected a woman speaker of parliament for the first time: Ethiopia (1995), Latvia (1995), Peru (1995), Jamaica (1996), Malta (1996) and Poland (1997).

According to the United Nations Division for the Advancement of Women (UN/DAW) *Fact Sheet on Women in Government* of 1996, the percentage of women in both ministerial and sub-ministerial levels ranges from sero (in about 15 countries), to 30 percent in two countries as distant and dissimilar as the Bahamas and Sweden. However, of the 15 countries with no women in government positions in 1996, eight were Arab states.

Statistical data on women in important judicial positions is difficult to obtain even at the level of the highest court. Worldwide statistics are therefore largely meaningless; the fact that Nigeria has not published its data for a number of years simply masks the fact that a number of women serve on that country's highest tribunals. To take the United States Supreme Court as an example, two of the current nine Justices are women—but this has not changed since 1995. And of the 1,181 federal judges in the USA, only 154 are women.

All these facts taken together are particularly ironic, since in both ancient Egypt and the West, justice has been symbolised by women—in the West, usually blindfolded to signify absolute impartiality. Yet since most law worldwide usually works in favor of men, however gender-blind or gender-neutral it may appear, the need for a gender perspective in the judiciary is critical, if only because laws and their interpretation and implementation often affect women and men differently.

In its study on women in local governments in different regions of the world, the International Union of Local Authorities (IULA) sets a representation rate of no more than 60 percent for either.

Latin America: Data compiled between 1992 and 1995 (after which, data is scant) showed an average rate for women of 7.5 percent for mayors and 3.8 percent for municipal councillors.

North America: USA figures from 1990 indicate an average figure of 17 percent for women mayors and 23 percent for women in local councils. Other statistics reveal that in January 1997, 12 of the nation's 100 largest cities had women mayors or city managers, and in March 1997, that 202 of the 975 US cities with more than 30,000 residents had women mayors.

In Canada, 18 percent of council members are women. In Quebec, a quota to equalise the number of seats for women and men resulted in an increase in the percentage of women mayors and councillors between 1985 and 1996, but a decline thereafter. IULA also observes that in Quebec and Montreal in particular, connections to the local women's movement played a key role in inspiring women to run for election.

The Caribbean: Trinidad and Tobago follows the pattern of higher female representation at the local level in comparison with the national: 21 percent in local councils and 14 percent at the mayoral positions.

Since 1995, both the number and level of women in decision-making has increased in the United Nations itself. For the first time a female Deputy Secretary-General was appointed, and for the first time, both the United Nations High Commissioner for Refugees and the World Health Organisation have been headed by women. These recent additions bring the total of women executive heads to five organisations— the others being UNICEF, the UN Population Fund and the World Food Programe. However, in non-governmental organisations (NGOs), we lack figures on women who are executive heads, even in those that deal; primarily with political participation. Such information is now vital because NGOs have been playing increasingly influential roles at the heart of civil societies across the world, in many instances stepping into the political, social and economic vacuums left by failed and failing states.

Given the available data, uneven as it may be, the following trends emerge:

7.8.1. Governments

— Despite the fact that many governments have adopted affirmative action measures and the rhetoric of gender balance, the threshold of 30 percent advocated by the Human Development Report 1995, as a prelude to the 50 percent that would reflect women's true global population position, remains remote in most of the world.

— In some countries, such as those of the Arab region, freedom of association remains a politically sensitive issue because of the predominance of authoritarian regimes alone— quite apart from the human rights principle of the equal rights of men and women to engage in political activities. Indeed, women's organisations encounter particular difficulties in the rising tensions between some governments and political Islamic groups (Islamists).

— Although differences in electoral systems appear to have marked impact on women's representation, the information collected thus far remains so heavily European and/or western, that it is difficult to advocate any specific electoral system as promoting women's participation in politics.

— Indeed, unless better-balanced information emerges on women in general and gendered statistics in particular, it is difficult to establish effective mechanisms to monitor women's access to senior levels of decision-making.

7.8.2. Political Parties

— The number of women in parliaments and in local governments around the world indicates that political parties have some way to go putting gender-conscious policies on their agendas and implementing these within their ranks.

7.8.3. The United Nations

— The rise of women to prominent leadership positions within the UN system points to progress in this realm, as is the increase in UN collection, assessment and dissemination of information on women in decision-making.

7.8.4. Civil Society

— Again, despite a growing wealth of anecdotal material, there remain grave shortcomings in systematic information collection. The rise in women's representation in community-based organisations in many countries worldwide, particularly during the last five years seems to indicate that women are increasingly seising opportunities for political participation where they can balance these activities with their traditional household responsibilities. Whether this will lead to greater activism at the national level and/or significantly change national political agendas remains to be seen.

7.8.5. Beijing Platform for Action in Practice

The Fourth World Conference on Women spurred a debate on matters of direct concern to women well before, during and after the actual meeting in Beijing. Although the Platform for Action is not legally binding, its signature by a vast variety of governments has generated significant moral force and the substantive and technical framework outline for a wide spectrum of initiatives in countries as diverse as Colombia, Japan, and Turkey. These have ranged from setting up special committees to pressure and monitor governments in implementing the Platform as a whole to multiparty collaborations to lobby governments on specific issues. In Poland, such efforts led to the liberalisation of existing anti-abortion law, in Turkey to amending the civil code and in Peru to setting up a commission to modify laws pertaining to women in Congress.

Mobilisation and motivation for discussions and initiatives aside, women's participation—at the very least in terms of numbers—remains hampered as long as wide gaps in the rates of political participation between the two genders, particularly when the definition of a "political space" is broadened to include domains such as the business sector, and the academia. Even in Sweden, despite the fact that women constitute 44 percent of MPs, they represent less than 10 percent of senior academic staff and the decision-making echelons of the business community. By contrast, in Egypt, although women MPs hold less than 2 percent of parliamentary seats, they occupy over 40 percent of high academic chairs— but less than 10 percent of executive positions in business. Although many African countries have witnessed little or no change, largely because of resource and management constraints, others, such as Uganda, South Africa and Kenya, are witnessing significant progress for women in position of power. However, Beijing appears to have had little impact for women politically in either Latin America or the Arab world, despite the vast differences between these two regions.

In this regard, it may be worth remarking that in sharing experience regions tend to compare themselves to the West and not to other developing countries. Latin America and the Middle East have many traits in common and might therefore profit immensely by sharing their respective experiences.

7.8.5.1. Affirmative Action Measures

Affirmative action measures, such as quotas and particular types of electoral systems (e.g. the proportional representation system) continue being used to rectify imbalances in political representation. However, the initial debacle on introducing quotas for women in the Indian Parliament—the bill was physically shredded before being tabled—indicates the aura of controversy that persists on the subject. Quotas are allegedly undemocratic because the women who benefit from them are (again, allegedly) not elected and are therefore unrepresentative. Others who oppose quotas argue that they demean women by viewing them as undeserving and incapable of fulfilling the demands of the position; quota-women are by definition token figures, unlikely to use their new positions to effect real change.

Quotas usually become more popular when presented as "a helping hand" for women against the multiplicity of obstacles they traditionally face in trying to enter the political arena. Other quota proponents hold that no group, female or male, can truly represent another and that failure to assist the less privileged in obtaining an opportunity to perform is in itself unjust. In addition, quota advocates argue that such measures in any domain are temporary means of correcting imbalance; the fact that in the political arena they are now used predominantly for women merely indicates that such an imbalance exists.

Research on the effects of electoral systems on women's representation is so far sketchy and predominantly Western. Studies carried out in Australia, Canada, Germany, New Zealand, Norway, the

United Kingdom, and the United States show a positive correlation between proportional representation (PR) systems and the number of women in the national legislature. Very few, if any, detailed and long-term studies on how electoral systems affect women's representation in the South are available.

In sum, we can conclude the following:

— The Beijing Platform for Action is an important tool for those working on enhancing women's political participation. Many of its recommendations serve as reference points for plans of action worldwide at levels ranging from the international to the local.

— With the exception of very few countries, women now occupy important political positions around the world, though the extent varies sharply from nation to another.

— The number of women in government remains, however, far below the 30 percent target specified by UNDP, despite significant progress.

— Information and data, particularly gender desegregated data, while impressive on women in parliaments and government (ministerial and sub-ministerial) remains low and seriously uneven, particularly on aspects such as local government and judiciaries, as well as NGOs and the private sector.

— Affirmative action strategies still need to be implemented in some areas, especially in the developing countries of the world.

7.9. Recent Initiatives for Women's Participation in Governance

In 1997, the Inter-Parliamentary Union (IPU) convened a conference entitled "Towards Partnership Between men and Women in Politics" in New Delhi (14–18 February), attended by parliamentary delegations from 80 countries, representatives of international parliamentary organisations, intergovernmental organisations and international NGOs. In July of that year, UNDP held an international conference in New York on "Governance for Sustainable Growth and Equity" that brought together more than 1000 ministers and other senior national officials from 147 countries, along with mayors and urban administrators, members of parliament, and representatives of civil society organisations. Women's political participation was a key feature of the agenda.

The IPU conference issued the New Delhi Declaration of recommendations to improve women's political participation, ranging in subject matter from attitudes through training in a variety of areas to increase both the presence and participation of women in decision-making bodies locally, nationally, regionally and internationally. Reiterating the principles of women's rights as human rights, along with the critical mass target of 30 percent, the Declaration also called upon political parties to facilitate the equal participation of both men and women, as well as to become more generally open to women's demands. Reserved seats were for political parties, as well as local and national representative institutions. The Conference also regarded proportional representation as the most promising approach for bringing women into decision-making forums.

Further, the Declaration emphasised the importance of women's education and political training, including the importance of facilitating campaign financing for women politicians; it therefore called for a compilation of a directory of worldwide institutions engaged in training with on these issues. It also underlined gender inequities in the labor market and the media and, in the latter regard, recommended an enhanced image of women politicians in the media to spur changes in traditional attitudes. The Declaration also stressed the need for setting up specialised national bodies and advisory boards, some within parliamentary structures as monitoring and advisory bodies. Last but not least, the Declaration stressed the need for international bodies to ensure gender-equal participation.

Structured in four simultaneous forums---respectively for senior national officials, mayors, parliamentarians and civil society organisations—the UNDP Conference on Governance for Sustainable Growth and Equity centred its gender recommendations on equalising (increasing up to 50 percent) women's representation at all levels of decision-making institutions and increasing the allocation of international resources for capacity-building to that effect. Another major recommendation stressed the need to remove obstacles to women's public participation and emphasised the responsibility of political parties in this regard, as well as that of civil society organisations, in ensuring the simultaneity of macro- and micro-level empowerment measures. The Conference also highlighted the need for mechanisms to translate recommendations to policies, as well as broadening the scope and themes of national social dialogues so as to include the concerns of media and academic circles.

Whereas the recommendations of the UNDP Conference tend to deal with the broader issues, those of the IPU examine of women's political engagement from the micro to the macro in detail, covering political parties, education, affirmative action, changing attitudes, training, parliaments, national commissions of women, international bodies, and directories of information—in short, the major challenges to women's political participation in the 21st century. The ensemble, however, reveals certain shortcomings, notably the following:

— They do not sufficiently emphasise certain information gaps and how these can be rectified;

— They do not argue strongly for comparative information-gathering to fill in not only gaps in data, but in qualitative areas, such as enhancing women's political contributions;

— They still tend to skirt the debates concerning quotas and other affirmative action measures, and thereby neglect opportunities to gain insights into alternative forms of promoting women's participation in political life;

They maintain an overemphasis on numbers.

7.10. Challenges of Women's De Jure Equality

Although the very disparity between de jure and de facto situations is significant in all human rights issues, the letter of the law remains one of the most important empowering instruments for the achieving rights. Few of the challenges to women's de jure equality in the 21st century are really new. Many, however, have taken on a different face— among these, in our own time, the challenge of electronic communication technology, which has become a critical tool of freedom of expression as well as economic empowerment.

Challenges differ from one country and region to another, often within individual countries. Political corruption and ensuing fears are major challenges in many parts of the world. It is probably most useful to look at challenges by sphere, notably socio-cultural, economic and political.

7.10.1. Socio-cultural

Despite the massive social science literature that has accumulated around the term "culture", notably within the last decade, our purposes here require little more than assuming that culture is a set of attitudes, rarely static and often unconscious, many of them historically conditioned. These can be local, ethnic or national and even global, particularly with regard to gender and class concerns. They shape people's sense of identity and the ways in which they behave, either as individuals or in groups. Far from being consistent, they may clash, even within an individual. To take only one simplistic example, a woman may act in one context or at one particular point in time to champion the rights of women in general and subsequently as an advocate of certain class interests that militate against equality between the genders within the labor market.

Women in particular play multiple roles. In most countries, they are perceived as having "primary" responsibilities as wives and mothers for which they receive no overt remuneration. They may also enter the labor market, formal or informal, beyond the immediate household economy. A political career usually emerges as a second or third job.

These perceptions are closely connected to a traditional understanding of space as private and public, women generally being relegated to the former, even to the exclusion of the latter. These notions are remarkably persistent and lie at the very heart of most of the difficulties women face not only entering politics, but achieving credibility and impact within this sphere. As Netumbo Nandi-Ndaiah, Namibia's Minister of Women's Affairs, remarked at the UNDP Conference on Governance for Sustainable Growth and Equity, "It is women who are managing day-to-day life in the family— making sure there is enough food for breakfast, for lunch, for dinner. Now if a woman is able to do this in her own family, why is she not able to ensure that the national cake is shared equally for the benefit of everybody? Because these are the skills that we would like to see in a good Minister of Finance."

The characterisation of politics as "dirty" arises partly from the pervasive public/private dichotomy, which tends to posit the home or "private" space as a haven from stresses outside, the wife/mother figure guaranteeing harmony within an atmosphere of ultimate trust and inclusion. One example of this myth is the idealisation of the mothers of Mafia members.

Even where they may possess considerable independent income, women in politics rely on a support network—and usually, the provision of a number of social services—based on family-friendly considerations that most countries lack, regardless of per capita GDP. Basic education constitutes another problem. According to the UNDP Human Development Report 1995, women outnumber men two to one among the developing world's 900,000 million illiterates and girls constitute the majority of the 130 million children without access to primary school. Further, because population growth has outstripped the expansion of women's education in many developing countries, the number of female illiterates has actually increased.

7.10.2. Economic

Economic and political development do not go hand in hand for women. The situation of a number of the oil-producing states is only the most glaring case in point. Even in Sweden, many women in politics suffer from entrenched, often subtle discriminatory attitudes. Nonetheless, poverty remains a major impediment largely because the daily struggle for survival precludes time for women's engaging in political activity. Worse still, poverty-stricken women do not yet seem to have benefited from women's entry into politics.

A number of women who might otherwise embark on political lives are discouraged by the lack of funds not only for financing electoral campaigns, but access to resources adequate to undertaking significant initiatives. These may entail extensive (and expensive) research, as well as outreach and public information efforts. A paradox of many of the strong recommendations made by international gatherings that both political parties and governments attempt to provide and/or set up funds for women in political life, is that women may end up confined to token funds, and possibly cut off from access to other resources.

7.10.3. Political

Research demonstrates that the type of electoral system plays an important role in determining whether or not women get properly involved on party lists or get elected—notably Proportional Representation. However, since most of the information available on this issue is specific to the Western world—and because each electoral system is affected by other cultural and economic considerations—no one particular system can be universally advocated.

In addition, because most powerful political parties reflecting the more general conditions in the rest of society, they do not easily accept or promote many women in their internal structures. Hence the current concerns being voiced about the viability and popularity of parties as vehicles for women's political advancement in the face of emerging alternative political entities, such as NGOs.

Moreover, lack of sufficient training and communication skills or media know-how remains a tremendous problem for women in developed and developing countries alike, particularly in this age of the media. The gravity of this issue is compounded by the fact that the media tend to feed on novelty. "Just being a woman politician is not enough to raise interest ... we need a story that is interesting and would attract attention" is not an uncommon view among media personnel in a number of countries, developing as well as developed.

Internet communications may well emerge as the determining variable in the years to come. Hence the importance of situating both women themselves and men with strong commitments to women's political advancement in institutions on the cusp of the newest communications systems. "Knowledge is power" is probably an even stronger injunction today than it was when the phrase came into wide circulation in 19th century Europe. Women who have limited access to common contemporary office facilities are at a distinct disadvantage in today's political world in terms of their capacity, efficiency and even local potential need, even in areas that appear to have little relevance to politics;

— Adjusting the discourse so as to emphasise the sharing of responsibilities rather than power takeovers;

— Comparing, comparing and comparing yet again experiences strategies and mechanisms from around the world.

Other lessons that remain to be formulated and implemented as practices are the following:

— Assessing impact in terms of means and ends and developing criteria for this purpose;

— introducing or developing shared training for women and men politicians, encouraging the sharing of experience not only between the sexes, but among both novices and seasoned veterans with respect to both failures and successes;

7.11. Practices to Building Women's Constituencies

7.11.1. Good Governance Practices

While no blueprints are universally valid, some practices appear to have had success in most parts of the world. Those that have been tried and tested at various levels can be summarised as follows:

— Gender-balanced representation within political parties and all other public institutions;

— Setting up of specialised national machinery for monitoring, implementing and, when necessary, creating gender equality policies;

— Setting up a woman's budget targeted to provide funds to secure gender equality measures and assist women in their political careers (e.g. campaign financing);

— Mainstreaming gender concerns at all levels of society, starting with poverty-alleviation;

— Adoption and implementation of affirmative action measures wherever there is a perceived

Is debatable because it is frequently subjective, women at all socio-cultural and economic levels have experiences that differ from those of men and that are reflected in different approaches, needs, insights and, often, goals. In her report, Public Life: Women Make a Difference, Virginia Willis argues that "the new political movement, the Greens, where women have from the beginning played a leading role, has tried new forms of politics and collaborative, non-hierarchical systems which also better reflect women's ways of working." Similarly, in

Sweden, Boman reports on a local council of a suburb which shows how an increase in women's representation to 40-48 percent led to changes in the political climate with male officials acknowledging and prioritising family obligations to broaden the context of decision-making, as well as debates that were more concise and focused, conducted in more accessible, concrete language.

There are many points of view on what constitutes an "impact". Policy-specific examples include the following:

— In the USA: a surge in day-care facilities and battered women's refuges. In addition, a number of private sector companies have developed diversity programes that include building women's leadership skills, mentoring, and family-friendly policies to facilitate the juggling of many roles that women occupy;
— In Australia: help pages in any telephone book include sections on domestic violence referral services, abortion counseling and rape crisis centres;
— In Norway: changes in the "politics of mother-hood" where care and career policies concerned with childcare institutions, working hours, as well as maternity leave, have generated an interest among political parties to adopt these as issues with which votes can be gained.

Once again however, with the exception of the South African case, there is a serious paucity of information on more methods of impacting, as well as similar examples from elsewhere in the world.

The question that should be kept in mind constantly is: To what extent has this kind of change taken place—if at all? Given current media biases, difficulties and obstacles may gain attention at the expense of consistent attempts to realise changes, often so subtle as to escape immediate notice. Among these biases are:

— Change in perception of women and men politicians, as well as in the expected division of labor between men and women in any society. How politicians are perceived often makes or breaks political careers.
— Change in discourse, such as shifts in emphasis in women's participation in areas traditionally seen as "men's affairs" or "hard politics" (defense, finance, foreign policy), in addition to

redefining and prioritising "soft" issues such as welfare, maternity leave and education.

— Change in coverage, notably in the writing of textbooks and history (the seed of many of the female stereotypes that discourage women from entering public life), as well as media content.

— Change in day-to-day workings of political institutions, including family-friendly timing and location of meetings, as well as the de facto exclusion of women from traditional male caucus spaces, such as bars and all-male clubs.

Perhaps the most important lesson of Beijing, however, is the need to stop mythologising women's political capacities. The idea that a world governed equally by women and men will not necessarily be one of greater justice or less violence. The association of women with the "safe" "peaceful" or "equitable" haven of the home is fundamentally a cultural assumption. However persistent and pervasive worldwide, it is—like all cultural assumptions—subject to change. Further, no previous era has been marked by change as rapid as ours in virtually every domain. This pace is unlikely to slow. Finally, the myth of women as guardians of the home has been exploded by research on household inequities and domestic violence worldwide, as well as used to deter women from entering public space.

What we do know at the moment is that men and women have much to learn from one another in politics. However rapid that learning process may become and however much we need to take action for its acceleration, the lessons require a great deal of internalisation in addition to conscious mastery. The process is therefore likely to take longer than the acquisition of factual knowledge. Consequently, in assessing progress since Beijing, it is probably a good thing to bear in mind a Chinese proverb:

7.12. Gender, Governance and Poverty

What is the "feminisation of poverty" that has taken so significant a place in so much debate about the status of women? Will "good governance" in itself serve to reduce it? Similarly, will poverty reduction necessarily serve the advancement of gender equality? Why ask these questions at all? Promoting choice and participation for women as well as for men has become increasingly pronounced in the general governance agenda—with, however, a tendency to assume that promoting participation for women and men revolves around the same mechanisms and that it will automatically promote women's interests. This assumption precludes recognising the gendered nature of institutions themselves.

Conventional approaches to poverty definition and measurement based on income- consumption measures have been widely criticised for failing to capture human development outcomes. The use of the household as the unit of analysis in poverty measurement has also been the subject of much criticism from gender analysts. It is perfectly possible for women to be deprived in rich households and also for increases in household income to result in greater gender inequality in well-being. According to Kabeer, gender inequality and poverty result from distinct, interlocking, social relations and processes. This implies that the social relations of gender may act to exacerbate or relieve poverty for women in one context or another.

Given the unreliability of household income-based measures as a guide to the well-being of both women and men, poverty should be studied in terms of ends as well as means. A broader understanding, rooted in Sen's entitlements and capabilities framework, has led to the development of a specific indicator—the Human Poverty Index or HPI—to monitor and compare experiences of human poverty over time (UNDP, 1997a; 1998). The HPI, alongside the HDI (Human Development Index) and GDI (Gender Development Index), provides the basis for comparing gendered experiences of well-being and deprivation, including those within the household.

However, although the HPI allows us to capture the magnitude of differences in actual well-being between men and women, it implicitly assumes those men and women experience deprivation in the same ways and face the same trade-offs. Yet lack of access to water, to take only one example, has different implications for both genders. Further, for women in a violent home, the trade-off between income and personal well-being is one that men do not face. A truly gendered understanding of well-being requires looking at additional factors,

own interests with those of other household members, and thereby leaving themselves vulnerable in the event of family breakdown.

All these issues, along with others, point to the limitations of traditional micro-credit programes in addressing women's poverty. Consequently, in the UNDP South Asian Poverty Alleviation Programe (SAPAP)—in which village development organisations form the basis for the savings and the allocation of loans by the organisations themselves—there is also investment in women's leadership and management skills (UNDP).

7.12.2. Governance and Poverty Reduction

The governance debate in development policy took off in the early 1990s, with different influences and interpretations of the issues. Narrow definitions of governance centre on economic and administrative governance (i.e. providing an enabling environment for private sector activity and reform of public administration); broader definitions encompass political governance, including the promotion of democratic political structures and human rights. In UNDP's definition, governance is 'the exercise of economic, political and administrative authority to manage a country's affairs at all levels. It comprises the mechanisms processes and institutions through which ciitizens and groups articulate their interests, exercise their legal rights, meet their obligations and mediate their differences.'.

The increasing convergence of the governance and poverty reduction agendas stems in part from rethinking the nature of well-being and also from a broadening interpretation of governance to encompass political accountability and popular participation. Thus, to the extent that improved governance structures and processes lead to greater participation of the poor, this is assumed to improve their well-being.

Bilateral agency members of the OECD-DAC (Organisation for Economic Cooperation and Development Assistance Committee) have made more explicit linkages between political and economic objectives and made more direct claims for the developmental potential of political reform. In recent UNDP literature, governance is increasingly stated as one of, if not the, key means to effective poverty reduction. Further, sustainable human development is posed as the goal of governance. Rights-based approaches to poverty reduction have been adopted by some development agencies, like that of the United Kingdom.

Similarly, according to UNDP, "Poverty needs to be redefined so as to include access to decision-making by both women and men and information on human rights". Current UNDP approaches to poverty reduction also stress the importance of empowerment as a means to address poverty, including that of women.

In linking the promotion of governance to poverty reduction, policy makers have tended to overemphasise participation as an aspect of accountability, rather than of effectiveness and impact. It is often unclear how the participation of the poor is expected to lead to the articulation of their interests in ways which can influence institutional rules and practices (effectiveness), and consequently to different decisions about resource use that lead to poverty reduction in a material sense (impact).

Typically, gender perspectives in the mainstream governance literature are limited to an examination of the need for more women in formal political life and strategies to achieve this, without consideration of the need for transformation of the institutions of power.

This weakness becomes particularly important when focusing on the links between improved governance and the gendered causes and consequences of women's poverty. Here, numbers alone may be necessary, but are certainly not a sufficient condition, either for the articulation of (poor) women's gender interests or for their achieving an impact on resource allocation decisions and processes.

Although governance is about "getting institutions right for development" governance policies rarely concentrate on "getting institutions right for women in development". Outside the family, where the gendering of roles and behaviors is explicit but often assumed to be "natural", there is a tendency to assume that institutions are neutral with respect to gender. Governance debates are no exception to this. However, "Familial norms and values are constantly drawn on in constructing the terms under which women and men enter and participate in public life and the market place". The public-private split that institutionalised women's exclusion from the public sphere and is also drawn on to reinforce gendered power relations in the public sphere. For example, women are confined to "typically" female tasks closely associated with their domestic roles, or more insidiously, subjected to sexual harassment or violence which both symbolically and literally threaten and contains women's identity as public actors.

Men's physical and historical dominance of the public sphere has meant that their needs and interests have become embedded in public institutions. Men's physical monopoly of public space means that everyday work patterns come to be structured around men's needs and capabilities, resulting in a gendered structuring of time and space in organisations. Ideologies and disciplines are also important in creating cognitive and cultural contexts that favor male interests. This is not immutable. However, confining reform efforts to measures to increase female representation in public life will have limited impact unless the broader constraints on women's meaningful participation are also addressed. It is important to recognise the interlocking forms of institutional exclusion faced by women, particularly poor women. This implies a need to rethink and extend the scope of the current governance debate, and of related interventions, in order to increase "gender accountability".

7.13. Enhancing Women's Participation

The practical limitations on women's participation in public and political debate are widely discussed in the development literature and elsewhere. The practical measures that may be necessary to include women in discussions and activities are well known (childcare provision, separate meetings where appropriate, consideration of women's workload and use of appropriate times and venues, language considerations) though less often actually implemented and adequately resourced. For poor women, these barriers are likely to be even greater.

Less discussed are the limitations on women's "voice". These relate to actual or perceived male resistance and silencing, internalised oppression and the difficulty of articulating women's interests within the existing framework of public debate. For poor women, the sense of powerlessness and exclusion is a product not just of their gender subordination, but of interlocking forms of exclusion linked also to class and race. Improvements in women's participation do not necessarily mean that they will be effective in articulating their gender interests in public space. Where women are present in only small numbers, they may be marginalised and find it difficult to promote group interests. Women's immediate preoccupations may also reflect practical concerns that flow from existing divisions of labor and power, rather than more strategic challenges to underlying power structures. For this reason alone, it may take time before women articulate their gender interests effectively in the most strategic forums.

Once individual women gain access to positions of relative power, the problem of their accountability to the grass roots or poor women whom they "represent" arises. There is a danger that women in positions of power will be co-opted, or allow their gender interests to be subsumed by class, caste or ethnic interests. This may be exacerbated by their "newness to the club"—creating feelings of being beholden to others for their position. There are also very real divisions between women; some women have more to gain from preserving the status quo since their (albeit limited) power rests on their standing in the hierarchy over other women.

Finally, as participation in and openness of public institutions increases, gender interests emerge alongside many other issues, among these, children's rights, consumer's rights, housing and pollution. So participation may lead to greater competition over resources and also greater scope for men to organise to resist women's efforts to promote their gender interests. On the other hand, it creates opportunities for building strategic alliances between different interest groups.

Accountability must also be assessed in terms of impact, i.e. changes in actual outcomes that improve women's lives, particularly those of poor women. Even where women are effective in articulating their gender interests, it does not always result in change. Certain areas of policy and decision-making (especially finance and economics, where decisions on resources are central) have been particularly resistant to incursions with a feminist agenda, in part because of their technical nature. Women, especially when in small numbers, are easily sidelined into "women's issues" in the social sectors, and may themselves feel more comfortable in such positions.

In addition, "unholy alliances" and "unruly practices" may impede women's efforts. "Unholy alliances" is a familiar term that connotes otherwise uncomfortable bedfellows—as in the concerted efforts of the Vatican and Islamist groups at the International

Conference on Population and Development (Cairo, 1994) and in the preparatory meetings for the Fourth World Conference on Women to resist the adoption of the term "gender" in the Beijing Platform for Action. "Unruly practices" refer to formal or informal decisions that subvert norms or established rules. For example, in Uganda, a proposed amendment to the land legislation drawn up by women's groups and accepted by Parliament in the course of its debate mysteriously disappeared from the text of the law released after its adoption Both forces often conspire with bureaucratic inertia and insufficient resources to conspire against women's impact. Because of entrenched gender biases, women working in state bureaucracies to promote gender interests find themselves in an ambivalent position working both "within and against" the state. Most importantly the public/private divide implicit in state institutions— in which meeting women's needs is often construed as conflicting with the privacy of the home—has proved a barrier to establishing more equitable practices.

All in all, while the issue of representation in formal political structures and arenas of decision-making is critical for women, a number of difficulties remain, notably in three areas:

(a) Sustaining gains in these areas;

(b) Ensuring that formal representation actually translates into meaningful participation; and

(c) Ensuring that participation translates into substantive change in policies or decisions for resource allocation, which requires that gender interests become institutionalised. While liberal political democracy may create spaces for discussion of gender concerns, it does not automatically ensure better representation of women or their interests.

7.13.1. Legal Frameworks and Systems

Internationally, the establishment and popularisation of human rights instruments and legal provisions which provide for equality as well as protection from abuse, have drawn attention to the extent of gender-based disadvantage and discrimination. In particular, the recognition of violence against women as a human rights violation has been a breakthrough and has stimulated efforts to address gender violence in development policy and programes.

United Nations interagency campaign to combat domestic violence against women in Latin America and the Caribbean.

However, the weakness of state interventions in promoting gender equality is widely acknowledged in the governance literature, and is attributed to the persistence of "customs and traditions [which] often undermine rules and regulations". Legal measures on their own are insufficient and need to be accompanied by efforts to change values through education, training and media, as well as affirmative action to promote women's representation in politics and also the legal system.

Moreover, the frequent failure of legislative reform to uphold women's gender interests at local level is not just an issue of outmoded cultural values. Religious, traditional and judicial authorities administering personal or customary law can bring considerable influence to bear on political processes locally and nationally such that constitutional or formal legal provisions for gender equality can be undermined. In South Africa, for example, even with a progressive Constitution including extensive commitments to gender equality, the political need to accommodate traditional authorities as part of the post-apartheid settlement has militated against strong action to challenge these institutions over gender questions. The recent Magaya vs. Magaya case is another example, from Zimbabwe, where the provisions of the Legal Age of Majority Act were overruled in favor of customary law, which favors male inheritance.

The failure of legal changes, even when accepted, to translate into meaningful change for poor women is also a result of their lack of capacity in the legal system. This results not only from women's lack of resources to access legal help, but from male dominance in the judicial system and from the social distance between poor women and legal systems, related to education and language. In cases involving domestic violence or sexual assault, unsympathetic or even abusive police responses, and fear of social ostracism, are added deterrents.

7.13.2. Macroeconomic Reform

The lack of consideration in macroeconomic policy of women's unpaid labor in the care economy has been described as a deeply embedded form of gender bias in macroeconomics. This "gender bias", combined with the lack of technical skills among women in politics in economic analysis, has limited the impact of gender concerns on macroeconomic policy processes. Greater efforts are now made to assess the likely social and gender impacts of economic policies, but there is still a tendency to see the solution in terms of improving market access of the poor, with little consideration of the gender-specific barriers that women face in market engagement. The case for promoting labor-intensive growth in order to promote opportunities for the poor, for example, is gender biased in overlooking the fact that poor women, especially in rural areas, are rarely underemployed. It is the productivity of and returns to women's labor, inside as well as outside the household, that calls for improvement—not just their opportunities for further work.

Flowing from the lack of gender analysis in economic policy is a failure to analyse the likely impacts on poor women of changes in public expenditure, a key component of economic reform. Recent emphasis by the World Bank and other agencies on the protection of social expenditures and their reallocation to basic services holds potential benefits for poor women. But it is unclear to what extent these gains have actually been realised in the face of downward pressures on total budgets and the collapse of free public service delivery in many countries. Much wider use of the tools for impact analysis of public expenditure, as well as more public scrutiny and debate over budgets *ex ante* as well as *ex post,* are needed in order to have a major impact here.

Recent initiatives from women in civil society, often working alongside women in government and with support from multilateral institutions, are beginning to make inroads into the domain of macroeconomic policy. In particular, the Women's Budget Initiative (WBI) in South Africa, learning from similar experiences in Australia has provided inspiration for the establishment of similar initiatives in a number of other countries, particularly in the Southern African region. South Africa is now also one of three pilot countries for a broader initiative to engender macroeconomic policy, formally under the aegis of government.

These initiatives are simultaneously addressing the issue of engaging women in economic policy debates, changing the rules and practices—through efforts to reform the budgetary process—and ensuring that actual resource allocation decisions take account of women's interests. Most importantly, perhaps, they are pushing for policies that give intrinsic value to human life, as well as adequate recognition of women's labor in producing and sustaining human life.

Other initiatives to monitor and influence the impact of macroeconomic regulatory frameworks on poor women include the work of the Council for the Economic Empowerment of Women in Africa (CEEWA) in Uganda. CEEWA have lobbied for changes to economic legislation (the recent Financial Institutions Act 1993 and Bank of Uganda Statute) enacted in the context of financial sector reform. These efforts are intended to ensure that such legislation does not institutionalise discrimination or biases against poor women who are the main beneficiaries of nonformal micro-enterprise finance. Networks of grassroots women's organisations in the informal sector have also been effective in influencing policy at both national and international levels leading to the adoption of the ILO Convention on Homeworking.

7.13.3. Public Sector Restructuring

Although no longer seen as providers of universally free services, or as having a monopoly on service delivery, governments are still widely held to have a central role as providers of a safety net for the poor and vulnerable. This includes providing an appropriate policy and institutional framework for poverty reduction efforts, collecting and using public revenues in ways which maximise their poverty impact and, increasingly, designing policies and delivering services in ways that empower the poor, or give them "voice".

Reform of the public administration is a key element of governance strategies. It encompasses a wide range of measures, including downsising and restructuring the civil service, introducing new human resources policies and management systems, and efforts to end or reduce corruption. Reform of the public sector often involves introducing competition into service delivery and contracting out service provision to voluntary sector or private providers, or service provision in partnership with non-government actors. While this can improve the quality of service provision and outreach to poorer groups, it has disadvantages from an accountability perspective.

Where a whole range of service providers are operating at a small-scale, localised level, it is hard to have a coordinated approach, particularly on strategic issues such as gender policy. A proliferation of service providers may also prove difficult to hold accountable, since there is no clear focus for complaint or lobbying and public administrations may find compliance hard to enforce. Where frontline personnel in service provision organisations (often women) have poor conditions of pay and work of, this can have very negative consequences on access to and quality of services available, due to absenteeism, demotivation and de facto 'privatisation'.

Research on the experiences of poor people has highlighted the problem of social distance between poor people (especially women users of social services) and providers or administrators of public services. This reinforces experiences of exclusion and powerlessness faced by many poor people. The disrespect of service providers towards the culture and views of poor clients sometimes encompasses verbal and even physical abuse and harassment, as in documented cases of nurses beating patients. Women and girls may be particularly susceptible to abuse and harassment of various kinds, such as sexual harassment of girls by male schoolteachers.

7.13.4. National Machineries

The main instrument through which support for women's gender interests has been mobilised within government structures to date is national machineries for women. These have made many positive achievements, most importantly legitimising the place of gender issues in development planning. However, these mechanisms suffer from a history of marginalisation and insecurity, under-resourcing, lack of technical capacity, overreliance on donor funding and, in some cases, lack of accountability to constituencies in civil society. The fact that many national machineries have been established during periods of fiscal restraint and government restructuring has made their claims on resources difficult to advance. In other words, there are serious questions about effectiveness and impact.

Some lessons have been learned. National machineries set up following democratic transitions (e.g. Philippines, Chile, South Africa, Uganda) have been relatively influential and effective because of the context of broad commitment to greater social equality and justice. Positive experiences also highlight the importance of broad and open processes of consultation, for example, in the development of national gender policies.

Latterly, mainstreaming strategies have become the focus of efforts to institutionalise gender in state bureaucracies. These are reaching beyond traditionally "female" arenas into "hard" ministries such as finance, planning and agriculture—which, in turn, has highlighted a lack of technical skills among gender advocates, as well as the need for heightened awareness of gender issues among technical staff in line ministries, where implementation responsibility should remain.

It is also unclear to what extent national machineries have prioritised the needs and interests of poor women. Given limited resources, this is critical. Certainly, there are positive examples: the Servicio Nacional de la Mujer (SERNAM) in Chile launched a major programe targeting poor female headed households in 1994/5; in South Africa, poor, African, rural women are a major stated focus of the Commission on Gender Equality, the statutory body charged with monitoring government and other actions to promote gender equality.

7.13.5. Decentralisation

Participation of the poor in the decentralised management of service delivery has been a major plank of governance efforts on the assumption that this will make service provision more accountable and response to the interests of the poor. Unlike central government, local authorities and agencies are perceived to be closer to the people and more directly accountable. But this assumption overlooks the possibility that at the local level, power elites may be more entrenched than at the national and more hostile to demands from marginalised groups.

Implicit in some of the governance literature is the idea that decentralisation is inherently favorable to women because it reduces logistical and other barriers to their participation and will lead to greater responsiveness of locally provided services to the needs of women as major users of these services. Recent moves to increase participation in local planning processes—such as the Law of Popular Participation in Bolivia, introduced in conjunction with decentralisation—are also seen as offering opportunities for the direct participation of women, among others, to influence the design of services to meet their needs.

However, women do not necessarily achieve greater representation at the local level as compared to national. There are both positive and negative examples here. In India, decentralisation has been used as a vehicle for promoting women's representation with a requirement to reserve one third of seats for women in local government, thus resulting in a huge increase in the numbers of women active in political life. Elsewhere, democratic transitions and national quotas adopted by political parties have ensured high levels of representation of women in Parliament, but this has not always been reflected at the local level, South Africa is a case in point. While women hold 27 percent of the South African Parliamentary seats, they attained only 19 percent of representation in local government elections. Outside formal local politics, women are often very involved in community action, but this can remain invisible because of its informal nature. Even where new participatory structures are put in place, which might enable more access for informal women's associations, other political imperatives, such as the ethnic politics of indigenous representation, may take precedence over gender interests.

Decentralisation of service delivery (e.g. of health services), when combined with an emphasis on increased cost-recovery, can also result in reduced access for the poor, reduced capacity for cross-subsidisation between services and localities and thus increased inequalities in service provision. Where the management of school provision has been decentralised or contracted out to the private sector, there is evidence of middle class capture and dominance leading to increased fees in good schools and thus the exclusion of children from poorer households.

Thus the responsiveness of decentralised services to women's needs appears to depend on available resources and competition over these, on the nature of local power structures, and on the degree of organisation and political visibility of women locally. Intergovernmental fiscal relations can be designed such that equity concerns are given a weighting in the allocation of resources from central to local government, but these tend to focus on interregional disparities. There may be instances where this benefits women for demographic reasons (e.g. where women predominate in poorer rural areas) but this is a blunt instrument. Where women are required to represent their interests at many different levels, this increases the difficulty of articulating aggregated interests that might have a major policy impact.

7.13.6. Markets and the Private Sector

Discussions of governance tend to focus more on the structures and processes related to public administration than on the market. This is perhaps consonant with the role of "good government" in underpinning market liberalisation in the context of macroeconomic adjustment. Discussions of market governance are thus relatively less developed in relation to the interests of the poor and other marginalised groups.

Nonetheless, feminist economists have analysed the embededness of markets in gendered institutions and the ways in which markets act as bearers of gender in relation not only to labor, but also financial and product markets. This reflects the social and spatial organisation of markets, in which women tend to be confined to individuated enterprises and restricted to certain points in the marketing chain or geographical spheres of operation. It also reflects gender ideology, whereby certain goods or skills are deemed to be "female" and therefore "inferior". Women's relative lack of access to formal financial services and their related reliance on informal sector finance can be understood in terms of gendered transaction costs in credit markets, linked to regulatory frameworks and institutional norms economic and social development.

A general problem with analyses of civil society in the governance literature is that is tends to be portrayed as virtuous, nonconflictual and functional in social development. Clearly, however, there are strong conflicts between interest groups (including gender-based interest groups; or groups with strongly opposed gender ideologies) in civil society, such that promoting civil society will not necessarily result in outcomes that increase gender accountability. Examples include welfare organisations linked to conservative religious groups or other groups that may have widespread networks of social provision (health care, schooling etc.) involving poor people, but that exclude girls and women, or relegate them to narrowly gendered roles.

There are a number of ways in which the constitution of civil society reflects gendered norms and practices. The spaces for women to mobilise in civil society may be relatively restricted, such that they belong to a narrow range of organisations that are gender-typed, gender-segregated or less politically influential. For example, poor women tend to be dominant as members of religious groups rather than trade unions, political parties and business associations, which have a more direct line into policy processes. Where women are active, it tends to be in mobilising support among women for organisational objectives, rather than organising around gender interests. Even women's organisations do not necessarily provide space for the articulation of gender interests; they may in fact promote highly conservative agendas. Explicitly feminist groups are often characterised as elitist, urban-based and middle-class. There are divisions between organisations focused on lobbying and advocacy and those engaged in direct service provision, the latter sometimes involved in more immediate demands from poor women.

Poor women are engaging in a variety of forms of community action and creating alternative organisations and movements, not necessarily motivated primarily by feminist agendas, but in response to processes of economic, social and political exclusion. However, rarely do these fragmented forms of organisation result in the articulation of aggregated gender interests in political movements of a durable nature. The problem is that the organisational forms in which women mobilise is often not recognised in political systems. And where networks or associations formed by women (e.g., around water use management; rotating credit associations) become formalised, positions of authority may be taken over by men.

In relation to poverty reduction objectives, the often presumed comparative advantage of NGOs and grassroots organisations in reaching the poor is not always based on rigorous analysis or evidence. Grassroots organisations and social movements may be genuinely participatory in their approach and some NGOs have been instrumental in developing and applying participatory methods of working with local communities. Nevertheless, there are many examples of NGOs dominated by charismatic leaders and run in an autocratic fashion.

Equally, research to date suggests that in the absence of specific goals of promoting gender equity, there is no necessary correspondence between management democracy in organisations and institutional comparative advantage. Consequently, NGOs do not necessarily provide a more congenial environmental for the institutionalisation of women's interests than state bureaucracies. Promotion of NGOs, or even women's organisations, then, should not be seen as an automatic panacea for improving gender accountability.

There remain many differences between women at all these levels in terms of their interests and priorities, as well as appropriate strategies to advance these. But there is also considerable evidence of networks and alliances developing around strategic issues, which link women internationally, as well as across the "domains"' of civil society, private sector and state.. There is much to be learned from the experiences of these networks and their attempts to hold international organisations accountable.

References

Norris, Pippa. Ed. 1997. *Women, Media, and Politics*. New York, USA: Oxford University Press.

Rule, Wilma and Joseph F. Zimmerman. 1994. Eds. *Electoral Systems in Comparative Perspective: Their Impact on Women and Minorities*. Westport: Greenwood Press.

UNESCO, 1993. *Women in Politics: Australia, India, Malaysia, Philippines, and Thailand*. (Guest Editor: Latika Padgaonkar). Bangkok.

Willis, Virginia. 1991. *Public Life: Women Make a Difference: Expert group Meeting on the Role of Women in Public Life* (Vienna, 21-24 May). New York: Division for the Advancement of Women.

Bibliography

Afshar, Haleh. ed. 1987. *Women, State and Ideology.* Studies from Africa and Asia. London and New York: Routledge.

Agnihotri, I. and V. Mazumdar. July 22, 1995. "Changing Terms of Political Discourse: Women's Movement in India, 1970s–1990s" *Economic and Political Weekly*, Vol. xxx, No. 29. pp. 1869–1878.

Ashworth, Georgina, 1996, *Gendered Governance: An Agenda for Change, Gender* in Development Monograph Series, Number 3, UNDP, New York

Balch, Jeff, Tendair Bare and Frances Gardiner. 1998. *Achieving the Advancement of Women in the Post-Beijing Era.* Cape Town and Amsterdam: AWEPA/ African-European Institute.

Barry, Trudie, Sneha Palnitkar . 1996. *Women and Local Politics in Mumbai and London : The quota Innovation*' Third IIAS International Conference (International Institute of Administrative Sciences) – Beijing, China 8 – 11, October, 1996.

Beall, Jo, 1996, *Urban Governance: Why Gender Matters, Gender* in Development Monograph Series, Number 1, UNDP, New York

Beckwith, Karen. 1992. "Comparative Research and Electoral Systems: Lessons from France and Italy." *Women and Politics* 12, no. 1: 1-33

Bjorkman, James W. 1987. "India: Party, Personality and Dynasty", in Alan Ware. ed. *Political Parties.* Oxford: Blackwell.

Brill, Alida. Ed. 1995. *A Rising Public Voice: Women in Politics Worldwide.* New York: The Feminist Press.

Buckley, Mary and Malcolm Anderson, eds. 1988. *Women, Equality and Europe.* London: Macmillan

Bukley, Mary and Malcolm Andersson. Eds. 1988. *Women, Equality and Europe.* London: Macmillan.

Chattopadhyaya, Kamaladevi. 1983. *Indian Women's Battle for Freedom.* New Delhi: Abhinav Press.

CWDS. 1995. *Towards Beijing: A Perspective from the Indian Women's Movement.* New Delhi.

Dahlerup, Drude. 1988. "From a Small to a Large Minority: Theory of Critical Mass", *Scandinavian Political Studies.* Vol. 11. No. 4. pp. 275–298.

Davidson, Alastair. 1989. "The Italian women's movement and the Italian Communist Party." Pp. 156-187 in *Politics of the future*, ed. ?. South Melbourne: ?.

Debbie Budlender & UNIFEM. 2004. *Budgeting to Fulfil International Gender and Human Rights Commitments*, Frontline Electronic Publishing Ltd, Harare.

Desai, Neera. 1991. 'Indian March Towards Equity – A Review of a Decade and half of Action and Policy on Women, *Janata : A Journal of Democratic Socialism,* Vol. 45, Nos. 36 - 40, Jan 6, 1991, pg.9 – 16.

Dodson, Debra L. 1991. *Gender and Policy Making: Studies of Women in Office*. New Jersey: Centre for the American Woman and Politics, Eagleton Institute, Rutgers University.

Folasade Ayorinde. 2005*Local Government Budget & Gender, A Guide Analysis of Kuje Area Council Budget, Abuja, Case Study of the Education & Health sectors*, Nigeria Gender Budget Network.

Gaspard, Françoise, ed. 1997. *Les femmes dans la prise de décision en France et en Europe* (Women in decision-making in France and Europe). Paris: L'Harmattan

Golandaz, H.M., 1996, *Human Resource Development for Better Cities with special reference to India*, Bombay, 1996

Haque, Syeda Obaida, 1996, *Urban Livelihood for Women*, Shakti Foundation, Bangladesh

Hoskyns, C. and S. Rai. 1996. "Gender, Class and Representation: India and the European Union", Paper presented at the 1996 Political Studies Association Conference. Glasgow, 10 April.

International Union of Local Authorities. 1998. *Women in Local Government. Stockholm: IULA.*

Inter-Parliamentary Union. 1997. *Men and Women in Politics: Democracy Still in the Making, A World Comparative Study*. Series Reports and Documents No.28. Geneva: Inter-Parliamentary Union.

Inter-Parliamentary Union. 1997. *Towards Partnership between Men and Women in Politics*: New Delhi (14-18 February). Series Reports and Documents No. 29. Geneva: Inter-Parliamentary Union.

Joshi, P. 1989. *Gandhi on Women.* New Delhi: Navjivan Press.

Karam, Azza Ed. 1998 *International IDEA Handbook on Women in Parliaments: Beyond Numbers*. Stockholm: International IDEA.

Karl, Marilee. 1995. *Women and Empowerment: Participation and Decision-Making*. London and New Jersey: Zed Books.

Karmhus, (Mayor) Ingebjorg, 1996, *Municipal Planning on Women's Terms*, Experiences from the Project, Leksvik Municipality, Norway

Karvonen L. and Per Selle. eds. 1995. *Women in Nordic Politics: Closing the Gap*. London: Dartmouth Press. Inter-Parliamentary Union. 1997. *Men and Women in Politics: Democracy Still in the Making*. Geneva.

Kumari, Ranjana and Anju Dubey, 1994, *Women Parliamentarians: A Study in the Indian Context*, Har-Anand Publications, New Delhi

Leijenaar, Monique. 1996. *How to Create a Gender Balance in Political Decision Making*. Brussels: European Commission.

Liddle, J. and R. Joshi. 1986. *Daughters of Independence*. New Delhi: Kali for Women.

Lovenduski, Joni. 1986. *Women and European Politics: Contemporary Feminism and Public Policy*. Amherst, MA: University of Massachusetts Press.

Nelson, Barbara J. and Najma Chowdhury, Eds. 1994. *Women and Politics Worldwide*, New Haven and London: Yale University Press.

Netherlands Ministry of Foreign Affairs 1998. "*Gender and Good Governance*". Conference held in Harare, Zimbabwe (May 1998). The Hague.

Norris, Pippa. Ed. 1997*: Women, Media, and Politics*. New York, USA: Oxford University Press.

Nuss, S.A., 1995, *List of Statistics on Women in Government, Public Sector Employment and Administration*, Judiciary United Nations Agencies and Conferences.

Okojie C.E & Amadi S.I (Eds). 2008*Gender Responsive Budgeting and Parliament: A Handbook for Nigerian Legislators*, a publication of the Centre for Democracy and Development (CDD) and Henrich Boll Foundation (HBF).

Patel, Vibhuti. 1986. *Getting a foothold in Politics, Reading in Women's Studies Series* : RCUES, SNDT, Bombay.

Phillips, A. 1991. *Engendering Democracy.* Cambridge: Polity.

Rai, S. M. 1995. "Women Negotiating Boundaries: Gender, Law and the Indian State". *Social and Legal Studies*, Vol. 4, No. 3, September.

Ramkumar V. 2008. *Our Money, Our Responsibility, A Citizens' Guide to MonitoringGovernment Expenditures,* The International Budget Project.

Richard Matland, "Enhancing Women's Political Participation: Legislative Recruitment and Electoral Systems", in Azza Karam. Ed. 1998. *Women in Parliament: Beyond Numbers*. pp. 65-90.

Rule, Wilma and Joseph F. Zimmerman. 1994. Eds. *Electoral Systems in Comparative Perspective: Their Impact on Women and Minorities*. Westport: Greenwood Press.

Sarkar, T. and U. Butalia. eds. 1995. *Women and Right-Wing Movements: Indian Experiences*. London: Zed Press.

Siddiqui, Kamal, (ed.), 1992, *Local Government in South Asia: A Comparative Study*, University Press Limited, Dhaka, Bangladesh

Thomson, Suteera, 1995, *Women in Decision-Making Positions: Politics and Administration,* Gender and Development Institute, Bangkok, Thailand

UNESCO, 1993. *Women in Politics: Australia, India, Malaysia, Philippines, and Thailand.* (Guest Editor: Latika Padgaonkar). Bangkok.

United Nations. 1991. *Women in Decision-Making: Case-Study on Greece*. New York: United Nations.

Vallance, Elizabeth. 1981. "Women in the House of Commons." *Political Studies* 29, no. 3: 407-414.

Willis, Virginia. 1991. *Public Life: Women Make a Difference: Expert group Meeting on the Role of Women in Public Life* (Vienna, 21-24 May). New York: Division for the Advancement of Women.

Index